P9-CLY-765

Cunningham's Encyclopedia of Magical Herbs

by
Scott Cunningham

1998
Llewellyn Publications
St. Paul, Minnesota 55164-0383, U.S.A.

FIRST EDITION, 1985
Twenty-fifth Printing, 1998

Cover art by Carol McEachron
Book design by Terry Buske
Original illustrations by Jack Adair and Bill Fugate

Library of Congress Cataloging-in-Publication Data
Cunningham, Scott, 1956–1993
    Cunningham's encyclopedia of magical herbs.
    Bibliography: p.
    Includes index.
    1. Magic. 2. Plants. I. Title. II. Title:
Encyclopedia of magical herbs.
BF1623.P5C86   1984   133.4'3   84-48091
ISBN 0-87542-122-9

Llewellyn Publications
A Division of Llewellyn Worldwide, Ltd.
P.O. Box 64383, St. Paul, MN 55164-0383

Printed in the United States of America

THERE ARE POWERS IN HERBS

Nature has provided a veritable magical pantry in the plants which cover our planet. For untold ages these plants have been utilized in magic—the practice of causing change by natural (albeit little-understood) powers.

In ancient times plants were Gods and Goddesses; spirits and magicians lived within gnarled oaks and whispered from flowers. Our ancestors discovered the forces present in plants and harnessed them to improve their lives.

Today the weeds and wildflowers that grace our cities and wildernesses, the ornamental and food plants in our gardens, even common house plants still possess incredible powers. Magical herbalism is the use of these powers.

Though the medicinal properties of plants are fairly well known—many of the most widely-prescribed drugs are synthesized versions of substances originally derived from plants—their occult powers are less accessible. Much of magic still lies in the shadow of secrecy.

This book is an attempt to continue the work done in MAGICAL HERBALISM— to bring to light the occult properties of plants. Over 400 herbs are discussed, with exact magical procedures for using them.

Far from concentrating on esoteric, unobtainable plants, many of those mentioned within are old friends. Onions, cashews, apples, rice, lettuce—as well as dill, basil, fennel, garlic and parsley are surveyed, and hundreds of others. Extensive tables, a cross-reference of folk names, a listing of herb suppliers, glossary, annotated bibliography and hundreds of illustrations make this an infinitely practical book.

About the Author

Scott Cunningham practiced elemental magic for over twenty years. He was the author of more than thirty books, both fiction and non-fiction, sixteen of them published by Llewellyn Publications. Scott's books reflect a broad range of interests within the New Age sphere, where he was highly regarded. He passed from this life on March 28, 1993, after a long illness.

To Write to the Publisher

If you would like more information about this book, please write to the publisher in care of Llewellyn Worldwide, and we will forward your request. The publisher appreciates hearing from you and learning of your enjoyment of this book and how it has helped you. Llewellyn Worldwide cannot guarantee that every letter can be answered, but all will be reviewed. Please write to:

Llewellyn Publications
c/o Llewellyn Worldwide
P.O. Box 64383, Dept. L122-9,
St. Paul, MN 55164-0383, U.S.A.

Please enclose a self-addressed, stamped envelope for reply, or $1.00 to cover costs.
If outside the U.S.A., enclose international postal reply coupon.

DEDICATION:

For Mom and Dad

Other Books by Scott Cunningham

The Complete Book of Incense, Oils and Brews
Cunningham's Encyclopedia of Crystal, Gem and Metal Magic
Earth, Air, Fire and Water: More Techniques of Natural Magic
Earth Power
Hawaiian Religion & Magic
Living Wicca: A Further Guide for the Solitary Practitioner
The Magic in Food
Magical Aromatherapy: The Power of Scent
Magical Herbalism
The Magical Household (with David Harrington)
Spell Crafts: Creating Magical Objects
   (with David Harrington)
The Truth About Herb Magic
The Truth About Witchcraft Today
Wicca: A Guide for the Solitary Practitioner

Video

Herb Magic

Biography

Whispers of the Moon by David Harrington and deTraci Regula

ACKNOWLEDGEMENTS:

My thanks go to these and many other individuals who shared information or offered criticism: Don Kraig, for suggestions on an early draft of this work; Ron Garst for spending a few evenings talking of oils and incenses; Ed and Marilee Snowden for (again) allowing me access to their library, as well as to Ms. Snowden for proofreading the final manuscript; Daniel Weime for sharing his herbal secrets and allowing some to be published here, and to all my friends who supported and encouraged me during the completion of this work.

TABLE OF CONTENTS

PREFACE

I was a young man when I began to write what was eventually to become *Magical Herbalism*. Frustrated at the lack of information concerning herb magic and at the surfeit of interest in my teachers and fellow occult students I set out to investigate this nearly lost art.

This search took me through worlds and experiences of which I had scarcely dreamt. Nights spent reading ancient books and manuscripts while sipping herbal teas led to practical application; I collected herbs by moonlight and brewed up spells on deserted beaches. Slowly the pieces fell into my hands. At last I gathered up the threads of the ancient ways and, from them, wove a system of herb magic.

The more I experienced herb magic the more I realized its true powers. It may well be the most ancient and yet the most practical form of magic, for its tools grow all around us, even in the concrete-laden cities in which so many of us live.

After witnessing the power of herbs I decided to write a book explaining these lost ways. Thus, *Magical Herbalism* was born. Five years and several drafts later it was published (Llewellyn, 1982).

During this process my research into and work with herb magic hadn't halted. Most of what I was learning could not be incorporated into *Magical Herbalism*, and so I decided that it had to wait for a later book. My early work was almost solely concerned with Old World plants, and this is reflected in *Magical Herbalism*. In recent years I have investigated the magical uses of plants of North and South America, the Near East, the Far East and Polynesia. (Some of these Polynesian plants have been included in this work, but the majority must wait for a future book on Hawaiian magic.)

With the amount of new information I had uncovered I soon realized that the second herbal would be a veritable encyclopedia of herb magic. Hence, this book.

The present work is not a guide to herb magic, only minimal information is given in these pages concerning it. That ground is covered in *Magical Herbalism*. Do you wish to attract a lover? Carry a bag of rose petals or an orris root. Want to stop a toothache? Chew an elder twig and drive it into a wall. This is the type of magic that abounds in these pages—quick, uncomplicated, non-ritualistic. All-purpose spells are presented in the first section of the book for use where needed.

While most of the magic presented here deals with everyday problems, more complex subjects are also broached in the text—invisibility, materialization of spirits, attaining immortality and so on. Such information is presented because it is traditional, interesting and romantic, not necessarily for its practical application. Similarly, the references to guarding against sea serpent bites and causing fairies to appear are included because such information fires the imagination, a necessity for effective magic.

This is not a book of quaintly impossible spells; it is an infinitely practical collection of herb magic which anyone can put to use.

I have limited myself strictly to the magical uses of herbs in this book; no medicinal information is presented here because there are a wealth of reliable guides available in this area. I have also bypassed the mythological and historical backgrounds of most of the plants except where relevant.

Those who seek destructive magic within these pages will be disappointed; none exists here, for such magic leads to its user's destruction.

A work of this type can never be completed; more secrets lie in waiting for discovery. It is the author's responsibility to decide when to stop nurturing and send a book out into the world to find its legs. I do so now, with the hope that it will stimulate others toward discovering and using the secrets of herb magic.

Part I

The Basics

The Powers of Herbs

How does it work? When people discover I'm a magical herbalist, this is one of two questions asked. The other usually refers to my state of mental health. Nonetheless, the first question is a valid one and has never been satisfactorily explained.

The basis of herb magic—and all magic—is *the power*. This power has worn many names and forms through the centuries; at times even its existence was kept secret; at others it was common knowledge.

The power is that which generated and maintains the universe. It is the power that germinates seeds, raises winds and spins our planet. It is the energy behind birth, life and death. Everything in the universe was created by it, contains a bit of it, and is answerable to it.

In other words, the power is the life-force, the stuff of creation. It is the very substance of existence itself.

The power as I see it has no name. It has been deified and anthropomorphized into a thousand-thousand Gods and Goddesses, spirits, demons and other unearthly beings. It has been only partially unexplained in the terms of science, which today is still 'discovering' some of its aspects. The power has played an important part in the evolution of the human race, for better or worse. All religions have tapped into it using different symbols and rites, and all magicians have wielded its powers.

Above the ritual and religion and magic the power exists, changeless in its eternal change. The power is in everything, and everything is in the power. (One of the problems of some modern religions is that they assert that the power is outside us, and not within.) Call it what you like, visualize it as you may, the power really is *the* power.

Definition: Magic is the practice of causing change through the use of powers as yet not defined or accepted by science.

I can cause change by accepted means (by calling a friend on the phone I can find out how she's doing); this is not magic. But when I do not have access to a phone, or my friend does not answer, I can make a sachet of thyme, yarrow

1

and bay, tie it around my neck, still my mind and, using my herb-fortified psychic powers, discover if she is alright. This is its practicality: magic can be used when no other means are available.

What methods are at the disposal of most people to guard their homes against theft? How can a lonely woman attract a love into her life? In what manner, beyond visiting doctors and buying medicines, can most people aid their bodies to combat illness?

Most people would not know how to answer the above questions save in the most physical ways; a lock, a new perfume and bedrest may be suggested as solutions. These are fine starts, but they can be supplemented with surer methods— they can be backed up with magic.

Magic is useful for solving these, and other common problems, but it becomes indispensible when dealing with occult matters. Need a glimpse into the future? Make a tea of rosebuds, drink it directly before going to bed, and remember your dreams. Or, wear some deerstongue wrapped in yellow cloth. Do you believe you're the target of a hex or curse? Doctors will direct you to the nearest psychiatrist; Witches and Magicians will tell you to sprinkle red pepper around your property and then bathe in mimosa flowers. Magic has many (but not quite all) of the answers.

There is an important point running through these words: magic, however simple it might seem, provides practical solutions to problems.

The power behind herb magic is formless, shapeless, eternal. It doesn't care whether you call on it in the name of a Witch Goddess or the Virgin Mary—or tap it within no religious framework at all. It is always there, present in abundance no matter where we are or where we travel in the universe.

Though the power is formless, it takes on many forms: a wildebeest has the power, so does a computer, or a dandelion. Some materials contain higher concentrations of the power than others; these include plants, gems and metals. Each substance also contain different types of power, or vibrational rates. The vibrations of a piece of pine wood, for example, are far different from those of a perfect, faceted diamond.

This vibratory rate is determined by several factors: chemical make-up, form, density and so on. The powers resident in herbs are determined by the plant's habitat, scent, color, form and other considerations. Similar substances usually possess similar vibrations.

Herb magic, then, is the use of herbs to cause needed changes. These plants contain energies—each as distinct as human faces. For maximum effects the herbs chosen for a spell should possess vibrations that match your need. Cedar is fine for attracting money, but wouldn't be of help in a fertility spell.

To practice herb magic you must know the powers of the plants. This book contains that information. To fulfill a need, just manipulate the herbs to give their powers direction. It is that simple.

Herb magic is easy because the powers (i.e., vibrations) lie *in the herbs themselves.* No outside forces need be called into play, for the power is resident within the organic matter. A few simple procedures are all that is necessary. These 'rites' include tying knots, boiling water, lighting candles, sewing and burying things in the Earth. More important than its simplicity, perhaps, is the fact that herb magic works.

How does it work? First, there must be a reason to call upon magical powers. This reason is a need. A desire often masquerades as a need, but in magic a 'desire' is not enough; there must exist an all-encompassing need.

The nature of the need determines which plants are used. Attracting love, for example, is a common magical need and several dozen plants do the job. (For a comprehensive listing of plants and their corresponding magical needs, see PART THREE of this book.)

Next, a spell or ritual may need to be devised; much herb magic doesn't need a complete spell but some of it does. This spell may be as simple as tying up the herbs in a piece of cloth, or placing them around the base of a candle, lighting the wick and visualizing your need. If you wish, your spell can be complex, involving boiling water in a cauldron over a mesquite wood fire at the edge of the desert while waiting for the Moon to rise, before throwing roots and leaves into the pot. All-purpose spells are included in CHAPTER THREE.

Third, the herbs can be enchanted (CHAPTER THREE) to ensure that their vibrations are attuned to the need.

Fourth, the spell is worked, in complete confidence and secrecy. Not that magic is anything to be ashamed of; but rather because mocking glances and disbelief only serve to cause you to doubt yourself and hinder your magic's effectiveness.

Fifth, once the spell has been worked, it should be forgotten. This allows it to 'cook' and bring your need into manifestation. (When baking a cake, if you look into the oven every few minutes the cake will be spoiled. In magic, as in cooking, keep the oven door shut!) Attempt to forget the spell completely.

And there you have it. This is how herb magic is worked. Does it sound

basic? It is. These are the first steps. As with any art the student may take magic further, exploring strange corners. Sensibly, few wish to venture too far from this familiar, homey magic. There are dark ways in herb magic as there are in every aspect of life. Those who wish to pursue such paths, to wreak havoc and control or kill other human beings, shall receive the heavy penalty for negative working.

The power is neutral. It cannot be divided into positive and negative energies. *Power is power.*

It is our responsibility as Magicians (wielders of the powers) to work with it toward beneficial ends. We need not become ascetic or saints to help others, or to improve our lives. All we need do is use herbs in loving ways.

Magic, as it was understood in long ago days, was a divine act. This is literally true; in magic we become one with and utilize the power, which has been fashioned into a multitude of deities.

It is an awesome feeling, and a greater responsibility, this wielding of power. The moment it is used for negative ends divinity quickly flees. However, when magic is used for positive ends our lives become richer and happier. When one embarks down the dark path of negativity, the suffering this causes to others spills into the Magician's life until, in the end, he or she is utterly destroyed.

Dramatic words? Perhaps—but their essence is true. For this reason no negative magic is included in this book. But to those who desire to help themselves and others with the old ways of herb magic, welcome!

Magical Ways

Though there isn't room here for a complete explanation of the methods and theories of magic, the following short essays discuss some of the most important points. For further information see *Magical Herbalism*.

TIMING

The ancients created magical systems with varying degrees of complexity. One area in which they excelled was the art of timing ritual acts in accordance with astronomical phenomena. Some of these systems were rigidly controlled by the phases of the Moon; others took the seasons into account, and in others still, the stars and their positions were all-important.

Some of these systems are still in use today, with good results. But any system can kill off spontaneity and hinder the effects of magic—even its very performance. Timing is important, true, but there should be only one inviolable rule: magic is used when needed.

If I have a headache which disturbs my sleep or work, I cannot wait for the Moon to enter the proper sign, or until Ursa Major rises; I need relief immediately.

This is a trifling example but it holds true for all magic. It is no use waiting three weeks to perform a money spell if your bills must be paid by the end of the week. I am not arguing that timing with the planets, stars, seasons, Lunar phases and so on does not provide *extra* power to spells: I am simply arguing against the *necessity* for such extra power. If the magic works it will work at *any* time of the day or night.

I can hear ghostly complaints from Magicians—'You can't perform love spells during the waning Moon.' 'Money spells fail unless performed on a Thursday during Spring while the Moon is in Taurus, at the third or tenth hour of the night.'

Such pronouncements are common in magic—usually from people who do little or no practical work. Spells need not have ideal astronomical, seasonal and weather conditions to be successful.

5

Those who wish to follow the old ways of timing magic with the Sun, Moon and stars can find this information in any good magical textbook, but it is by no means a necessity.

If you need courage before facing a job interview, don't look at the phase of the Moon—grab some thyme and get on with it!

Though some instances of magical timing are mentioned in this book, especially regarding the collection of specific plants, they may be followed, or not, as you please, with almost identical results.

TOOLS

Herb magic requires blessedly few tools compared to other types of magic. A mortar and pestle set is necessary to grind herbs and seeds, and a large wooden or ceramic bowl will be needed for enchanting herbs. Keep a large glass or enamelled pot (avoid metals) exclusively for brewing infusions or 'potions'. Simple sewing supplies (needles, pins, scissors, cotton thread, thimbles) will come in handy in making sachets and poppets, and a good stock of various colors of cotton or wool cloth and yarn will be needed.

Candles and herbs, of course, are necessities, as is a censer (incense burner), candleholders, charcoal blocks and jars in which to store your herbs.

THE ALTAR

This is also called the spell table or work table, but I like the sound of 'altar' which is far less akward, even though it gives a religious association to magic which may not always be deserved. However, 'altar' will be used throughout this book.

A great deal of magic does not need the presence of an altar, but certain rites do. When performed at home, the altar is the place where spells are cast. It can also be used as a work table where herbs are enchanted, sachets composed and where, in general, all magical work is done.

An altar may be any flat surface on which you can place candles, an incense burner, herbs, and any other materials needed for a spell. It can be the top of a coffee table or dresser, or a section of the floor. Wherever you can find a place is sufficient.

Some people who wish to acknowledge their religious beliefs place symbols of their faith on the altar. Statues and holy books are common, but any objects with which you feel comfortable may be placed on the altar, such as lucky charms, fossils, rocks, shells, and so on. Such natural objects may actually empower your magical further.

I cannot stress too strongly the advisability of performing magic outdoors when possible. Indoor spells work, of course, and most of us have to substitute a living room or bedroom for a forest clearing or lonely beach. Magic must be practical.

Outdoor altars aren't always necessary; when they are necessary, they usually consist of a cleared section of ground, a flat rock, or a tree stump, but ingenuity can aid the Magician here. The altar is simply a place to perform magic, and is limited only by your imagination.

VISUALIZATION

The most 'advanced' magical technique needed in herb magic is visualization; i.e. forming a picture in your mind of your need*

Many books have been written on this subject, for students often complain that they have difficulty visualizing clearly. Usually, the ability is present but hindered by inhibitions.

Can you, at this moment while reading this book, see your mother's face? What about that of your closest friend, or worst enemy?

This is visualization. In magic visualization is used to direct the power by forming a picture of your need; a car, a love, employment, and so on. If you need an object, visualize yourself owning it; if a job, see yourself working; and if love is needed, visualize a ring slipping onto your finger, or any symbol you associate with love.

The need must be visualized as if you have already obtained it, or as if it has already come to fruition. Use your creativity and natural visualization talents to really see your need. Don't think of the reasons behind your need; simply *see* it in concrete terms.

As with everything from golf to cooking, practice makes perfect. Even if you're never capable of completely visualizing your need, magic will work as long as the intention is there.

---

* See *Creative Visualization* by Denning & Phillips. Llewellyn Publications.

OTHER CONSIDERATIONS

This is a convenient heading for a variety of short topics, as evidenced by the diversity of material below.

When possible, bathe before performing magic. A sachet of purification herbs added to the water can be a great help, also.

Dress in clean, comfortable clothing or nothing at all, as you wish. Some practitioners wear robes and jewelry but this isn't necessary.

It is also not necessary to abstain from sex, food or liquids prior to magic. Do so if you wish but it simply isn't a requirement.

Most of the magic in this book is down-to-Earth and deals with everyday problems. However, for important spells, especially those that deal with other human beings, perform a divination to make certain that the spell is necessary before using magic. Information and techniques of divination are included in my book *Earth Power* (Llewellyn, 1983) as well as *Magical Herbalism*.

As a rule of thumb don't cast spells for others unless you have their permission. One way to avoid such problems is to make up sachets and similar items for them (direction in CHAPTER THREE) and give them as presents. Explain their uses and powers and the other person involved can choose to bring those vibrations into his or her life or not, according to their wishes.

Above all, have fun with herb magic. Although you should be serious when actually enchanting herbs and visualizing, don't view every aspect of herb magic solemnly. It should be enjoyable.

MAGICAL PRINCIPLES

1. Magic is natural.
2. Harm none—not even yourself—through its use.
3. Magic requires effort. You will receive what you put into it.
4. Magic is not usually instantaneous. Spells require time to be effective.
5. Magic should not be performed for pay.
6. Magic should never be used in jest or to inflate your ego.
7. Magic can be worked for your own gain, but only if it harms none.
8. Magic is a divine act.
9. Magic can be used for defense but should never be used for attack.
10. Magic is knowledge—not only of its way and laws, but also of its effectiveness. Do not believe that magic works—*know it!*
11. Magic is love. All magic should be performed out of love. The moment anger or hatred tinges your magic you have crossed the border into a dangerous world, one that will ultimately consume you.

Spells and Procedures

ENCHANTING HERBS

Prior to actually using herbs in magic, they can be enchanted. Enchantment (in a magical context) aligns the vibrations of the plants involved with your magical need. Thus it is a process which increases the effectiveness of the herbs.

Enchantment may be performed on a single herb or a mixture, but should not be done until moments before the herb is to be used. When several herbs are needed for a spell they may be enchanted together as a mixture or singly as each herb is introduced into the mixture.

A preliminary enchantment may be performed if the herb is collected from the wilds or a garden. While actually cutting the herb for a specific spell the need should be stressed, as should the plant's role in fulfilling that need, i.e.:

I gather you, rosemary, herb of the Sun, to
increase my mental powers and concentration.

This begins the process of enchantment, although it is preliminary only.

The equipment is simple: a plain wooden or ceramic bowl, two candle-holders, and a supply of colored candles.

Place the bowl in the center of the altar, the candleholders with correctly colored candles on either side (see APPENDIX I for colors and their magical uses). The herbs to be enchanted should be placed around the bowl in their containers.

Light the candles and still your mind. Unplug the phone and lock the door. If you wish, darken the room of artificial illumination. Enchant herbs (and perform all magic) only when you are alone and will be free from interruption.

ATTUNEMENT:

Pour the needed amount of dried herb into the bowl. Sit or stand calmly and gaze into the herb. Sense its vibrations awaiting within the leaves and flowers and stems; see them emerging from the plant or lying in wait. Psychics can see

9

the vibrations leaving the plants in various forms, such as sharp jagged lines, lazy spirals or blazing comets. Lean toward the bowl and place your power hand (see GLOSSARY) within it, touching the herb. Leave it motionless for a few seconds. Visualize your need strongly.

ENCHANTMENT:
Run your fingers through the herb. Still strongly visualizing your need, send it into the herb. Feel your fingertips charging the herb with energy. If you find trouble holding the image in your mind chant simple words that match your need, such as;

> *Yarrow, yarrow, make love grow.*

Chant this endlessly under your breath. As you run your fingers through the herb feel them infusing the plant with your need.

When the herb is tingling with power (or when you sense that the enchantment is complete) remove your hand. The plant has been enchanted.

If there are other plants to be used in a mixture, add them one at a time, re-enchanting the mixture with each addition.

If you wish to enchant herbs to be used separately, remove the enchanted herb from the bowl and wipe it clean with a dry towel. Replace the candles with colors appropriate to the new herb and repeat the procedure.

When making incense, infusions, sachets, poppets and the like powder or grind herbs (if needed) before enchanting.

If roots or branches are to be enchanted, simply hold in your power hand, visualizing and/or chanting, or lay it on top of the bowl between the candles.

In earlier days to 'enchant' meant to sing or chant to. Once you have sung your song of need to the herbs, they are ready for use.

Of course enchantment isn't absolutely necessary, but it is a method of obtaining better results. The wise herbalist will never omit enchantments.

MAGICAL PROCEDURES
This section details the actual methods of working with herbs that are mentioned in PART II of this book. Where the text directs you to 'carry rosemary,' for instance, it should be made into a sachet. These procedures are not necessary in every instance.

Sachets:
Herbs to be carried or placed in the house (over doors, windows, etc.) should be made into sachets. A sachet is a small bag or piece of cloth in which herbs are contained. In voodoo magic this is often called a 'charm bag' or 'root bag.' They are exceedingly easy to make.

Take a small amount of material (square, round or triangular shaped) of the appropriate color. Felt works well and is relatively inexpensive.

Place the enchanted herbs (usually no more than a tablespoon or so) on the center of the material. Gather the ends together and tie with a piece of cord or yarn of a matching color. As you knot the cord firmly visualize your need. (In actual fact, do this during the entire procedure.) Make two more knots and the sachet is finished. The smaller sachets are, the easier they are to carry in the pocket. Household sachets may be made larger since they aren't carried.

Poppets:

This is also known as the 'voodoo doll', although it has been in magical use at least 4,000 years and was only lately associated with voodoo. Though they have been made out of roots, potatoes, lead, bark, paper and other materials, in magical herbalism poppets are usually fashioned of cloth and herbs. The poppet is a doll made to represent the person to be aided through magic.

Poppets are most often made to speed healing, and are also fashioned to draw money, love, and all the various magical needs. For best results *do not* construct a poppet representing another person; only yourself.

Poppets are easy to make: draw a rough outline of a human figure (about eight inches long). Transfer this outline to a piece of cloth doubled-over of the appropriate color. Cut it out so that you have two identical pieces of cloth. Pin these together and begin to sew them around the edges. When three-quarters of the doll is stitched, fill it with the appropriate enchanted herbs. For instance, if I need help in overcoming a cold, I'd stuff the poppet with crushed eucalyptus leaves.

Once the poppet is completed hold it in your power hand and visualize your need. State in plain words that you have fashioned the poppet to aid you in becoming healthy, to draw money, etc.

The herbs within the poppet will go to work in manifesting your need. The poppet filled with healing herbs (for example) represents you 'filled' with health.

Place the poppet on the altar. Burn candles of the proper colors and stare at the poppet, visualizing your need. Store the doll in a safe place when not in use.

After it has done its job, pick it apart and bury the herbs and cloth.

Infusion:

The infusion is the origin of the 'potion' so identified with Witches. It is simply a process of soaking herbs in hot water.

There are some refinements, however. Use no metal pots when boiling water or during the steeping process, for they interfere with the herb's powers. Keep the liquid covered during infusion so that little steam is lost. Finally, enchant all herbs prior to infusion.

Use one teaspoon dried herb to every cup of water. Heat water until just boiling. Pour over the herb and cover. Let steep 9 to 13 minutes. Strain and cool before using.

Infusions are drunk as teas, of course, but they are also added to baths, rubbed onto furniture and floors, and used to anoint the body. Needless to say, never make an infusion of a poisonous plant.

Baths:

Baths are often used in herb magic, for they are an easy way to spread an herb's power over the entire body.

There are two methods; one, make a sachet (use about one-half to one cup of the appropriate enchanted herb) of cheesecloth. Drop this into the warm bath water.

A better method entails the preparation of an infusion (see above). Add the strained liquid to the tub.

Essential oils are also sometimes added to baths. Just a few drops are all that is necessary for most oils; too much may irritate the skin. (See APPENDIX III for oils and their magical powers.)

Ointments:

An old form of herb magic as well as medicine, an ointment is simply any fatty substance to which powdered herbs and/or oils have been added. A good example of this is found in the text under MALLOW. In the past, lard was generally used as the base, but today vegetable shortening is usually substituted. It certainly smells better.

To a cup of shortening or lard, add three tablespoons of the enchanted, powdered herb(s). Pound or mash them together while visualizing until well-mixed, then place in an air-tight container to store.

An alternative method is to melt the base over low heat. Add the herbs and steep for about 9 minutes or until the herb is 'fried'. Strain and allow the ointment to cool before use.

A third method is even easier; melt the lard or shortening, add drops of the appropriate oils, and cool.

Using the ointment is easy: simply apply to the body at the pulse points (wrists, neck, etc.). Such ointments are best stored in air-tight containers in a cool place.

Oils:

Though extracting oils by steam distillation and other methods is almost prohibitively expensive, we are spared this cost by the wide availability of essential oils and synthetics on the market today. Many so-called 'essential oils' are actually

synthetic; this does not negate their use in magic, however. If they smell good, use them.

Though oils aren't covered in this book, a list of them by their uses can be found in APPENDIX III. For commercial suppliers of oils, see APPENDIX II.

Essential oils are used in numerous ways. They are worn on the body, rubbed onto candles, dabbed onto sachets and poppets, added to baths, burned on charcoal blocks and smeared onto roots.

Incense:

Incense composition and use is an art form in itself. Basically, an incense is any combination of plant materials, perhaps combined with essential oils and a base, which are mixed together and burned or smouldered on charcoal. (This type of incense is known as 'raw' or 'granular.' It is usually used in magic, rather than the stick or cone forms.)

In magical use, incense is burned for its vibrations alone as a kind of spell, while visualizing. But it can also be used as a background while performing other types of magic.

In composing your own incense formulae remember that 'more' is not always better. Any recipe requiring over 9 substances is probably too complicated. Simply choose a few plants appropriate to your need. For a love incense, for instance, I might choose lemon balm, cardamom, cinnamon, ginger and vanilla. The herbs are reduced to powder form with the mortar and pestle and then enchanted. The resultant mixture is ready for use.

To use incense, ignite a charcoal block (see APPENDIX II) and place in a heat-proof container. An incense burner is fine, as is a dish half-filled with salt or sand. Sprinkle a small amount of incense on the glowing charcoal every few minutes during your spell.

Remember, however, that many sweetly-scented plants smell quite differently when burning, so don't be surprised if your incense isn't pleasant. The important factors here are the vibrations and not the scents.

FOUR ALL-PURPOSE SPELLS

These spells are designed to be used when no other is available or desired. As with any part of magic they can be altered to suit your tastes and imagination. Most of them should be done outside, but with a little thought they can be performed inside as well.

Though they are related to the four elements* each spell can be used for any magical need, alone or in conjunction with other spells. For example, if I wished to attract a love, I might wear a sachet and then throw herbs onto a roaring ocean, as in the Water spell.

Feel free to make up your own spells when working with herbs; it's perfectly alright and the spell can be tailor-made.

The Earth Spell:

Place the appropriate enchanted herbs in a bag and take to a wild place. With your hands, dig a small hole in the Earth and pour the herbs into it. Visualize your need strongly. Cover the herbs over and leave the area. It is done.

The Air Spell:

Stand in an open place atop a hill or mountain, far from tall trees, buildings, and other hills. Hold the appropriate enchanted herbs in your power hand and, facing North, blow a little of them to that direction. Turn East and repeat the spell, then do so to the South. At the West blow all the herbs far from your hand. Visualize your need strongly all the while, stating it in words if you wish.

---

* See *Earth Power* by Scott Cunningham. Llewellyn Publications.

The Fire Spell:

Write or make a symbol of your need on a piece of paper cut into a triangle. While visualizing your need, place the appropriate enchanted herbs in the center of the paper and crumble it tightly so that the herbs are trapped inside the paper. Anoint with oils if you wish.

Build a roaring fire in an outside pit or indoor fireplace. Throw the herb packet into the fire. As it touches the flames firmly visualize your need. Continue to do so until the packet has been consumed by the flames.

The Water Spell:

Take the appropriate enchanted herbs to a river, spring, lake or seashore. Hold them tightly in your power hand and visualize your need. With a sweeping motion, scatter the herbs onto the water. The power has been sent.

Magical Intentions

Magical intentions are simply magical needs; love is one, money another, and protection a third. This chapter briefly discusses some of the most common magical intentions.

Herbs appropriate to each intention are listed in PART III.

PROTECTION

From the overwhelming number of herbs used for this purpose it is obvious that protection is (and has been) of the utmost concern for many people. Most of the protective herbs mentioned in this book are general in their effects; they guard their bearer against physical and psychic attacks; injury, accidents, poison, snakebite, lightning strikes, wicked spirits, the evil eye and so on. In other words, they are protective in a general way.

Naturally, they won't do you much good once something has happened— protective herbs should be preventatives. This doesn't mean that if you wear a protective root or carry a sachet you'll breeze through life unfettered with annoyances. But carrying some of these herbs will certainly help screen out potentially harmful situations.

In today's world we should guard ourselves with every available means. Protective herbs are one of these. They create a type of force-field around your home, possessions or self. When carried they also increase the effectiveness of your body's natural defenses.

An ounce of prevention, after all, is worth a pound of cure.

LOVE

Ah love; the endless quest for companionship, warmth, sexual contact, emotional fulfillment and someone to talk to over coffee in the morning.

Love magic should be of one type—to attract an unspecified person into your life. Thus, simply stated, love herbs will place you in situations where you will meet people, help you to overcome shyness (if necessary), and communicate that you are more than in the mood for love.

Love herbs (as opposed to lust herbs—see below) extend their gentle, emotional vibrations far and wide in searching for a love. Generally they attract persons in the same frame of mind; love herbs put out the call and those who are interested will answer it.

This is on a subconscious level, of course. No one will walk up to you and say, "Hi. I just couldn't help but notice your love vibrations." But if you use these herbs people will pay more attention to you, and you will meet new friends. From these you may find a love.

Love herbs should not be used to magically force or persuade another human being to love you. Not only is this manipulation of a free soul (how would you feel if someone did it to you?) it also won't work. Love is something that grows from shared experiences and quiet conversation, glances in darkened rooms, interwoven fingers and nights out on the town. Even if it begins with a burst of infatuation, real love is the mellowed product of time.

The most love herbs can do (if one does use them to entrap another person) is to confuse the victim's emotions. At first it might seem to be love to both of you, but it quickly disintegrates into something far less appealing: emotional slavery. Capturing a person with love magic of this sort is little short of psychic rape.

The safest course is to use love herbs to bring several people into your life. The rest is up to you.

EXORCISM

This ancient form of magic comes in handy today—not necessarily to drive demons from people or buildings, but to clear away the negativity that daily living so amply provides.

Purification herbs are simply less-powerful exorcism herbs and usually do not rid a place of evil entities.

HEALING

There are many herbs which aid the body's healing processes. Some of these are multi-purpose and others specific. All can be mixed into sachets which, when carried, help the body's healing powers. Some are used in incense form, others added to the bath.

However, when a serious condition or severe symptoms occur, obtain medical attention immediately. Herb magic—as with all magic—must be backed up with appropriate and timely actions in the physical world. For example, you cannot perform a spell to pass a test and expect to do so without studying. Similarly, don't expect magic to heal you unless at the same time you take care of yourself physically. This means getting medical help when needed.

HEALTH

As with most types of magic, prevention is better than cure, so if you're prone to bad health it might be wise to carry some of these herbs at all times. Replace them regularly (every three months or so).

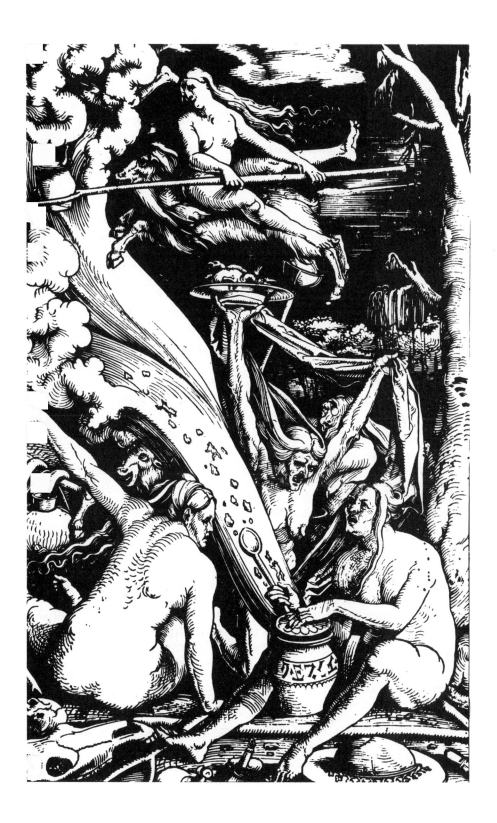

HEX-BREAKING

Many of the requests for information I receive through the mail concern ways of breaking hexes and lifting curses. 99% of these people are not now, and never will be, the target of curses or hexes. Contrary to popular belief, evil magicians don't lurk behind each tree ready to hex everyone out of existence.

When people feel that they have been hexed, cursed, jinxed or psychically attacked, an ordinary cause can usually be traced for the supposed hex. No matter how certain these people are of their condition, they are simply victims of life and their own fears and worries. A run of accidents, mishaps, illnesses, financial and emotional losses, even car trouble will provide the basis for imaginary hexes.

Although most hexes are imaginary, some are not. Additionally, it is a well-attested fact that the mind has a powerful effect on the body. If a person believes him or herself hexed, its physical effects (if any) will usually manifest.

Thus many herbs are used for their traditional ability to remove evil spells and curses. They work—whether a hex exists or not.

FIDELITY

Although magically forcing your loved one to remain faithful is violating one of the precepts of magic (harm none), there are herbs which can be used to gently remind him or her of you, and to guard against unwanted temptations. Use them with love and care.

LUCK

Luck is simply the knack for being in the right place at the right time, saying the right things, and acting on instinct. If a person is not naturally 'lucky' such an ability can be acquired through the use of herbs. How this 'luck' will manifest is left unstated, but luck herbs are usually utilized when a person has had a run of 'bad' luck—and wishes to change this to good.

Luck herbs give you the power to make your own 'good' luck.

LUST

These plants have been used for centuries to create a sexual desire in those near them. Not surprisingly, they are commonly used to arouse another person's lust, perhaps against their will.

However, they are also used as love herbs are, to attract others who desire sexual contacts, and this is certainly less manipulatory than the former use.

MANIFESTATIONS

Some types of magic specialize in raising spirits and 'daemons' to vis—ible appearance, usually within a circle or triangle. These herbs have long been burned so that the smoke can be used by the spirit as a medium in which to materialize.

This magic, though dangerous and difficult to perform, is nonetheless traditional, and so I've included such herbs in this book.

MONEY

These plants increase a person's financial scene; they will not create dollar bills out of thin air. The money may come in the form of unexpected gifts or legacies, but usually it will manifest as a raise in pay, a better job, a good investment, a loan suddenly re-paid to you, and so on.

Magic performed to gain money is quite commonly practiced. However, few people actually need money—they need what money can buy. If I needed enough money to pay my bills, for example, I would use these money herbs while visualizing my bills as being marked 'paid in full' and then disappearing. Give the power direction and it shall flow.

WISHES

Throughout this book I've stressed that magic should be used when needed, perhaps as a last-resort when all other methods have failed. However, we all have wishes that might not be as pressing as a need. These wishes may be emotionally and physically important, however, and so magic can be used to make them 'come true,' and herbs can help this along.

וֹהוֹהִי

PLANTÆ CVIQVE SVAS VIRES DEVS INDIDIT, ATQVE
PRÆSENTEM ESSE ILLVM, QVÆLIBET HERBA DOCET.

The
Herbs

Part II

THEOPHRASTVS   DIOSCORIDES

Each plant is covered by an article of varying amounts of information. For convenience much of this information is summarized in the briefest possible form; thus half of each listing is basically a recitation of nomenclature, planetary and elemental rulers, and so on.

Here is a look at each item:

The first listing is the *common name,* which is simply the most widely-known.

The next is the *scientific name* for both genus and species (if known). This is of the utmost importance, for several herbs share common names and can be easily confused with one another. With this information exact identification can be made and mistakes avoided.

Following are *folk names* by which the plant has been known, if any. Since this information is cross-indexed with the common names a person who knows acacia only as *Egyptian thorn* can locate it with ease, by using the FOLK NAME cross-reference at the back of the book.

Next, the *gender* of the plant is listed. This somewhat confusing aspect of magical herbalism is simply an old way of categorizing herbs by their basic type of vibration. In *Magical Herbalism* I used the terms 'hot' and 'cold' (as did earlier herbalists) to avoid sexist connotations, but this is even more confusing. I still find distaste in identifying bay, for instance, as 'male' and willow as 'female.' Therefore, the terms 'masculine' and 'feminine' are used to denote each plant's gender.

The masculine herbs are those which are possessed of strong, fiery vibrations. These are the herbs which are actually used for protection, purification, hex-breaking, exorcism, lust, to maintain sexual potency, health, strength, courage, and so on. Also any that strengthen the mind.

The feminine herbs are plants which are quieter, subtler, softer in their effects. Thus they are used to attract love, increase beauty, recapture youth, aid in healing and developing psychic powers, increase fertility, draw wealth, promote

·happiness and peace, aid sleep and spirituality and cause visions.

This is, again, a form of classification which has been included because of its traditional importance. It is a useful tool in determining magical uses.

The plant's *ruling planet* is next, if known. While this is not the place to explain planetary magic the heavenly bodies (including the Sun and Moon) have long been associated with various types of magical needs. Here is a quick list:

> SUN: Legal Matters, Healing, Protection
> MOON: Sleep, Prophetic Dreams, Fertility, Peace, Healing
> MERCURY: Mental Powers, Divination, Psychic Powers, Wisdom
> VENUS: Love, Friendship, Fidelity, Beauty, Youth
> MARS: Courage, Strength, Lust, Sexual Potency, Exorcism, Hex-Breaking, Protection
> JUPITER: Money, Prosperity, Legal Matters, Luck
> SATURN: Visions, Longevity, Exorcisms, Endings

The *ruling element* follows, where known. The theory of the four elements, the building blocks of the universe (another method of dividing up the power) is explained more fully in *Earth Power*. However, in brief, four elements (Earth, Air, Fire and Water) are within all things in varying amounts.

This includes herbs. Each, naturally, has its own use in magic:

> EARTH: Money, Prosperity, Fertility, Healing, Employment
> AIR: Mental Powers, Visions, Psychic Powers, Wisdom
> FIRE: Lust, Courage, Strength, Exorcism, Protection, Health
> WATER: Sleep, Meditation, Purification, Prophetic Dreams, Healing, Love, Friendships, Fidelity

As you can plainly see by the above tables the gender, planet and element of each plant are intimately related and, to the expert, provide a wide range of magical information.

Since many plants have been associated with divinities through the centuries, *deities* specifically connected with the plant are listed, if any. This provides yet another clue to the plant's use in magic, for each divinity has one or more influences attributed to them. Venus, as a Goddess of love, is a well-known example; herbs sacred to the Goddess Venus may be used in love spells.

A summation of each herb's *powers* follows for easy reference. This listing may not contain all of the various uses mentioned in the text, however.

If the plant has been used in a religious capacity in any way relevant to herb magic this is listed under *ritual uses.*

Finally, *magical uses* begins the main bulk of each discussion.

Where any of the information isn't available or relevant, it has been omitted.

(Note: If any herb is known to be poisonous in one or more of its parts, the word 'POISON' appears to the right of the common name. These herbs should never be used internally or applied to the skin. Never use any herb internally unless specifically directed to do so. This way you will avoid accidental poisoning.)

ACACIA *(Acacia Senegal)*
Folk Names: Cape Gum, Egyptian Thorn, Gum Arabic Tree
Gender: Masculine
Planet: Sun
Element: Air
Deities: Osiris, Astarte, Ishtar, Diana, Ra
Powers: Protection, Psychic Powers
Ritual Uses: The wood is used as fuel in sacred fires in India, and is also used in building temples.
Magical Uses:

A sprig of the tree placed over the bed wards off evil, as it does when tucked into the turban in Eastern countries.

When the wood is burned with sandlewood the psychic powers are stimulated.

Acacia is also used in money and love spells, although in the latter case the outcome would be a platonic love.

ADAM AND EVE ROOTS *(Orchis* spp.)
Gender: Feminine
Planet: Venus
Element: Water
Power: Love, Happiness
Magical Uses:

Carry the two roots in a small bag at all times to attract a love. If you wish to be free from amatory competitors, also carry the two roots sewn into a small bag. Given to a couple they ensure continued happiness.

ADDER'S TONGUE *(Erythronium americanum)*
Folk Names: American Adder's Tongue, Serpent's tongue, Adder's Mouth
Gender: Feminine
Planet: Moon
Element: Water
Powers: Healing
Magical Uses:

Soak some adder's tongue in cold water and apply it to a wound or bruise (wrap it in a piece of cloth) until the herb grows warm. Next, bury the wet herb in a muddy place. The wound will be cured.

AFRICAN VIOLET *(Saintpaulia ionantha)*
Gender: Feminine
Planet: Venus
Element: Water
Powers: Spirituality, Protection
Magical Uses:
The purple-colored flowers and plants are grown in the home to promote spirituality within it.

The plants are also slightly protective when grown.

AGARIC *(Amanita muscaria)* **POISON**
Folk Names: Death Angel, Death Cap, Magic Mushroom, Redcap Mushroom, **Sacred** Mushroom
Gender: Masculine
Planet: Mercury
Element: Air
Deity: Dionysus
Powers: Fertility
Ritual Uses: There is speculation that at least some of the mystery religions of classical times centered their secret rituals around the use of the *amanita*.
Magical Uses:
Place on the altar or in the bedroom to increase fertility. Unfortunately, the *amanita* is so virulently poisonous that it is unwise to use it.

AGRIMONY *(Agrimonia eupatoria)*
Folk Names: Church Steeples, Cocklebur, Garclive, Philanthropos, Sticklewort, Stickwort
Gender: Masculine
Planet: Jupiter
Element: Air
Powers: Protection, sleep
Magical Uses:
Use in all protection sachets and spells, also to banish negative energies and spirits. It protects against goblins, evil and poison.

Agrimony has also long been used to reverse spells sent against the magician; i.e. it not only breaks hexes, it also sends them back to the hexer.

Agrimony placed under the head will make one sleep as if dead, according to ancient lore, but don't use this for insomnia: the sleeper won't awaken until the herb is removed.

At one time agrimony was used to detect the presence of Witches.

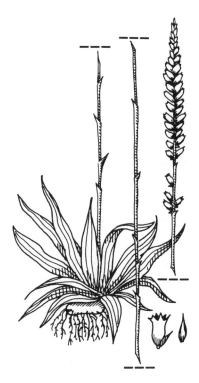

AGUE ROOT *(Aletris farinosa)*
Folk Names: Ague Grass, Bitter Grass, Black-Root, Crow Corn, Stargrass, Starwort, True Unicorn Root, Unicorn Root
Powers: Protection
Magical Uses:

Sprinkle around your home to keep evil at bay, or carry in a sachet for the same purpose.

Also, use in hex-breaking and uncrossing rituals and mixtures.

ALFALFA *(Medicago sativa)*
Folk Names: Buffalo Herb, Lucerne, Purple Medic
Gender: Feminine
Planet: Venus
Element: Earth
Powers: Prosperity, Anti-Hunger, Money
Magical Uses:

Keep in the home to protect from poverty and hunger. It is best placed in a small jar in the cupboard or pantry. Also, burn alfalfa and scatter the ashes around the property for this purpose.

Alfalfa is also used in money spells.

ALKANET *(Anchusa spp.)*
Gender: Feminine
Element: Water
Powers: Purification, Prosperity
Magical Uses:

Alkanet is burned as an incense to

purify the area of negativity, and is also used to attract prosperity in all its forms.

ALLSPICE *(Pimenta officinalis or P. dioica)*
Gender: Masculine
Planet: Mars
Element: Fire
Powers: Money, Luck, Healing
Magical Uses:

Allspice is burned as an incense to attract money or luck, and is also added to such mixtures.

Allspice is also used to promote healing.

ALMOND *(Prunus dulcis)*
Gender: Masculine
Planet: Mercury
Element: Air
Deities: Attis, Mercury, Thoth, Hermes
Powers: Money, Prosperity, Wisdom
Magical Uses:

Almonds, as well as the leaves and wood of the tree, are used in prosperity and money spells. Additionally, climbing an almond tree is said to ensure success in business ventures.

Eating almonds will cure or combat fevers as well as give the partaker wisdom. Five almonds eaten before drinking prevents intoxication.

Magical wands are made of almond wood, for it is a plant of Air, which is the elemental ruler of the magic wand, in some traditions.

Finally, placing almonds in your pocket will lead you to treasures.

ALOE *(Aloe vera, A. spp.)*
Folk Names: Burn Plant, Medicine Plant
Gender: Feminine
Planet: Moon
Element: Water
Powers: Protection, Luck
Magical Uses:

The aloe, a popular house plant, is

also protective. It guards against evil influences and prevents household accidents. In Africa the aloe is hung over houses and doors to drive away evil, as well as to bring good luck.

In Mexico, large wreathes made of whole garlic bulbs strung on wire are festooned with pictures of saints, packets of magical herbs, lodestones, rock salt, pine nuts as well as clumps of freshly-cut aloe. These are hung up in the home for protection, luck, money, and so on.

ALOES, WOOD *(Aquilaria agallocha)*
Folk Names: Lignum Aloes
Gender: Feminine
Planet: Venus
Element: Water
Powers: Love, Spirituality
Magical Uses:
    Although almost totally unavailable

today, wood aloes have been used in magic for so many centuries that some mention of it has to be made here.

Anciently, it was used to attract good fortune in Egypt, and burned as incense in magical evocatory rites during the Renaissance. It possesses high spiritual vibrations, and will bring love if carried or worn.

Modern magical herbalists use wood aloes as a strengthening herb, by adding a small amount to other mixtures to intensify their powers.

ALTHEA *(Althaea officinalis)*
Folk Names: Marshmallow, Mortification Root, Sweet Weed, Wymote
Gender: Feminine
Element: Water
Powers: Protection, Psychic Powers
Magical Uses:

Althea has long been used in protection rites, and it also is a good psychic power-stimulator. Burn as incense for this purpose, or carry in a sachet.

Althea is also known to be a good 'spirit-puller', i.e. it brings good spirits in during rituals when placed on the altar. This is a popular voodoo practice.

ALYSSUM *(Alyssum spp.)*
Folk Names: Alison, Madwort
Powers: Protection, Moderating Anger
Magical Use:

Dioscorides recommended the alyssum as an amulet, for it has the power to 'expell charms.' Hung up in the house it protects against fascination, that magical process which is also known as 'glamour.'

Alyssum also has the power to cool down an angry person if placed in the hand or on the body, and was even said to cure hydrophobia (rabies).

AMARANTH *(Amaranthus hypochondriacus)*

Folk Names: Flower of Immortality, *Huauhtli* (Aztec), Love-Lies Bleeding, Red Cockscomb, Velvet Flower
Gender: Feminine
Planet: Saturn
Element: Fire
Deity: Artemis
Powers: Healing, Protection, Invisibility
Ritual Uses: The amaranth was used in pagan burial rituals. It was also once outlawed by Spanish colonial authority in Mexico because it was used by Aztecs in their rituals.
Magical Uses:

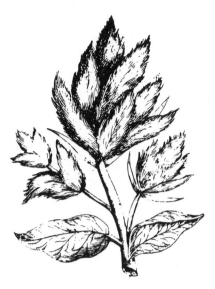

A crown of amaranth flowers worn on the head speeds healing. To make sure that you are never struck by a bullet, pull up a whole amaranth plant (including roots) preferably on a Friday during the Full Moon. Leave an offering to the plant and then fold it, roots and all, in a piece of white cloth. Wear this against your breast and you'll be 'bullet-proof.'

The dried amaranth flowers have been used to call forth the dead, and are also carried to 'cure the affections', i.e. to mend a broken heart.

A wreath of amaranth worn confers invisibility.

ANEMONE *(Anemone pulsatilla)*
Folk Names: Meadow Anemone, Pasque Flower, Passe Flower, Wind Flower
Gender: Masculine
Planet: Mars
Element: Fire
Deities: Adonis, Venus
Powers: Health, Protection, Healing
Magical Uses:

Gather the blossoms when first seen in the spring, wrap them up in a red cloth and wear or carry to prevent disease.

Grow red anemones in the garden to protect both it and the home.

Use the blossoms in all healing rituals.

ANGELICA *(Angelica Archangelica)*
Folk Names: Archangel, Masterwort
Gender: Masculine
Planet: Sun
Element: Fire
Deity: Venus
Powers: Exorcism, Protection, Healing,
    Visions
Magical Uses:

Grown, the plant is protective. Use in all protection and exorcism incenses. Sprinkle the four corners of the house with angelica to ward off evil, or do this around the perimeter of the house. Added to the bath angelica removes curses, hexes and any spells that may have been cast against you.

The root was carried in the pocket as a gambling talisman among some American Indian tribes.

Angelica is also used in healing incenses and mixtures, and smoking the leaves is said to cause visions.

ANISE *(Pimpinella anisum)*
Folk Names: Anneys, Aniseed
Gender: Masculine
Planet: Jupiter
Element: Air
Powers: Protection, Purification, Youth
Magical Uses:

Fill a small pillowcase with anise seeds and sleep on it. This will ensure that you have no nightmares.

Use in protection and meditation incenses. Fresh anise leaves placed in a room will drive off evil, and they are sometimes placed around the magic circle to protect the magician from evil spirits. It also averts the evil eye.

Anise seed is also used in purification baths, especially with bay leaves.

It is used to call forth spirits to aid in magical operations, and a sprig hung on the bedpost will restore lost youth.

APPLE *(Pyrus* spp.)

Folk Names: Fruit of the Gods, Fruit of the Underworld, Silver Branch, The Silver Bough, Tree of Love

Gender: Feminine

Planet: Venus

Element: Water

Deities: Venus, Dionysus, Olwen, Apollo, Hera, Athena, Aphrodite, Diana, Zeus, Iduna

Powers: Love, Healing, Garden Magic, Immortality

Ritual Uses:

August 13 was Diana's Festival in Greece (Venus' in Rome) and on this day a ritual meal was prepared, part of which consisted of apples still hanging on their boughs.

Wiccan altars are often piled high with apples on Samhain for the apple is considered to be one of the foods of the dead. For this very reason Samhain is sometimes known as 'Feast of Apples'.

The apple is a symbol of immortality. A branch of the apple which bore buds, flowers and fully-ripened fruit (sometimes known as the Silver Bough), was a kind of magical charm which enabled its possessor to enter into the land of the Gods, the Underworld, in Celtic mythology.

In the old English ballad, *Thomays the Rymour* (Thomas the Rhymer), the Fairy Queen warns Thomas against eating any of the apples and pears which hung in her garden, for to eat the food of the dead ensures there will be no return to the world of the living.

In some Wiccan traditions, the apple is a symbol of the soul, and so they are buried on Samhain so that those, who will be reborn in the spring will have food during the cold winter months.

Magical Uses:

The apple has long been used in spells of love. The blossoms are added to love sachets, brews and incenses, and they are

infused in melted pink wax, then strained out, to make candles suitable to burn for attracting love.

A simple apple love spell consists of cutting an apple in half and sharing it with your loved one. This ensures that you will be happy together.

A similar spell directs you to hold an apple in your hands until warm, and then give it to your intended. If he or she eats it your love will be returned.

Apples are also used in love divinations, which were so popular among unmarried women in Europe for many centuries. Simply cut an apple in two and count the number of seeds. If they are even, marriage will soon occur. If one of the seeds is cut it may be a stormy relationship. If two are cut, widowhood is foretold. However, if an uneven number of seeds are found the woman will remain unmarried in the near future.

One last apple love spell. Take an apple 'before it falls from the tree' and write upon it with a sharp knife the following:

Aleo + Deleo + Delato

As you do this say the following words:

I conjure thee, apple, by these
names which are written on thee,
that what woman (or man) toucheth
and tasteth thee, may love me and
burn in my love as fire melteth wax.

Then give the apple to whom you will— but be warned, for this (like much love magic) borders on manipulation.

For healing, cut an apple into three pieces, rub each on the affected part of the body, and then bury them. Do this during the waning of the Moon to banish illnesses.

To insure that you do not contract a fever, eat an apple.

If you are a gardener, pour cider onto freshly-turned earth to give it life just before planting. Also pour libations on roots just before tree rituals. And if you

grow apples, bury thirteen leaves of an apple tree after harvest to ensure a good crop of apples next year.

The Norse, as well as many other peoples, ate apples to gain immortality through wisdom, and the wood of the apple tree can be made into charms for longevity.

Apple wood also makes excellent magical wands, especially suited to emotional magic, as well as love rites.

Use apple cider in place of blood where it is called for in old recipes.

Apples can be fashioned into poppets or magical figures for use in spells, or images can be carved from the wood itself.

Before eating any apple, rub it to remove any demons or evil spirits which might be hiding inside. (You can't be too careful!)

Finally, unicorns live beneath apple trees (as well as those of the ash), and so if you know of an apple orchard, quietly go there on a misty day. You may see a single horn upraised and a horse-like animal quietly munching sweet, magical apples.

APRICOT *(Prunus Armeniaca)*
Gender: Feminine
Planet: Venus
Element: Water
Deity: Venus
Powers: Love
Magical Uses:

Eat the fruit to obtain a sweet disposition, or use the juice in love spells and 'potions'.

The leaves and flowers can be added to love sachets, and the pits are carried to attract love.

ARABIC, GUM *(Acacia vera)*
Folk Names: Arabic, Egyptian Gum, Indian Gum

Gender: Masculine
Planet: Sun
Element: Air
Powers: Spirituality, Purification
Magical Uses:

Add to incenses for good vibrations, or smoulder alone on charcoal. Purifies the area of negativity and evil.

ARBUTUS *(Arbutus unede)*
Gender: Masculine
Planet: Mars
Element: Fire
Deity: Cardea
Powers: Exorcism, Protection
Magical Uses:

The Romans used it to chase away evil, and also to protect little children. It is also used in exorcisms, and has been since the time of ancient Greece.

ASAFOETIDA *(Ferula foetida)*
Folk Names: Assyfetida, Devil's Dung, Food of the Gods
Gender: Masculine
Planet: Mars
Element: Fire
Powers: Exorcism, Purification, Protection
Magical Uses:

Burn small amounts in exorcism and protection incenses. Also use in protection sachets, but only if you want to smell odd. Destroys manifestations of spirits if thrown onto a fire or into the censer during magical rites.

Sometimes used as an amulet to keep away colds and fevers, and for this purpose is usually worn around the neck.

Unfortunately, though asafoetida is undoubtedly powerful, it also has a particularly horrid odor. Just the slightest suggestion of the fragrance has caused vomiting. Use with care.

ASH *(Fraxinus excelsior* or *F. americana)*
Folk Name: Nion

PARADISI IN SOLE
Paradisus Terrestris.
Or
A Garden of all sorts of pleasant flowers which our
English ayre will permitt to be noursed vp:
with
A Kitchen garden of all manner of herbes, roots, & fruites,
for meate or sause vsed with vs.
and
An Orchard of all sorte of frutebearing Trees
and shrubbes fit for our Land
together
With the right ordering planting & preseruing
of them and their vses & vertues
Collected by John Parkinson
Apothecary of London
1629

Gender: Masculine
Planet: Sun
Element: Fire
Deities: Uranus, Poseidon, Thor, Woden, Neptune, Mars, Gwydion
Powers: Protection, Prosperity, Sea Rituals, Health

Ritual Uses:

The ash, to the ancient Teutons, represented Ygdrasill, or the world tree, which was their conception of the universe, and was therefore reverenced.

Magical Uses:

Carve a piece of ash wood into a solar cross (equal-armed) and carry as a protection against drowning while at sea. It is also used in sea rituals, for it represents the power which resides in water.

The leaves of the ash when placed beneath the pillow induce prophetic dreams.

It is, as with most trees, considered to be protective. A staff of ash hung over the doorposts wards off malign influences, and at one time a garter made of the green bark was worn as a protectant against the powers or sorcerers and conjurers. The leaves are also scattered to the four directions to protect a house or area, and are used in protective sachets and spells.

Healing wands are sometimes fashioned of ash wood, and a few ash leaves placed in a bowl of water next to the bed, left overnight, will prevent illnesses. The water should be discarded each morning and the rite repeated each night.

If any person or animal has been bitten by a snake, make a circlet of ash twigs and tie it around the victim's neck (whether it be human or otherwise) and it will cure them. (Of course, it would not hurt to get the snakebite kit and call a doctor as well.) This spell probably works because snakes have an innate fear of the ash tree; they will not crawl over its wood.

If you burn ash wood at Yule, you will receive prosperity, and poppets may be carved from the roots of the ash.

The ash attracts lightning, so don't stand beneath one during an electrical storm.

If you wish your new-born to be a good singer, bury it's first nail parings under an ash tree.

And to gain the love of the opposite sex, carry the leaves.

ASPEN *(Populus* spp.)
Folk Names: European Aspen
Gender: Masculine
Planet: Mercury
Element: Air
Powers: Eloquence, Anti-Theft
Magical Uses:

Use in anti-theft spells, and plant an aspen in your garden or field to be protected from thieves.

Place an aspen leaf under your tongue if you wish to become eloquent.

ASTER *(Callistephus chinensis)*
Folk Names: China Aster, Michaelmas Daisy, Starwort
Gender: Feminine
Planet: Venus
Element: Water
Deity: Venus
Power: Love
Ritual Uses:

The aster was sacred to all the gods, and was placed on temple altars during festive occasions by the classical Greeks.
Magical Uses:

Use in love sachets, or carry the bloom to win love. Also grow in the garden with a wish for love.

AVENS *(Geum urbanum)*
Folk Names: Assaranaccara, Bennet, Blessed Herb, Clove Root, Colewort, Golden Star, Goldy Star, Harefoot,

Herb Bennet, Minarta, Pesleporis, Star of the Earth, Way Bennet, Yellow Avens

Gender: Masculine
Planet: Jupiter
Element: Fire
Powers: Exorcism, Purification, Love
Magical Uses:

Add to exorcism incenses and mixtures, or sprinkle around the area to be exorcised. Also used in purification rites.

When worn or carried as an amulet, it protects against the attacks of all venemous beasts.

Employed by male American Indians to gain the love of the opposite sex.

AVOCADO *(Persea americana)*
Folk Names: *Ahuacotl* (Aztec: 'Testicle Tree'), Alligator Pear, Persea
Gender: Feminine
Planet: Venus
Element: Water
Powers: Love, Lust, Beauty
Ritual Uses: The Egyptians revered the persea.
Magical Uses:

Eat the fruit of the avocado to become infused with lust, as the ancient Aztecs did.

Grow a plant from the pit of an avocado in your home to bring love into it.

Magical wands made of avocado wood are potent all-purpose instruments.

Carry the pit to promote beauty.

BACHELOR'S BUTTONS *(Centaurea cyanus)*
Folk Names: Devil's Flower, Red Campion
Gender: Feminine
Planet: Venus
Element: Water
Deity: Robin Goodfellow
Power: Love
Magical Uses:

Women wear this flower on their

breast to attract the love of a man. Or, take a flower and put it in your pocket. It will lose or retain its freshness in accordance with bad or good success in amatory pursuits.

BALM, LEMON *(Melissa officinalis)*
Folk Names: Bee Balm, Lemon Balsam, Melissa, Sweet Balm, Sweet Melissa
Gender: Feminine
Planet: Moon
Element: Water
Powers: Love, Success, Healing
Magical Uses:

From Arabian herb magic comes the information that lemon balm can be used to influence love. Soak the herb in wine for several hours, strain and share with a friend. Or, carry the herb with you to find love.

It is also used in magical healing, and Pliny said that its powers were so great that if it was attached to a sword that had made a wound the blood would be immediately staunched. Though sword-wounds are rare today, the lemon balm is still used in healing incenses and sachets.

It can also be used in spells to ensure success, and if you keep bees, rub this herb on the hives; it will attract new bees and keep the old ones there.

BALM OF GILEAD *(Commiphora opobalsamum)*
Folk Names: Balessan, Balsam Tree, Balsumodendron Gileadensis, Bechan, Mecca Balsam
Gender: Feminine
Planet: Venus
Element: Water
Powers: Love, Manifestations, Protection, Healing
Magical Uses:

Carry the buds of the balm of Gilead to mend a broken heart, or to attract a new love. Also steep them in red wine for

a simple love drink.

Burn as a material basis for spirits, and also carry for protective and healing purposes.

BAMBOO *(Bambusa vulgaris)*
Folk Names: Common Bamboo, *Ohe* (Hawaiian)
Gender: Masculine
Deity: Hina
Powers: Protection, Luck, Hex-Breaking, Wishes
Ritual Uses:

Bamboo is used in divination in Chinese temples. Bits of the wood are thrown to the worshipper by the priest. According to the way they fall, the omen is interpreted as good or bad.

Magical Uses:

Carve your wish on a piece of bamboo and bury in the ground in a secluded place. Or, carve a symbol of protection, like a five-pointed star (pentagram), on a length of bamboo and plant it in the ground to protect your home.

Grown near the house, bamboo gives it and its residents good fortune. Also, bamboo is placed over the door because, since its wood never changes color, it is lucky.

Bamboo is used to break hexes, either by carrying it in a sachet, growing a plant near the house, or crushing the wood to a powder (called bamba wood) and burning.

The Chinese use the bamboo as a charm against evil spirits. To call up good spirits, make a flute out of bamboo. Carve the name of the spirit (if any) and play an improvised melody.

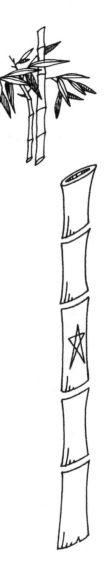

BANANA *(Musa sapientum)*
Folk Names: *Maia* (Hawaiian)
Gender: Feminine
Planet: Venus
Element: Water
Deity: Kanaloa

Powers: Fertility, Potency, Prosperity
Ritual Uses:

In sacrifices to the Gods, a banana stalk was sometimes used as a substitute for a human, both in Hawaii and Tahiti. Until the *kapu* (code of taboos) in Hawaii was broken in 1819, certain kinds of bananas were among foods forbidden to women on pain of death. The banana plant is also used in contemporary voodoo rites, in which it represents the gods, since both they and the banana's flowers are hermaphroditic.

Magical Uses:

The banana is used to increase fertility, and also to cure impotency. Perhaps because of these magical powers, if a bride is married under a banana tree she cannot help being lucky.

The leaves, flowers and fruits of the banana are used in money and prosperity spells, due to the tree's fruitfulness.

Curiously enough, an old belief tells us that a banana should never be cut, only broken.

BANYAN *(Ficus benghalensis)*
Folk Names: Arched Fig, Indian Fig Tree, Indian God Tree, Vada Tree
Gender: Masculine
Planet: Jupiter
Element: Air
Deity: Maui
Powers: Luck
Ritual Uses: The banyan is reverenced by the Hindus, and the tree is planted outside around their temples. It is also connected with the worship of Maui in Hawaiian and Polynesian religions.
Magical Uses:

To simply sit beneath or look at a banyan tree brings good luck, and to be married under one ensures the couple's happiness.

BARLEY *(Hordeum* spp.)
Gender: Feminine
Planet: Venus
Element: Earth
Powers: Love, Healing, Protection
Magical Uses:

Use the grain or barley water in love spells.

If you have a toothache, it can be cured with barley. Wind a barley straw around a stone, visualizing your pain into the stone. Now throw it into a river or any running water, and see your pain being washed away.

Barley may be scattered on the ground to keep evil and negativity away.

BASIL *(Ocimum Basilicum)*
Folk Names: Albahaca, American Dittany, 'Our Herb.' St. Joseph's Wort, Sweet Basil, Witches Herb
Gender: Masculine
Planet: Mars
Element: Fire
Deities: Vishnu, Erzulie
Powers: Love, Exorcism, Wealth, Flying, Protection
Magical Uses:

The scent of fresh basil causes sympathy between two people, and this is why it is used to sooth tempers betwixt lovers. It is added to love incenses and sachets, and the fresh leaves are rubbed against the skin as a kind of natural love perfume. In Eastern Europe it was once thought that a young man would love any woman from whose hand he accepted a sprig of basil.

Basil is also used in love divinations. Place two fresh basil leaves upon a live coal. If they lie where you put them and burn quickly to ashes, the marriage (or relationship) will be harmonious. If there is a certain amount of crackling the life of the pair will be disturbed by quarrels. And if the leaves fly apart with

fierce crackling the projected relationship is undesireable.

Do you want to know if someone is chaste or promiscuous? Simply lay a sprig of fresh basil on their hand. It will immediately wither if that person is 'light of love.'

Basil brings wealth to those who carry it in their pockets, and is used to attract customers to a place of business by placing some in the cash register or on the doorsill.

The basil is also used to ensure that one's mate remains true. Sprinkle basil powder over your body thoroughly while he or she is asleep, especially over the heart, and fidelity will bless your relationship.

Basil is strewn onto floors, because where it is, no evil can live. It is also used in exorcism incenses and in purification baths. Small amounts are sometimes placed in each room of the house to bring protection.

Basil is also used to keep goats away from your property, to attract scorpions, and to prevent inebriation.

Witches were said to drink about ½ cup of basil juice before flying off into the air.

Basil can also be used to diet, but only by a second party's help, and without the dieter's knowledge. According to an ancient spell, a woman (or a man, presumably) will not be able to eat a bite from any dish if, secretly, basil has been placed beneath it.

Basil given as a gift brings good luck to a new home.

BAY *(Laurus nobilis)*

Folk Names: Baie, Bay Laurel, Bay Tree, Daphne, Greecian Laurel, Laurel, Laurier d'Apollon, Laurier Sauce, Lorbeer, Noble Laurel, Roman Laurel, Sweet Bay

Gender: Masculine
Planet: Sun
Element: Fire
Deities: Aesculapius, Apollo, Ceres, Faunus, Eros
Powers: Protection, Psychic Powers, Healing, Purification, Strength
Ritual Uses:

The ancient priestesses of Apollo chewed bay leaves to induce a prophetic state, and also inhaled their fumes. Bay leaves are used as decorations at Yule.

Magical Uses:

Bay is used in clairvoyance and wisdom brews, although its taste is strong. Bay leaves are placed beneath the pillow to induce prophetic dreams, and are also burned to cause visions.

It is a protection and purification herb *par excellence* and is worn as an amulet to ward off negativity and evil, burned or scattered during exorcism rituals, placed in the windows to protect against lightning, and hung up to prevent poltergeists from working any mischief in the house. A sprig of bay is used to sprinkle water during purification ceremonies, and the tree planted near the home protects its inhabitants against sickness. Bay leaves mixed with sandalwood can be burned to remove curses and evil spells.

To ensure that a love will stay, the couple should break off a twig from the tree, then break this in two, each keeping a half.

Bay leaves give strength to those engaged in wrestling and athletic sports if worn at the time of competition.

Wishes are written on bay leaves which are then burned to make them come true, and a bay leaf held in the mouth wards off bad luck.

BEAN *(Phaseolus* spp.)
Folk Names: Poor Man's Meat
Gender: Masculine

Planet: Mercury
Element: Air
Deities: Demeter, Cardea
Powers: Protection, Exorcism, Wart Charming, Reconciliations, Potency, Love

Ritual Uses:

The bean's flower is white, and hence sacred to the Goddesses of old Europe. According to tradition only the highest-ranking priestess in Scotland could either plant or cook the bean. Beans, along with pork, were offered to Cardea in Rome on June 1st. They are also associated with the Underworld and the dead; and in ancient Rome they were distributed and eaten during funerals.

Magical Uses:

In general, beans were used in classical times (and still are) as a charm against evil sorcerers. Put a bean in your mouth and spit it out at the person. Dried beans are carried as an amulet against negativity and evil magic. They are also used in rattles to scare away spirits, especially those who have entered into bodies and made those people sick. To avert evil spirits, say very quickly three times in one breath, 'Three blue beans in a blue bladder. Rattle, bladder, rattle'.

If a couple is quarreling, the woman should carry three lima beans strung on a silk thread for two days. The couple will quickly smooth over their difficulties.

Beans help cure impotency if they are carried or eaten. This is due to the fact that they resemble testicles.

A bean love spell: a woman should place seven beans of any kind in a circle on the ground. Next, she must have the man of her choice step into the circle or walk over it. If this can be done, he will be attracted to her. (But this might also be manipulatory.)

To cure warts, rub a dried bean on each wart during the waning Moon. As you do

this say:
> *As this bean decays,*
> *So wart, fall away!*

BEDSTRAW, FRAGRANT *(Galium triflorum)*
Folk Names: Cleavers, Madder's Cousin
Gender: Feminine
Planet: Venus
Element: Water
Power: Love
Magical Uses:

Fragrant bedstraw is worn or carried to attract love.

BEECH *(Fagus sylvatica)*
Folk Names: Bok, Boke, Buche, Buk, Buke, Faggio, Fagos, Faya, Haya, Hetre
Gender: Feminine
Planet: Saturn
Powers: Wishes
Magical Uses:

Take a stick of beech, scratch or carve your wishes onto it, bury it in the ground and leave it there. Your wish will come true if it is to be.

Carry the wood or leaves to increase creative powers.

BEET *(Beta vulgaris)*
Gender: Feminine
Planet: Saturn
Element: Earth
Power: Love
Magical Uses:

If a man and woman eat of the same beet, they will fall in love.

Beet juice is used as an ink in love magic, and is also a blood substitute.

BELLADONNA *(Atropa belladonna)* **POISON**
Folk Names: Banewort, Black Cherry, Deadly Nightshade, Death's Herb, Devil's Cherries, Divale, Dwale, Dwaleberry, Dwayberry, Fair Lady, Great Morel, Naughty Man's Cherries, Sor-

cerer's Berry, Witch's Berry
Gender: Feminine
Planet: Saturn
Element: Water
Deities: Hecate, Bellona, Circe
Ritual Uses:

The priests of Bellona, according to ancient tradition, drank an infusion of belladonna prior to worshipping Her and invoking Her aid. Bellona is the Roman Goddess of war.

Magical Uses:

Today belladonna is little-used in herb magic due to its high toxicity—all parts of the plant are extremely poisonous and there are still reports of death resulting from accidental ingestion of nightshade.

In the past it was used to encourage astral protection and to produce visions, but safer alternatives are available today and belladonna is best avoided.

BENZOIN *(Styrax benzoin)*
Folk Names: Ben, Benjamen, Gum Benzoin, Siam Benzoin, Siamese Benzoin
Gender: Masculine
Planet: Sun
Element: Air
Powers: Purification, Prosperity
Magical Uses:

Burn benzoin to purify, and add to purification incenses. A fine 'clearing' herb.

Make an incense of benzoin, cinnamon and basil, and burn to attract customers to your place of business.

Often used as a base for incenses.

Benzoin can be substituted for storax, to which it is related.

BERGAMOT, ORANGE *(Mentha citrata)*
Folk Names: Bergamot, Orange Mint
Gender: Masculine
Planet: Mercury
Element: Air
Powers: Money

Magical Uses:

The leaves of the orange bergamot are slipped into wallets and purses to attract money. Fresh leaves are also rubbed onto money before spending it to ensure its return.

Also used in 'success' rituals and spells.

BE-STILL *(Thevetia nereifolia)* **POISON**
Folk Names: Trumpet Flower, Yellow Oleander
Powers: Luck
Magical Uses:

In Sri Lanka, the seeds are known as 'lucky beans' and are worn as talismans or charms to attract luck.

(Not Shown)

BETONY, WOOD *(Betonica officinalis)*
Folk Names: Bishopwort, Lousewort, Purple Betony
Gender: Masculine
Planet: Jupiter
Element: Fire
Powers: Protection, Purification, Love
Magical Uses.

Betony has long been celebrated as a protective and purificatory herb. The pseudo-Apuleius said that the plant protected the wearer's soul as well as the body, and that when placed beneath the pillow it shielded the sleeper from visions and dreams. Betony is added to purification and protection mixtures and incenses, and it is traditional on Midsummer to burn it on a bonfire and then jump through the smoke to purify the body of ills and evil.

Betony is also grown in gardens to protect the home, and is scattered near doors and windows. This forms a kind of protective wall around the property through which no evil can pass.

Betony is also a good plant to carry when making love advances, and is said to reunite quarelling couples if the plant is added to food.

Additionally, betony prevents intoxication if carried, strengthens the body when worn, and is a cure for the mysterious disease known as 'elf-sickness'.

BIRCH *(Betula alba)*
Folk Names: Beithe, Bereza, Berke, Beth, Bouleau, Lady of the Woods
Gender: Feminine
Planet: Venus
Element: Water
Deity: Thor
Powers: Protection, Exorcism, Purification
Magical Uses:

Birch twigs have been used to exorcise spirits by gently striking possessed people or animals, since the birch is a purificatory or cleansing herb.

The tree is also used for protection, and Russians used to hang a red ribbon around the stem of a birch to rid themselves of the evil eye. The birch also protects against lightning.

The traditional broom of the Witches was made of birch twigs, and cradles were once manufactured from birch wood to protect their helpless charges.

BISTORT *(Polygonum bistorta)*
Folk names: Dragonwort, Easter Giant, English Serpentary, Osterick, Passions, Patience Dock, Red Legs, Snakeweed, Sweet Dock
Gender: Feminine
Planet: Saturn
Element: Earth
Powers: Psychic Powers, Fertility
Magical Uses:

Carry bistort if you wish to conceive. Burn with frankincense to improve psychic powers, or when using divination.

The infusion sprinkled about a place will drive out poltergeists.

Bistort is carried in money attracting sachets and is added to wealth and money incenses.

BITTERSWEET *(Celastrus scandens;*   **POISON**
  Solanum dulcamara)
Gender: Masculine
Planet: Mercury
Element: Air
Powers: Protection, Healing
Magical Uses:

Some bittersweet placed beneath the pillow will help you in forgetting a past love.

The bittersweet is also used to protect against and to remove evil from both humans and animals, by tying a small piece of the herb somewhere on the body.

Tied to the neck, bittersweet cures vertigo or dizziness of the head, according to Culpeper.

BLACKBERRY *(Rubus villosus)*
Folk Names: Bly, Bramble, Bramble-Kite, Bumble-Kite, Cloudberry, Dewberry, Goutberry, High Blackberry, Thimbleberry
Gender: Feminine
Planet: Venus
Element: Water
Deity: Brigit
Powers: Healing, Money, Protection
Ritual Uses:

Blackberry was considered to be sacred to some of the old Pagan deities of Europe, and was used in worship. To the present day, blackberry pies are baked on Lughnasadh (August 2) by some of the Wiccans in commemoration of the harvest, seen poetically as the death of the God.
Magical Uses:

A bramble bush that forms a natural arch is a great aid to magical healing. On a sunny day, crawl through the arch backward and then forward three times, going as nearly east to west as possible. This will cause boils, rheumatism, whooping cough and even blackheads to disappear.

The blackberry leaves are used in spells of wealth, as are the berries themselves, and the vines are protective if grown.

The blackberry plant is also used to heal scalds by dipping nine blackberry leaves in spring water and then laying them against the wound gently, while saying the following chant three times to each leaf (27 times in all):

Three ladies came from the east,
One with fire and two with frost.
Out with fire, in with frost.

This is an old invocation to Brigit, the ancient Celtic Goddess of poetry, healing and smithcraft.

BLADDERWRACK *(Fucus visiculosus;* various other plants)

Folk Names: Bladder Fucus, Cutweed, Kelp, Sea Spirit, Seawrack, Seetang

Gender: Feminine

Planet: Moon

Element: Water

Powers: Protection, Sea Spells, Wind Spells, Money, Psychic Powers

Magical Uses:

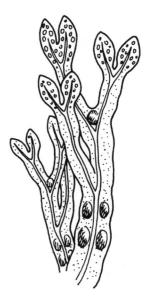

Seaweeds generally give protection to those at sea, or those who are flying over it. Therefore, intercontinental travellers should carry this plant. It is also used in sea spells to summon the spirits of the sea, by throwing it onto the waves and calling them. This will gain their favor and they will aid your magic.

Kelp is used to summon the winds, stand on the shore and hold a long strand of the fresh seaweed in your hand, whip it around in the air above your head in a clockwise direction and whistle. The winds will come.

Make an infusion of the plant and scrub the floors and doors of a place of business to attract customers and bring good vibrations into the store. Also use in all money spells. A particularly potent spell entails simply filling a small jar with whiskey, placing some kelp in it, capping tightly, and placing this in the kitchen window. This will ensure a steady flow of money into the household.

Bladderwrack is also used in sachets to increase psychic powers and carried to protect against mental derangement.

BLEEDING HEART *(Dicentra spectabilis or D. formosa)*
Gender: Feminine
Planet: Venus
Element: Water
Powers: Love
Magical Uses:

Crush the flower. If the juice is red, your love has a heart full of love for you. But if it is white, he or she doesn't love you. When grown, the plant brings love.

The bleeding heart, when grown indoors has the reputation of producing negative vibrations. To forestall this, plant a coin in the soil and all will be right.

BLOODROOT *(Sanguinaria canadensis)* **POISON**
Folk Names: King Root, Red Root
Gender: Masculine
Planet: Mars
Element: Fire
Powers: Love, Protection, Purification
Magical Uses:

The root is carried or worn to draw love. It is also carried to avert evil spells and negativity. Place near doorways and windowsills so the home will be protected. The darkest red roots are considered to be the best, and are known as 'king roots', or 'he roots'.

BLUEBELL *(Campanula rotundifolia)*
Folk Names: Harebell
Powers: Luck, Truth
Magical Uses:

If you can turn a bluebell inside out without tearing or damaging it, you will eventually have the one you love.

The next time you see a bluebell, pick it and repeat the following words:

January—Snowdrop

February—Primrose

March—Violet

April—Daisy

May—Hawthorn

June—Honeysuckle

The Flowers of the Months, from an old English Calendar, 1866

> *Bluebell, bluebell, bring me some*
> *luck before tomorrow night.*

Slip it into your shoe to seal the spell.

Anyone who wears a bluebell is compelled to tell the truth in all matters.

BLUEBERRY *(Vaccinum frondosum)*
Folk Names: Bilberry
Power: Protection
Magical Uses:

Place some blueberries beneath the doormat to keep undesireables away from your property, or from entering your home. This protects against evil as well.

Make blueberry pies or tarts and eat when under psychic attack; this gets the protection inside you and increases the herb's effectiveness.

BLUE FLAG *(Iris versicolor)* **POISON**
Folk Names: Flag Lily, Fleur-de-Lys, Iris, Liver Lily, Poison Lily, Poison Flag, Snake Lily, Water Flag, Water Iris
Gender: Feminine
Planet: Venus
Element: Water
Powers: Money
Magical Uses:

Carry the root for financial gain. The root is also placed in cash registers to increase business.

BODHI *(Ficus religiosa)*
Folk Names: Bo-Tree, Peepul Tree, Pipul, Sacred Tree
Gender: Masculine
Planet: Jupiter
Element: Air
Deities: Buddha, Vishnu
Powers: Fertility, Protection, Wisdom, Meditation
Ritual Uses:

The plant is sacred to Vishnu who, like Buddha, was said to have been born beneath it. In the East, sacred fires are fed

July—Water Lily

August—Poppy

September—Morning Glory

October—Hop

November—Chrysanthemum

December—Holly

with its wood. Since Buddha also sat beneath this tree in meditation for six years, it is sacred to Him, and the heart-shaped leaves still tremble remembering the divine vibrations.

Magical Uses:

If you feel evil near, simply circle this tree several times and the evil shall flee in terror.

Barren women walk naked beneath a bodhi tree to become fertile.

Use the leaves in meditation incenses and all mixtures designed to give wisdom.

BONESET *(Eupatorium perfoliatum)*

Folk Names: Agueweed, Crosswort, Feverwort, Indian Sage, Sweating Plant, Teasel, Thoroughwort, Wood Boneset

Gender: Feminine

Planet: Saturn

Element: Water

Powers: Protection, Exorcism

Magical Uses:

The plant wards off evil spirits. Make an infusion and sprinkle about the house to drive away evil.

BORAGE *(Borago officinalis)*

Folk Names: Bugloss, Burrage, Herb of Gladness

Gender: Masculine

Planet: Jupiter

Element: Air

Powers: Courage, Psychic Powers

Magical Uses:

Carry the fresh blossoms to strengthen your courage, or place one in your buttonhole for protection when walking outdoors.

A tea of borage induces psychic powers.

BRACKEN *(Pteridium aquilinum)*

Gender: Masculine

Planet: Mercury

Element: Air

Powers: Healing, Rain Magic, Prophetic Dreams

Magical Uses:

If you burn bracken outside, rain will fall.

Bracken is also used for protection, healing and fertility. If the root is placed beneath the pillow it causes solutions of problems to appear in dreams.

BRAZIL NUT *(Bertholletia excellsa)*

Gender: Masculine

Planet: Mercury

Element: Air

Powers: Love

Magical Uses:

Brings good luck in love affairs if carried as a talisman.

BRIONY *(Bryony* spp.)

Folk Names: Gout Root, Ladies' Seal, Mad Root, Snake Grape, Tamus, Tetterberry, Wild Hops, Wild Vine, Wood Vine

Gender: Masculine

Planet: Mars

Element: Fire

Powers: Image Magic, Money, Protection

Magical Uses:

The briony root is often used as a substitute for the rare mandrake root in various image magic operations.

Money placed near a briony root will increase, as long as it is left there. The root is also hung in houses and gardens as a protection against the effects of bad weather.

BROMELIAD *(Crypanthus* spp.)

Folk Names: Chameleon Star, Earth Star

Gender: Masculine

Planet: Sun

Element: Air

Power: Protection, Money

Magical Uses:

Grow a bromeliad in the home for

money and luxuries. The plants are also protective, and so are a good choice of house plants.

BROOM *(Cytisus scoparius)* POISON
Folk Names: Banal, Basam, Besom, Bisom, Bizzon, Breeam, Broom Tops, Brum, Genista Green Broom, Irish Broom, Irish Tops, Link, Scotch Broom
Gender: Masculine
Planet: Mars
Element: Air
Powers: Purification, Protection, Wind Spells, Divination
Magical Uses:

Broom is used in purification and protection spells, and is hung in the home to keep evil out. Also, an infusion of broom sprinkled through the house exorcises poltergeists.

Although the infusion was once used as a drink to increase psychic powers, this can be dangerous because the plant is slightly poisonous; carry instead for this purpose.

To raise the winds, throw broom into the air while invoking the spirits of the Air, preferably from a mountain-top. To calm the winds, burn broom and bury the ashes.

If you do outdoor spells (which is the best place to perform magic) sweep the ground with broom prior to your workings, if it grows nearby.

BUCHU *(Agathosma betulina; Barosma betulina)*
Folk Names: Bookoo, Bucoo, Buku, Oval Buchu, Short Buchu
Gender: Feminine
Planet: Moon
Element: Water
Powers: Psychic Powers, Prophetic Dreams
Magical Uses:

An infusion of buchu, drunk, enables one to foretell the future.

Frankincense mixed with buchu is burned directly before retiring to produce prophetic dreams. Only a small amount should be burned, and this must be in the bedroom.

BUCKTHORN *(Rhamnus* spp.)
Gender: Feminine
Planet: Saturn
Element: Water
Powers: Protection, Exorcism, Wishes, Legal Matters
Magical Uses:

Branches of the buckthorn, placed near doors and windows, drive away all enchantments and sorceries, according to Dioscorides.

A charming legend concerning the buckthorn vows that if one sprinkles buckthorn in a circle and then dances within it under a full Moon, an elf will appear. The dancer must notice the elf and say, 'Halt and grant my boon!' before the creature flees. The elf will then grant one wish. I cannot make any guarantees this will happen, however.

Buckthorn is also used in legal matters (carried or worn to court, etc.) and as a general good luck generator.

BUCKWHEAT *(Fagopyrum* spp.)
Folk Names: Beechwheat, Brank, French Wheat, Saracen Corn
Gender: Feminine
Planet: Venus
Element: Earth
Powers: Money, Protection
Magical Uses:

Grind the seeds (make flour) and sprinkle around your house in a circle to keep evil from it. Or, use to form magic circles on the floor around you while performing magic.

Add a few grains of buckwheat to money incenses, and keep some in the kitchen to guard against poverty.

BURDOCK *(Arctium lappa)*

Folk Names: Bardana, Beggar's Buttons, Burrseed, Clotbur, Cockleburr, Great Burdock, Happy Major, Hardock, Hurrburr, Personata

Gender: Feminine

Planet: Venus

Element: Water

Powers: Protection, Healing

Magical Uses:

Cast around the home to ward off negativity. Add to protection incenses and use in such spells. Gather burdock roots in the waning Moon, dry and then cut them into small pieces. String these on red thread like beads and wear for protection against evil and negativity.

The leaves of the burdock, when laid to the soles of the feet, help to cure gout.

CABBAGE *(Brassica oleracea)*

Gender: Feminine

Planet: Moon

Element: Water

Powers: Luck

Magical Uses:

Cabbage should be planted in the garden the first thing after a couple has been married, if they wish to have good luck in their marriage and garden.

CACTUS

Powers: Protection, Chastity

Magical Uses:

Cacti of all kinds are protective, owing to their spines. Grown indoors, they protect against inwanted intrusions and burglaries, and also absorb negativity. Outside, one cactus should be placed facing each direction, next to the house, to further protect it.

Cactus spines are sometimes used in Witch bottles, and to mark symbols and words on candles and roots. These are then either carried or buried to release the power.

CALAMUS *(Acorus calamus)* **POISON**
Folk Names: Gladdon, Myrtle Flag, Myrtle Grass, Myrtle Sedge, Sweet Cane, Sweet Flag, Sweet Grass, Sweet Root, Sweet Rush, Sweet Sedge
Gender: Feminine
Planet: Moon
Element: Water
Powers: Luck, Healing, Money, Protection
Magical Uses:

The seeds are strung as beads and used for healing, or the powdered root is used in healing incenses and sachets.

Small pieces of the root kept in all corners of the kitchen protect against hunger and poverty.

Growing the plant brings good luck to the gardener, and calamus is also used to strengthen and bind spells.

CAMELLIA *(Camellia japonica)*
Gender: Feminine
Planet: Moon
Element: Water
Powers: Riches
Magical Uses:

The camellia brings riches and luxury, and so is used in spells of this kind. Place the fresh blossoms in vessels of water on the altar during money and prosperity rituals.

CAMPHOR *(Cinnamomum Camphora)*
Gender: Feminine
Planet: Moon
Element: Water
Powers: Chastity, Health, Divination
Magical Uses:

Sniff to lessen sexual desire. Also place beside the bed for this purpose.

A bag of camphor (or the bark of a camphor tree) hung around the nect, prevents the contraction of colds and flu.

Camphor is sometimes used in divinatory incenses; unfortunately, true camphor is all but unavailable in the United

States, so synthetics usually have to suffice.

CAPER *(Capparis spinosa)*
Gender: Feminine
Planet: Venus
Element: Water
Powers: Potency, Lust, Love
Magical Uses:

A man who suffers from impotency has but to eat some capers and he will be cured.

The caper is also used in love and lust formulae.

CARAWAY *(Carum carvi)*
Gender: Masculine
Planet: Mercury
Element: Air
Powers: Protection, Lust, Health, Anti-Theft, Mental Powers
Magical Uses:

The caraway serves as protection against Lilith, as well as all manner of evil spirits, entities and plain old negativity. It is often carried for this purpose. Any object which holds some caraway seeds is theft-proof.

The seeds are also used to encourage fidelity, and are placed in sachets and talismans to attract a mate. When baked into cookies, bread, or cakes they are lust-inducing. Chewing the seeds is helpful to gain the love of one you desire.

They also strengthen the memory and a small bag of the seeds placed in a child's bed protects it from illness.

CARDAMON *(Elettario Cardamomum)*
Gender: Feminine
Planet: Venus
Element: Water
Deity: Erzulie
Power: Lust, Love
Magical Uses:

The ground seeds are added to

warmed wine for a quick lust potion. They are also baked into apple pies for a wonderful amatory pastry, and are added to love sachets and incenses.

CARNATION *(Dianthus carophyllus)*
Folk Names: Gillies, Gilliflower, Jove's Flower, Nelka, Scaffold Flower, Sops-In-Wine
Gender: Masculine
Planet: Sun
Element: Fire
Deity: Jupiter
Powers: Protection, Strength, Healing
Magical Uses:

Worn during Elizabethan times to prevent coming to an untimely death on the scaffold, carnations can be used in all-purpose protective spells.

Carnations are placed in convalescent rooms to give the healing patient strength and energy, and are also used in healing spells. Place fresh carnations (red are best) on the altar during healing rituals and add the dried blossoms to sachets and incenses for the same purpose.

CAROB *(Jacaranda procera; Prosopis dulcis)*
Folk Names: Caaroba, Caroba, Carobinha, Chocolate
Powers: Protection, Health
Magical Uses:

Carry or wear to maintain good health, and to guard against evil.

CARROT *(Dancus carota)*
Folk Names: Bird's Nest, Philtron
Gender: Masculine
Planet: Mars
Element: Fire
Powers: Fertility, Lust
Magical Uses:

The seeds, eaten, help women become pregnant.

Carrots are eaten to promote lust

and to cure impotence.

CASCARA SAGRADA *(Rhamnus Pur-shiana)*
Folk Name: Sacred Bark
Powers: Legal Matters, Money, Protection
Magical Uses:

Sprinkle an infusion of cascara sagrada around your home before going to any court proceeding. It will help you win your case.

Cascara sagrada is also used in money spells, and worn as an amulet against evil and hexes.

CASHEW *(Anacardium occidentale)*
Gender: Masculine
Planet: Sun
Element: Fire
Power: Money
Magical Uses:

Cashews are used in prosperity and money spells.

CASTOR *(Ricinus communis)* **POISON**
Folk Names: Palma Christi, Palms Christi Root
Power: Protection
Magical Uses:

Castor beans are good protection against the evil eye, as well as all negativity. They absorb evil.

CATNIP *(Nepeta cataria)*
Folk Names: Cat, Catmint, Catnep, Catrup, Cat's Wort, Field Balm, Nepeta, Nip
Gender: Feminine
Planet: Venus
Element: Water
Deities: Bast
Powers: Cat Magic, Love, Beauty, Happiness
Magical Uses:

Given to your cat, catnip creates a

psychic bond between the two of you. It is also intoxicating to the cat.

Catnip is used in love sachets, usually in conjunction with rose petals. If you hold catnip in your hand until it is warm, then hold anyone else's hand, they will forever be your friend, as long as you keep the catnip you used for the spell in some safe place.

Grown near the home or hung over the door, catnip attracts good spirits and great luck.

Catnip is also used in spells designed to enhance beauty and happiness.

Large catnip leaves are pressed and used as bookmarks in magical texts.

CAT TAIL *(Typha* spp.)
Gender: Masculine
Planet: Mars
Element: Fire
Powers: Lust
Magical Uses:

If a woman doesn't enjoy sex, but wishes to, she should carry some cat tail with her at all times.

CEDAR *(Cedrus libani* or *C.* spp.)
Gender: Masculine
Planet: Sun
Element: Fire
Powers: Healing, Purification, Money, Protection
Magical Uses:

The smoke of the cedar is purifying, and also cures the predeliction to having bad dreams. Twigs of the cedar are burned and smouldered, or made into incense, to heal head colds, they are placed upon the hot rocks in sweat baths for purification by some American Indians.

Cedar hung in the home protects it against lightning strikes. A cedar stick carved into three prongs is placed prongs up into the ground near the home to protect it against all evil.

A piece of cedar kept in the wallet or purse draws money, and cedar is used in money incenses.

Cedar is added to love sachets and is burned to induce psychic powers.

(Note: Juniper is often used in place of cedar.)

CELANDINE *(Chelidonium majus)*

Folk Names: Celydoyne, Chelidoninum, Devil's Milk, Garden Celandine, Greater Celandine, Kenning Wort, Swallow Herb, Swallow-Wort, Tetterwort

Gender: Masculine

Planet: Sun

Element: Fire

Powers: Protection, Escape, Happiness, Legal Matters

Magical Uses:

Celandine aids in escaping unwarranted imprisonment and entrapments of every kind. Wear next to the skin and replace every three days for this purpose.

Celandine also imparts good spirits and joy if worn; and it cures depression.

Wear to court to win the favor of the judge or jury, or as a protective herb.

CELERY *(Apium graveolens)*

Gender: Masculine

Planet: Mercury

Element: Fire

Powers: Mental Powers, Lust, Psychic Powers

Magical Uses:

Chew the seeds to aid in concentration, or use in spell pillows to induce sleep. Burned with orris root, celery seeds increase psychic powers.

The stalk, along with the seeds, induces lust when eaten.

Witches supposedly are celery seeds before flying off on their brooms so that they wouldn't become dizzy and fall!

CENTAURY *(Centaurium* spp.)
Folk Names: Christ's Ladder, Feverwort
Gender: Masculine
Planet: Sun
Element: Fire
Powers: Snake-Removing
Magical Uses:
    The smoke from burning or fuming centaury drives off snakes.

CHAMOMILE *(Anthemis nobilis)*
Folk Names: Camomyle, Chamaimelon, Ground Apple, *Heermannchen* (German), *Manzanilla* (Spanish), Maythen, Roman Camomile, Whig Plant
Gender: Masculine
Planet: Sun
Element: Water
Powers: Money, Sleep, Love, Purification
Magical Uses:
    Chamomile is used to attract money, and a handwash of the infusion is sometimes used by gamblers to ensure winnings.
    It is used in sleep and meditation incenses, and the infusion is also added to the bath to attract love.
    It is also a purificatory and protective herb. When sprinkled around the property, it removes curses and spells cast against you.

CHERRY *(Prunus avium)*
Folk Names: Sweet Cherry
Gender: Feminine
Planet: Venus
Element: Water
Powers: Love, Divination
Magical Uses:
    The cherry has long been used to stimulate or attract love. A beautiful Japanese spell to find love is simple: tie a single strand of your hair to a blossoming cherry tree.
    More complex is the following love spell. This is the type of complicated spell which can be simplified if desired. Collect

as many cherry stones as years you are old. Drill a hole through no more than one stone each night, beginning on the night of the New Moon. Do not drill any holes during the waning Moon. This means that the most you can drill in one month is fourteen stones. When you have finished drilling, wait until the next New Moon. Thread them on a piece of red or pink thread and tie this around the left knee each night for fourteen nights. Sleep with it on and remove each morning. This will bring you a husband or wife.

To find out how many years you will live, run around a tree full of ripe cherries, then shake it. The number of cherries that fall represents the number of years left. (Be sure to shake the tree hard!)

Cherry juice is also used as a blood substitute where called for in old recipes.

CHESTNUT *(Castanea* spp.)
Gender: Masculine
Planet: Jupiter
Element: Fire
Powers: Love
Magical Uses:
Use chestnuts in love spells, or feed to a loved one.

CHICKWEED *(Stellaria media)*
Folk Names: Adder's Mouth, Indian Chickweed, Passerina, Satin Flower, Star Chickweed, Starweed, Starwort, *Stellaire* (French), Stitchwort, Tongue Grass, Winterweed
Gender: Feminine
Planet: Moon
Element: Water
Powers: Fidelity, Love
Magical Uses:
Carry or use in spells designed to attract a love or to maintain a relationship.

CHICORY *(Cichorium intybus)*
Folk Names: Succory, Wild Cherry, Wild Succory
Gender: Masculine
Planet: Sun
Element: Air
Powers: Removing Obstacles, Invisibility, Favors, Frugality
Magical Uses:

Chicory is used to remove all obstacles that might crop up in your life. It is carried for this purpose.

At one time it was thought to make its possessor invisible, and to open locked boxes and doors if held against the locks. But for these last two purposes, chicory has to be gathered with a gold knife in perfect silence at noon or midnight on Midsummer.

If you anoint your body with chicory juice, you will obtain favors from great persons. It is also carried to promote frugality.

CHILI PEPPER *(Capsicum* spp.)
Folk Name: Red Pepper
Gender: Masculine
Planet: Mars
Element: Fire
Powers: Fidelity, Hex-Breaking, Love
Magical Uses:

If you feel your mate is looking for greener pastures, buy two large dried chili peppers. Cross them and tie together with a red or pink ribbon. Place this beneath your pillow and this should help keep fidelity in your marriage.

If you've been cursed, scatter red pepper around your house to break the spell.

Red pepper is also used in love powders to enflame the beloved, or to ensure that the love you find will be spicy.

CHINA BERRY *(Melia azederach)* **POISON**
Powers: Luck
Magical Uses:

    The seeds are used as good-luck charms, and are also carried to bring a change into your life.

CHRYSANTHEMUM *(Chrysanthemum* spp.)
Folk Name: Mum
Gender: Masculine
Planet: Sun
Element: Fire
Power: Protection
Magical Uses:

    Drink an infusion of chrysanthemums to be cured of drunkenness.

    Wearing the flowers protects against the wrath of the Gods, and when grown in the garden chrysanthemums protect it from evil spirits.

CINCHONA *(Cinchona ledgeriana* or *C. succirubra)*
Powers: Luck, Protection
Magical Uses:

    Carried, a piece of the bark gives luck as well as protection from bodily harm and evil.

CINNAMON *(Cinnamomum zeylanicum)*
Folk Names: Sweet Wood
Gender: Masculine
Planet: Sun
Element: Fire
Deities: Venus, Aphrodite
Powers: Spirituality, Success, Healing, Power, Psychic Powers, Lust, Protection, Love
Ritual Uses:

    Cinnamon oil was used as part of a holy anointing oil by the ancient Hebrews. The leaves of the cinnamon tree were woven into wreaths which were used to decorate ancient Roman temples. The Egyptians used cinnamon oil during the mumification process.

Magical Uses:

Cinnamon, when burned as an incense, raises high spiritual vibrations, aids in healing, draws money, stimulates psychic powers and produces protective vibrations. Cinnamon is also used in making sachets and infusions for these purposes.

CINQUEFOIL *(Potentilla canadensis* or *P. reptans)*

Folk Names: Crampweed, Five Finger Blossom, Five Finger Grass, Five Fingers, Goosegrass, Goose Tansy, Moor Grass, Pentaphyllon, Silver Cinquefoil, Silverweed, Sunkfield, Synkefoyle

Gender: Masculine

Planet: Jupiter

Element: Fire

Powers: Money, Protection, Prophetic Dreams, Sleep

Magical Uses:

The five points of the leaves represent love, money, health, power and wisdom, and so if carried cinquefoil grants these.

It is also hung up at the door, or placed on the bed, for protection. An infusion of the leaves is used to bathe the forehead and hands, nine times, to wash away hexes and curses.

If you find a cinquefoil sprig with seven leaflets, place it under your pillow. You will dream of your future lover or mate. If a bag of cinquefoil is suspended from the bed you will have restful sleep all night.

Carried, cinquefoil gives eloquence when asking for favors of officials, and usually ensures that the favor is granted. It is thus used in court cases.

Cinquefoil is also added to purificatory bath sachets.

CITRON *(Citrus medica)*
Gender: Masculine
Planet: Sun
Element: Air
Powers: Psychic Powers, Healing
Magical Uses:

If eaten, the citron increases psychic powers.

It is also used in healing spells and incenses.

CLOTH-OF-GOLD *(Crocus angustifolia)*
Powers: Understanding Animal Languages
Magical Uses:

The cloth-of-gold gives the power to understand the language of birds and beasts. You must be barefooted with washed feet when gathering it, and clad in white. Offer a sacrifice of bread and wine, and pluck it tenderly. Wear the plant for these powers.

CLOVE *(Syzygium aromaticum* or *Caryophyllus aromaticus)*
Gender: Masculine
Planet: Jupiter
Element: Fire
Powers: Protection, Exorcism, Love, Money
Magical Uses:

Burned as an incense, cloves attract riches, drive away hostile and negative forces, produce spiritual vibrations, and purify the area.

Cloves are burned as an incense to stop others from gossiping about you.

Worn or carried, cloves attract the opposite sex and bring comfort to the bereaved.

CLOVER *(Trifolium* spp.)
Folk Names: Honey, Honeystalks, Shamrock, Three-Leaved Grass, Trefoil, Trifoil
Gender: Masculine
Planet: Mercury

Element: Air
Deity: Rowen
Powers: Protection, Money, Love, Fidelity, Exorcism, Success
Magical Uses:

TWO LEAVED:

If you find a two-leaved clover, you shall soon also find a lover.

THREE-LEAVED:

Trefoil, or the three-leaved clover, is worn as a protective amulet.

FOUR-LEAVED:

The four-leaved clover, if worn, helps men avoid military service. It also protects against madness, strengthens psychic powers, enables you to detect the presence of spirits, and leads the wearer to gold, money or treasures.

If two people eat a four-leaved clover together, mutual love will result.

Seven grains of wheat laid on a four-leaved clover will enable one to see fairies.

If you put a four-leaved clover in your shoe before going out you will increase your chances of meeting a rich new love.

FIVE-LEAVED:

The five-leaved clover is powerful for attracting money, and should be worn for this purpose.

WHITE-CLOVER:

White clover is used to work against hexes, and is worn or scattered around the premises for this.

RED CLOVER:

This clover, added to the bath water, aids you in dealing with financial arrangements of every kind.

Red clover is also used in lust potions and the infusion is sprinkled to remove negative spirits.

IN GENERAL:

Clover keeps snakes away from your property, if grown there. When placed in the left shoe, and then forgotten, clover keeps evil from you. Worn over the right breast it brings success in all undertakings.

If you have been disappointed in love, wear clover near your heart in a piece of blue silk to help you through.

CLUB MOSS *(Lycopodium clavatum)*
Folk Names: Foxtail, Lycopod, Selago, Vegetable Sulfur, Wolf Claw
Gender: Feminine
Planet: Moon
Element: Water
Powers: Protection, Power
Magical Uses:
The herb, when gathered correctly, gives protection, power and blessings from the Gods. Take a purification bath in a running stream, offer bread and wine to the plant, then uproot it with the little finger or a silver blade. Then it will be powerful.

COCONUT *(Cocos nucifera)*
Gender: Feminine
Planet: Moon
Element: Water
Powers: Purification, Protection, Chastity
Magical Uses:
Coconut has long been used in chastity spells, as well as in protection rituals.

A coconut can be halved, drained of its juice, filled with appropriate protective herbs and sealed shut, then buried to protect your property.

Hang a whole coconut in the home for protection.

COHOSH, BLACK *(Cimicifuga racemosa)*
Folk Names: Black Snake Root, Bugbane, Rattle Root, Squaw Root
Gender: Masculine
Powers: Love, Courage, Protection, Potency
Magical Uses:
Use black cohosh in love sachets

and add an infusion to the bath to help in cases of impotency.

The herb, carried, helps to strengthen courage in the meek. An infusion of the herb sprinkled around a room or added to the bath, drives away evil presences.

COLTSFOOT *(Tussilago Farfara)*
Folk Names: Ass's Foot, British Tobacco, Bull's Foot, Butterbur, Coughwort, *Pas d'ane* (French), *Sponnc* (Irish)
Gender: Feminine
Planet: Venus
Element: Water
Powers: Love, Visions
Magical Uses:

Add to love sachets and use in spells of peace and tranquility.

The leaves, when smoked, can cause visions.

COLUMBINE *(Aquilegia canadensis)*
Folk Names: Lion's Herb
Gender: Feminine
Planet: Venus
Element: Water
Powers: Courage, Love
Magical Uses:

Rub your hands on the herb to induce courage and daring, or carry it with you.

The seeds are used as a love perfume; when pulverized, they are rubbed onto the hands and body to attract love. Both sexes can use this spell.

COMFREY *(Symphytum officinale)*
Folk Names: Assear, Black Wort, Boneset, Bruisewort, Consolida, Consound, Gum Plant, Healing Herb, Knit Back, Knit Bone, Miracle Herb, Slippery Root, Wallwort, Yalluc
Gender: Feminine
Planet: Saturn
Element: Water

Powers: Safety during Travel, Money
Magical Uses:

Worn or carried, comfrey protects and ensures safety during travel. Also, tuck some into your suitcases so that they aren't lost or stolen.

The root is also used in money spells.

COPAL *(Bursera odorata)*
Gender: Masculine
Planet: Sun
Element: Fire
Powers: Love, Purification
Magical Uses:

Copal is added to love and purification incenses, especially in Mexico.

A piece of copal can represent the heart in poppets.

CORIANDER *(Coriandrum sativum)*
Folk Names: Chinese Parsley, Cilantro, Cilentro, Culantro
Gender: Masculine
Planet: Mars
Element: Fire
Powers: Love, Health, Healing
Magical Uses:

Coriander has long been used in love sachets and spells. Add the powdered seeds to warm wine to make an effective lust potion.

The seeds are used for healing, especially easing headaches, and are worn for this purpose.

If pregnant women eat coriander, their future child will be ingenious.

CORN *(Zea Mays)*
Folk Names: Giver of Life, Maize, Sacred Mother, Seed of Seeds
Gender: Feminine
Planet: Venus
Element: Earth

Powers: Protection, Luck, Divination
Ritual Uses:

The Corn Mother, or Goddess, is a deity of plenty and of fertility, long worshipped throughout the East and North America. The Zunis utilize different colors of corn in their religious rituals. Blue corn meal is used to bless and is scattered as an offering.

Magical Uses:

Reach into a bin of corn, pull out any ear, count the grains. Allow twelve grains of corn for each year and it will tell your age.

An ear of corn is placed within the cradle to protect the baby against negative forces.

A bunch of cornstalks hung over the mirror brings good luck to the household, and a necklace made of dried red corn kernels prevents nosebleed.

Pollen from corn was used to make rain by ancient Meso-American peoples, probably by tossing it into the air.

At one time, in the mountains of the United States, if a birth was difficult red corncobs were burned on the doorstep of the cabin (or even under the bed) to speed up the process.

COTTON *(Gossypium barbadense)*
Gender: Feminine
Planet: Moon
Element: Earth
Powers: Luck, Healing, Protection, Rain, Fishing Magic
Magical Uses:

If a piece of cotton is placed in the sugar bowl, good luck will follow, as it will if cotton is thrown over the right shoulder at dawn. In this latter case, the good luck will come before the day is over.

Cotton is placed in an aching tooth to stop the pain.

Cotton planted or scattered in the

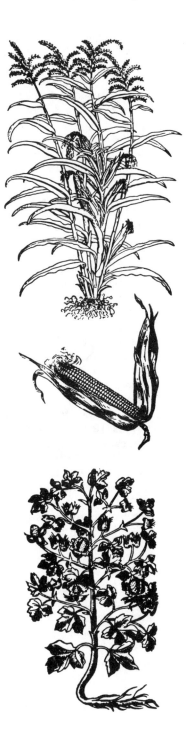

yard keeps ghosts away, and cotton balls soaked in vinegar and placed on the windowsills keep evil at bay.

To bring back a lost love, place some pepper in a piece of cotton and sew this into a sachet. Wear to make its magic work.

Cotton is the best kind of cloth (next to wool) to use for making sachets, or for any time cloth is needed in magic.

If you go fishing on a windy day, take twenty cotton seeds with you. Lay them at the edge of the water and you shall have at least one bite.

Burning cotton causes rain.

COWSLIP *(Primula veris)*
Folk Names: Arthritica, Artetyke, Buckles, Cuy, Drelip, Fairy Cup, *Frauenschlussel* (German), Herb Peter, Key Flower, Key of Heaven, Lady's Key, Lippe, Our Lady's Keys, Paigle, Paralysio, Password, Peggle, Plumrocks
Gender: Feminine
Planet: Venus
Element: Water
Deity: Freya
Powers: Healing, Youth, Treasure-Finding
Magical Uses:

A bit of cowslip placed beneath the front porch will discourage visitors, if you don't wish to have company.

Cowslip, when carried or worn, will preserve youth, or restore it when lost.

The odor of cowslip is healing, and a bunch of the flowers held in the hand will help you find hidden treasure.

CROCUS *(Crocus vernus)*
Gender: Feminine
Planet: Venus
Element: Water
Powers: Love, Visions
Magical Uses:

The plant, when grown, attracts love.

Burn crocus along with alum in a censer, and you may see the vision of a thief who has robbed you. This was done in ancient Egypt.

CUBEB *(Piper Cubeba)*
Gender: Masculine
Planet: Mars
Element: Fire
Power: Love
Magical Uses:
   The berries are used in love sachets and spells.

CUCKOO-FLOWER *(Orchis morior* or *O. spp.)*
Gender: Feminine
Planet: Venus
Element: Water
Powers: Fertility, Love
Magical Uses:
   The fresh tubers of the cuckoo-flower are used in love spells, and are worn to promote conception. If a large tuber is used for the latter purpose, the child will be male; if small, female.

CUCUMBER *(Cucumis sativus)*
Folk Names: Cowcucumber
Gender: Feminine
Planet: Moon
Element: Water
Powers: Chastity, Healing, Fertility
Magical Uses:
   The fruit of the cucumber, when eaten, hinders lust.
   The peel bound onto the forehead relieves headache pain, while the seeds are eaten to promote fertility.

CUMIN *(Cumimum Cyminum)*
Folk Names: *Cumino, Cumino Aigro*
Gender: Masculine
Planet: Mars
Element: Fire
Powers: Protection, Fidelity, Exorcism,

Anti-Theft

Magical Uses:

In Germany and Italy, cumin is put into bread to keep wood spirits from stealing it. Cumin seed also possesses the 'gift of retention'; i.e., it will prevent the theft of any object which retains it.

Cumin is burned with frankincense for protection and scattered on the floor, sometimes with salt, to drive out evil. It is also worn by brides to keep negativity away from the wedding.

It is used in love spells, and when given to a lover it will promote fidelity. Cumin seed is steeped in wine to make a lust potion.

Cumin when carried, gives peace of mind, and if you plan to grow the plant yourself, bear in mind that you must curse while sowing the seed to obtain a good crop!

CURRY *(Murraya Koenigii)*

Gender: Masculine

Planet: Mars

Element: Fire

Power: Protection

Magical Uses:

Burn curry (a specific plant, not the mixture of spices used in cooking) at nightfall to keep evil influences away.

(Not Shown)

CYCLAMEN *(Cyclamen* spp.)

Folk Names: Groundbread, *Pain-de-Porceau* (French: Sow Bread), Sow-Bread, Swine Bread

Gender: Feminine

Planet: Venus

Element: Water

Deity: Hecate

Powers: Fertility, Protection, Happiness, Lust

Magical Uses:

Cyclamen, when grown in the bedroom protects the sleeper, and where grown, it is said that no noxious spells

can have effect.

Cyclamen is also used to promote conception, raise the passions, and the blossoms are used to remove grief of the heart.

CYPRESS *(Cupressus sempervirens)*
Folk Names: Tree of Death
Gender: Feminine
Planet: Saturn
Element: Earth
Deities: Mithras, Pluto, Aphrodite, Ashtoreth, Artemis, Apollo, Cupid, Jupiter, Hekat, Hebe, Zoroaster
Powers: Longevity, Healing, Comfort, Protection
Ritual Uses:

The ancient Minoans worshipped the cypress as a divine symbol, and spread the cult to cyprus from Crete. Cypress wood was used to make coffins in Egypt.

Magical Uses:

Cypress should be used at times of crisis, especially at the death of a friend or relative. It eases the mind and allays grief if worn or carried to funerals.

The tree is quite protective when grown near the home and boughs of cypress are used in protective and blessing capacities.

Since the cypress is the symbol of eternity and immortality, the wood has long been carried to lengthen life.

To make a healing wand of cypress, slowly cut, over a three-month period, a branch from a cypress tree. This is known as a 'healing stock' and should be used only in healing rituals. Make passes over the sick person, touch the afflicted area and then plunge the tip into a fire to cleanse it. Also used in invocations to the gods. The root and 'cones' of the cypress are also healing, as is the greenery when dried and burned as incense.

Throw a sprig of cypress into a grave to give the deceased luck and love

in the hereafter.

A mallet of cypress wood was once used to discover thieves, but as far as is known, the exact procedure is lost.

DAFFODIL *(Narcissus* spp.)
Folk Names: Asphodel, Daffy-Down-Dilly, Fleur de Coucou, Goose Leek, Lent-Lily, Narcissus, Porillon
Gender: Feminine
Planet: Venus
Element: Water
Powers: Love, Fertility, Luck
Magical Uses:

The flower is placed on the altar during love spells, or is carried for this purpose.

Placed in the bedroom, the fresh flowers increase fertility.

If a daffodil is plucked and worn next to the heart, good luck shall surely come your way.

DAISY *(Chrysanthemum leucanthemum* — American Daisy; *Bellis perenis* — European Daisy)
Folk Names: Bairnwort, Bruisewort, Eyes, Field Daisy, *Llygady Dydd* (Welsh: Eye of the Day), Maudlinwort, Moon Daisy
Gender: Feminine
Planet: Venus
Element: Water
Deities: Freya, Artemis, Thor
Powers: Lust, Love
Magical Uses:

It is said that whoever picks the first daisy of the season, will be possessed of 'a spirit of coquetry' beyond any control.

Sleep with a daisy root beneath your pillow and an absent lover may return to you.

Worn, the daisy brings love.

DAMIANA *(Turnera diffusa* or *T. aphro-disiaca)*
Folk Names: Mexican Damiana
Gender: Masculine
Planet: Mars
Element: Fire
Powers: Lust, Love, Visions
Magical Uses:

Damiana is used in lust infusions as well as lust spells. It is also burned to produce visions.

DANDELION *(Taraxacum officinale)*
Folk Names: Blowball, Cankerwort, Lion's Tooth, Piss-a-Bed, Priest's Crown, Puffball, Swine Snout, White Endive, Wild Endive
Gender: Masculine
Planet: Jupiter
Element: Air
Deity: Hecate
Powers: Divination, Wishes, Calling Spirits
Magical Uses:

To find out how long you will live, blow the seeds off the head of a dandelion. You will live as many years as there are seeds left on the head.

To tell the time: blow three times at the seed head. The number left is the hour.

The root, when dried, roasted and ground like coffee, is used to make a tea. This infusion will promote psychic powers. This same tea, steaming and placed beside the bed, will call spirits.

To send a message to a loved one, blow at the seed head in his or her direction and visualize your message.

Dandelion, buried in the northwest corner of the house, brings favorable winds.

DATURA *(Datura* spp.*)* **POISON**
Folk Names: Devil's Apple, Ghost Flower, Jimsonweed, Love-Will, Mad Apple, Madherb, Manicon, Stinkweed, Sor-

cerer's Herb, Thornapple, *Toloache*, Witches' Thimble, *Yerba del Diablo* (Spanish: Herb of the Devil)

Gender: Feminine
Planet: Saturn
Element: Water
Powers: Hex-Breaking, Sleep, Protection
Ritual Uses:

Datura has been used in shamanic practices and religious rites for untold centuries. The Aztecs considered the plant to be sacred.

Magical Uses:

Datura is used to break spells by sprinkling it around the home. It also protects against evil spirits.

If insomnia persists night after night, it may be cured by placing some datura leaves into each shoe and then setting the shoes under the bed with the toes pointing toward the nearest wall.

A few datura leaves placed on the crown of a hat protects the wearer from apoplexy as well as sunstroke.

Datura is extremely poisonous—do not eat. Sensitive skin may be irritated simply by touching the plant.

DEERSTONGUE *(Frasera speciosa; Liatris odoratissima)*
Folk Names: Vanilla Leaf, Wild Vanilla
Gender: Masculine
Planet: Mars
Element: Fire
Powers: Lust, Psychic Powers
Magical Uses:

Worn or carried, it attracts men. Deerstongue is also sprinkled on the bed for this purpose.

It aids the psychic powers if worn.

DEVIL'S BIT *(Scabiosa succisa)*
Gender: Masculine
Powers: Exorcism, Love, Protection, Luck

Magical Uses:

When worn around the neck, devil's bit drives away evil spirits, and offers protection to the wearer.

Devil's bit is also used to attract women and to bring luck.

DEVIL'S SHOESTRING *(Viburnum alnifolium)*
Powers: Protection, Gambling Luck, Power, Employment
Magical Uses:

This herb wards off evil when worn around the neck, and protects its bearer against accidental poisoning.

Gamblers carry devil's shoestring as a good luck charm.

Cut the root into small pieces, place in a jar filled with whiskey and spirits of camphor. When you need power of any kind, take out a piece of root and rub your hands with it. Then use the root in the appropriate way (i.e., if money is desired, place near money or in the wallet).

A piece of devil's shoestring carried in the pocket while seeking employment (or while having problems at work) will either help you get hired, or will smooth out the difficulties. Also carry when asking for a raise in pay.

DILL *(Anethum graveolens)*
Folk Names: Aneton, Dill Weed, Dilly, Garden Dill
Gender: Masculine
Planet: Mercury
Element: Fire
Powers: Protection, money, Lust, Love
Magical Uses:

The herb is protective when hung at the door and carried in protective sachets. Placed in the cradle it protects children. And if it is placed over the door no one ill-disposed or envious of you can enter your house.

Dill, owing to the number of seeds

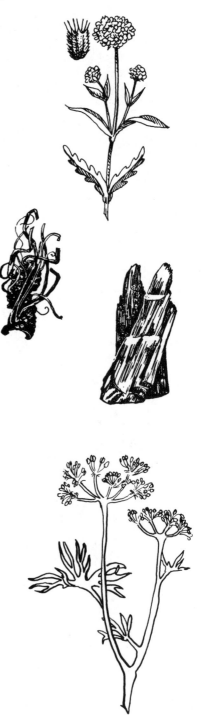

the plant produces, is used in money spells.

Added to the bath it makes the bather irresistible, and dill stimulates lust if eaten or smelled (which is why dill pickles are so popular).

Smell dill to cure hiccoughs.

DITTANY OF CRETE *(Dictamus origanoides)*
Gender: Feminine
Planet: Venus
Element: Water
Powers: Manifestations, Astral Projection
Magical Uses:

Dittany, when burned, is an excellent base for manifestations of spirits; the wraiths appear in the smoke rising from the censer.

Dittany is also mixed with equal parts of vanilla, benzoin and sandalwood to make an astral projection incense. Burn a small amount prior to making the attempt.

The juice of the dittany drives away venemous beasts, so smear some onto your body before venturing out where they live.

DOCK *(Rumex* spp.)
Folk Name: Yellow Dock
Gender: Masculine
Planet: Jupiter
Element: Air
Powers: Healing, Fertility, Money
Magical Uses:

The seeds of the common dock are used in money spells, and money incenses. They are also made into an infusion, which is sprinkled about the place of business to attract customers.

When the seeds of the dock are tied to the left arm of a woman they help her to conceive a child.

DODDER *(Cuscuta glomurata* or *C. europaea)*
Folk Names: Beggarweed, Devil's Guts, Fireweed, Hellweed, Lady's Laces, Love Vine, Scaldweed, Strangle Tare, Witches Hair
Gender: Feminine
Planet: Saturn
Element: Water
Powers: Love Divination, Knot Magic
Magical Uses:

Pluck the dodder, throw it over the shoulder back onto the host plant (dodder is a parasite), and then return to the plant the next day. If the dodder has attached itself to the plant again, the person in question loves you. If not, no.

Use the 'laces' as cords for knot magic (don't tie the knots too tightly).

DOGBANE *(Apocynum androsaemifolium)*
Powers: Love
Magical Uses:

Use the flowers of the dogbane in love mixtures.

DOGWOOD *(Cornus florida)*
Folk Names: Boxwood, Budwood, Dogtree, Florida Dogwood, Flowering Cornel, Flowering Dogwood, Green Osier, Virginia Dogwood
Powers: Wishes, Protection
Magical Uses:

Place the sap of the dogwood onto a handkerchief on Midsummer Eve. This will grant any wish you may have, if you faithfully carry the handkerchief.

Dogwood leaves (or the wood) are also placed in protective amulets.

DRAGON'S BLOOD *(Daemonorops draco; Dracaena* spp.)
Folk Names: Blood, Blume, *Calamus Draco, Draconis Resina, Sanguis Draconis,* Dragon's Blood Palm
Gender: Masculine

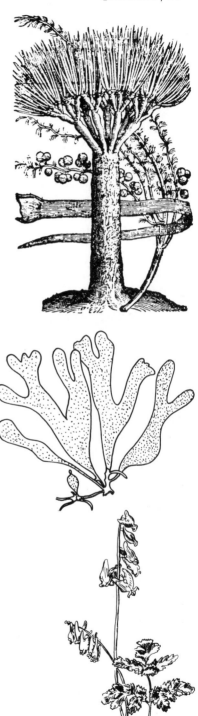

Planet: Mars
Element: Fire
Powers: Love, Protection, Exorcism, Potency
Magical Uses:

This resin from a palm tree is burned to entice errant lovers to return. This is usually done by women seated near an open window, looking outside, at night.

A stick of dragon's blood placed under the pillow or mattress will cure impotency.

The dried resin is a powerful protectant when carried, sprinkled around the house, or smouldered as incense. It will also drive evil and negativity away when burned.

A pinch of dragon's blood added to other incenses increases their potency and power.

To quiet a noisy house, powder some dragon's blood, mix it with sugar and salt, and place in a bottle. Cover this tightly and secure it somewhere in your house where it won't be found. You'll have peace and quiet.

DULSE *(Rhodymenia palmata)*
Gender: Feminine
Planet: Moon
Element: Water
Powers: Lust, Harmony
Magical Uses:

Add to beverages to induce lust. Sprinkled around the home it encourages harmony.

Dulse is also used in sea rituals; it is usually thrown onto the waves to placate the spirits of the sea. Dulse is also tossed from high places to contact the wind spirits.

DUTCHMAN'S BREECHES *(Dicentra cucullaria)*
Powers: Love

Magical Uses:
Wear the root of the Dutchman's Breeches to attract love.

EBONY *(Diospyros lotus)*
Folk Names: *Lama* (Hawaiian), Obeah Wood
Powers: Protection, Power
Magical Uses:
Ebony wood is protective and so is used in making amulets. Ebony wands gives the magician pure, unadulterated power.

Don't stand beneath this tree in a storm!

ECHINACEA *(Echinacea augustifolia)*
Folk Names: Black Sampson, Coneflower, Rudbeckia
Powers: Strengthening Spells
Magical Uses:
Enchinacea was used by American Indians as an offering to spirits to ensure and strengthen spells.

EDELWEISS *(Leontopodium alpinum)*
Powers: Invisibility, Bullet-Proofing
Magical Uses:
Made into a wreath and worn, edelweiss confers invisibility.

To be protected against daggers and bullets, pull up a whole edelweiss by its roots during the day on a Friday of the Full Moon. Wear it wrapped in white linen.

Edelweiss also grants your heart's desire; you need only grow and care for the plant.

ELDER *(Sambucus canadensis)*
Folk Names: Alhuren, Battree, Boure Tree, Bour Tree, Eldrum, Ellhorn, *Frau Holle* (German), *Hildemoer* (German), *Hollunder* (German), Hylder, Lady Ellhorn, Old Gal, Old Lady, Pipe Tree, Rob Elder, *Sureau*

(French), Sweet Elder, Tree of Doom, *Yakori bengeskro* (Romany—Devil's Eye)

Gender: Feminine
Planet: Venus
Element: Water
Deities: Holda, Venus
Powers: Exorcism, Protection, Healing, Prosperity, Sleep

Ritual Uses:

The elder was used in burial rites in ancient British long barrows. It is sacred to many Mother Goddess figures, due to its white flowers. Witches and spirits were thought to live within the elder; this was why it 'bled' red sap when cut. Before felling an elder the following formula was recited:

'Lady Ellhorn, give me of thy wood,
And I will give thee of mine,
When I become a tree.'

This is recited kneeling before the tree, prior to making the first cut, and allows the Witch or spirit within the tree time to vacate.

Magical Uses:

If worn, elder wards off attackers of every kind. Hung over doorways and windows it keeps evil from the house. It also has the power to force an evil magician to release any enchantments or spells they may have cast against you. The berries, when carried, protect against evil and negativity. Grown in the garden, elder protects the household against the ravages of sorcery, and shields it from lightning.

To bless a person, place, or thing, scatter the leaves and berries of the elder to the four winds in the name of the person or object to be blessed. Then scatter some more elder over the person or object itself, and it is done.

To lose a fever, poke an elder twig into the ground while keeping completely silent. Toothaches may be alleviated by chewing on an elder twig, and then

placing it into the wall while saying:
Depart thou evil spirit!
Toothaches were once thought to be
caused by evil spirits.

To prevent rheumatism, tie a twig
of elder into three or four knots and
carry in the pocket.

Warts can be cured by rubbing
them with a green elder twig and then
burying it to rot in the mud.

Grown near the home, the elder
gives prosperity to the household, and
the sticks placed about the house protect against robbers and snakes.

Elder is used at weddings to bring
good luck to the couple, and pregnant
women kiss the tree for good fortune
for the coming baby.

Place elderberries beneath your
pillow if you have difficulty sleeping.
They'll allow you to slumber peace-
fully.

Carry elder to preserve you
against the temptation to commit
adultery.

Make flutes from the branches and
call forth spirits with their music. Best
done at midnight in a deserted place far
from the haunts of humans.

Many think it dangerous to burn
elder wood, and some Gypsies strictly
forbade its use as a firewood. However,
magicians have used its wood in fashioning magic wands for centuries.

ELECAMPANE *(Inula Helenium)*
Folk Names: *Alantwurzel* (German),
Alycompaine, *Aunee* (French), Elf
Dock, Elfwort, Horseheal, Nurse Heal,
Scabwort, Velvet Dock, Wild Sun-
flower
Gender: Masculine
Planet: Mercury
Element: Air
Powers: Love, Protection, Psychic Pow-
ers

Magical Uses:

Worn, elecampane attracts love. Sew up some of the leaves or flowers in pink cloth, or make a sachet.

It is also carried for protection, and the herb smouldered on charcoal aids in sharpening psychic powers, particularly when scrying.

ELM *(Ulmus campestris)*
Folk Names: Elven, English Elm, European Elm
Gender: Feminine
Planet: Saturn
Element: Water
Deities: Odin, Hoenin, Lodr
Powers: Love
Magical Uses:

Once known as 'Elven' due to its popularity among elves, elm is now used to protect against lightning strikes, as well as to attract love when carried.

ENDIVE *(Cichorium endivia)*
Gender: Masculine
Planet: Jupiter
Element: Air
Powers: Lust, Love
Magical Uses:

Endive, to be used in magic, is best gathered in the following manner: dig it up on June 27 or July 25 with a piece of gold or a stag's horn. But no matter how gathered, endive is worn as a talisman to attract love. It is used fresh, and should be replaced every three days.

It is also served in salads to stir lust in the partakers.

ERYNGO *(Eryngium* spp.)
Folk Names: Sea Holly
Gender: Feminine
Planet: Venus
Element: Water
Powers: Traveler's Luck, Peace, Lust, Love

Magical Uses:

Eryngo is carried or worn by travelers for safety and luck during their journeys.

This herb also has the power of causing peace if strewn about a place or given to a couple who are quarreling.

Once eaten to provoke lust, eryngo is also used in love spells of all types.

EUCALYPTUS *(Eucalyptus* spp.)
Folk Names: Blue Gum Tree, Stringy Bark Tree
Gender: Feminine
Planet: Moon
Element: Water
Powers: Healing, Protection
Magical Uses:

The leaves are used to stuff healing poppets and are carried to maintain good health. To relieve colds, ring green candles with the leaves and pods and burn them to the socket, visualizing the person (or yourself) as being completely healthy. Also hang a small branch or twig of eucalyptus over the sick bed.

String the immature (green) pods on green thread and wear to help heal sore throats. Placed beneath the pillow, the pods guard against colds.

The leaves are also carried for protection.

EUPHORBIA *(Euphorbia* spp.) **POISON**
Folk Names: Crown of Thorns, Spurge, Wolf's Milk
Gender: Feminine
Planet: Saturn
Element: Water
Powers: Purification, Protection
Magical Uses:

In Anman, a branch of the euphorbia is brought into a house to cleanse it after childbirth. The euphorbia is also an extremely protective plant, grown indoors

or out.

The milky white juice is sometimes used in magical oils and salves, but is extremely poisonous and should not be used carelessly.

EYEBRIGHT *(Euphrasia officinalis)*

Folk Names: Euphrosyne, Red Eyebright

Gender: Masculine

Planet: Sun

Element: Air

Powers: Mental Powers, Psychic Powers

Magical Uses:

Brewed into a tea and drunk, eyebright clears the mind and aids the memory.

The infusion applied to the eyelids on cotton pads induces magical clairvoyance, but it must be persisted in before results are achieved.

Carry to increase psychic powers. Also, use when you need to see the truth in a matter.

FENNEL *(Foeniculum vulgare)*

Gender: Masculine

Planet: Mercury

Element: Fire

Deities: Prometheus, Dionysus

Powers: Protection, Healing, Purification

Ritual Uses:

The thyrsus, which figured in Dionysian ceremonies, was often made of giant fennel stalks with pine cones attached to the ends.

Magical Uses:

Grown around the home, fennel confers protection. Wearing a piece of fennel in the left shoe will prevent wood ticks from biting your legs. Fennel is also hung up at windows and doors to ward off evil spirits, and the seeds can be carried for the same reason.

Fennel is used in purification sachets, as well as healing mixtures.

FENUGREEK *(Trigonella foenum-grae-cum)*
Folk Names: Bird's Foot, Greek Hay-Seed
Gender: Masculine
Planet: Mercury
Element: Air
Deity: Apollo
Powers: Money
Magical Uses:

To bring money into the household, a few fenugreek seeds can be added to the mop water (or a small amount of a fenugreek infusion). Also, half-fill a small jar with fenugreek and leave open in the house to attract money. Add a few seeds every couple of days until the jar is full; then empty the fenugreek out and begin again. Return the spent herb to the ground.

FERN
Gender: Masculine
Planet: Mercury
Element: Air
Deities: Laka, Puck
Powers: Rain-Making, Protection, Luck, Riches, Eternal Youth, Health, Exorcism
Magical Uses:

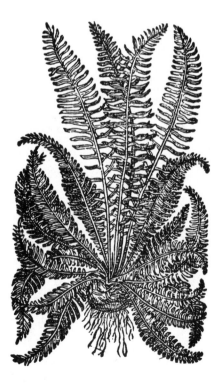

The fern is included in vases of flowers for its protective properties, and is also planted at the doorstep as well. Inside the home, fern is also protective.

Dried fern is thrown upon hot coals to exorcise evil spirits. When burned out of doors, fern causes rain to fall. The smoke from burning fern also drives away snakes or noisome creatures.

Carried or worn, fern has the power to guide its bearer to discover treasures, and the person who breaks the first fern frond of spring will have good luck.

If you ever find yourself in a spot covered with ferns, exactly at midnight, where no sounds of any kind can be heard, Puck will appear and give you a

purse of gold. When done intentionally, this is known as 'watching the fern'.

If you bite the frond of the first fern of the spring you will be guarded from toothache, at least until the next spring.

Fern sap, if you can obtain any, is said to confer eternal youth if drunk. The 'seed' is carried for invisibility.

FEVERFEW *(Chrysanthemum parthenium)*
Folk Names: Featherfew, Febrifuge Plant
Gender: Masculine
Planet: Venus
Element: Water
Power: Protection
Magical Uses:

Carry with you for protection against colds and fevers, as well as accidents.

FIG *(Ficus carica)*
Folk Name: Common Fig
Gender: Masculine
Planet: Jupiter
Element: Fire
Deities: Dionysus, Juno, Isis
Powers: Divination, Fertility, Love
Magical Uses:

Small phallic images are carved from fig wood and carried by women who wish to conceive. They are also used by men to overcome infertility or impotency. Fresh figs are eaten for the same results.

Write a question on a fig leaf. If the leaf dries slowly, the answer is yes, or it is a good omen. If it dries quickly just the opposite.

A fig (such as the popular *Ficus benjamina*) grown in the home is protective and brings the inhabitants good luck. Grown in the bedroom it aids in restful sleep, and in the kitchen ensures the family will never go hungry.

To charm any man or women, give

them a fig. They will be spellbound by
your presence, as long as they like figs.

Before leaving home on a journey,
place a branch of the fig tree before your
door, so that you will return home safely
and happily.

FIGWORT *(Scrophularia nodosa)*
Gender: Feminine
Planet: Venus
Element: Water
Powers: Health, Protection
Magical Uses:

Hung from the neck, the figwort
keeps the wearer healthy and protects
against the evil eye. The plant is also
smoked over Midsummer fires and then
hung in the home for its protective
powers.

FLAX *(Linum usitatissimum)*
Folk Names: Linseed
Gender: Masculine
Planet: Mercury
Element: Fire
Deity: Hulda
Powers: Money, Protection, Beauty, Psy-
chic Powers, Healing
Ritual Uses:

Flax was used in rituals to Hulda,
the Teutonic Goddess who first taught
mortals to cultivate flax, and to spin it
into linen thread and weave it into cloth.
Magical Uses:

Flax seeds are used in money spells.
A few can be placed in the pocket, wallet
or purse, or a jar should be placed on the
altar and a few coins, plus some flax seed,
added. This should be repeated each day
to attract money. A bit of flax in the shoe
wards off poverty.

The blue flax flowers are worn as a
preservative against sorcery. To protect
yourself while asleep, mix equal parts
flax seed and mustard seed and place this
mixture next to your bed. On the other

side of the bed place a pan of cold water. You will be guarded during your slumber.

Alternatively, a combination of red pepper and flax seed, kept in a box somewhere in the house, prevents evil from entering.

To ensure that your child grows up to be a beautiful or handsome adult, let him or her dance among growing flax at the age of seven years.

Sprinkle the altar with flax seed while performing healing rituals, or include it in healing mixtures. To help cure lumbago, tie a hank of flax around the loins.

If you suffer from dizziness, this is a somewhat drastic cure: run naked, after sunset, three times through a field of flax. While you do this the flax will take to itself your dizziness and you'll be cured. You may get a cold, but you won't be dizzy!

FLEABANE *(Inula dysenterica)*
Gender: Feminine
Planet: Venus
Element: Water
Powers: Exorcism, Protection, Chastity
Magical Uses:

Fleabane has been used since ancient times to exorcise evil spirits, and to protect against their entry to the home. To do this simply tie some fleabane, along with a few leaves of St. John's Wort, wheat, and some capers, into a sachet and hang over the lintel of the door.

Fleabane seed placed on the sheets causes chastity.

FOXGLOVE *(Digitalis purpurea)* **POISON**
Folk Names: Cow-Flop, Deadmen's Bells, Digitalis, Dog's Finger, Fairy Fingers, Fairy Petticoats, Fairy Thimbles, Fairy Weed, Floppy-Dock, Floptop, Folk's Gloves, Fox Bells, *Foxes Glofa*, The Great Herb, Lion's Mouth, Lusmore,

Lus na mbau side *(Irish Gaelic),* Our Lady's Glove, Witches Bells, Witches Thimbles
Gender: Feminine
Planet: Venus
Element: Water
Powers: Protection
Magical Uses:

Grown in the garden it protects it, as well as the home. In the past, housewives in Wales used the leaves of the foxglove to make a black dye, which they used to paint crossed lines on their cottage's stone floors. This was done to keep evil from entering the house.

Foxglove is poisonous; do not take internally.

FRANKINCENSE *(Boswellia carterii)*
Folk Names: Incense, Olibans, Olibanum, Olibanus
Gender: Masculine
Planet: Sun
Element: Fire
Deities: Ra, Baal
Powers: Protection, Exorcism, Spirituality
Ritual Uses:

The ancient Egyptians burned frankincense at sunrise to honor Ra. To this day it is included in the composition of some of the incenses used in Catholic churches.
Magical Uses:

When burned, frankincense releases powerful vibrations which not only uplift those of the area, but also drive out all evil and negativity. Frankincense is therefore used in incenses of exorcism, protection, purification and consecration. It is also burned to induce visions and to aid meditation, and is added to sachets for luck, protection and spiritual growth. Rosemary may be used as a substitute for frankincense.

FUMITORY *(Fumaria officinalis)*
Folk Names: Beggary, Earth Smoke, Fumiterry, Fumus, *Fumus Terrae, Kaphnos*, Nidor, *Scheiteregi, Taubenkropp*, Vapor, Wax Dolls
Gender: Feminine
Planet: Saturn
Element: Earth
Powers: Money, Exorcism
Magical Uses:

An infusion of fumitory sprinkled around your house and rubbed onto your shoes once a week will draw money to you quickly.

Fumitory has been burned to exorcise evil spirits for centuries.

FUZZY WEED *(Artemisia dracunculus)*
Powers: Love, Hunting
Magical Uses:

This plant, part of the family which includes mugwort and wormwood, was used by American Indians to attract love. For this purpose it was rubbed onto the clothing and body.

Fuzzy weed was also carried to bring good luck on the hunt, once an integral part of survival.

GALANGAL *(Alpina officinalis or A. galanga)*
Folk Names: Chewing John, China Root, Colic Root, East India Catarrh Root, Galingal, Galingale, Gargaut, India Root, Kaempferia Galanga, Low John the Conqueror, *Rhizoma Galangae*
Gender: Masculine
Planet: Mars
Element: Fire
Powers: Protection, Lust, Health, Money, Psychic Powers, Hex-Breaking
Magical Uses:

Galangal has been used for many different magical needs. Worn or carried it protects its bearer and draws good luck. Placed in a sachet of leather with silver it brings money. Powdered galangal is burned to break spells and curses. It is also carried or sprinkled around the home to promote lust.

Worn, galangal aids psychic development and guards the bearer's health.

If galangal is unavailable, ginger, which is part of the same family, can be substituted.

GARDENIA *(Gardenia* spp.*)*
Gender: Feminine
Planet: Moon
Element: Water
Powers: Love, Peace, Healing, Spirituality
Magical Uses:

The fresh blossoms are placed in sickrooms or on healing altars to aid in the process. The dried petals are also added to healing incenses and mixtures.

Dried gardenia is also scattered around a room to induce peaceful vibrations and is also added to Moon incenses.

Gardenias are used in love spells, and to attract good spirits during rituals. They are possessed of very high spiritual vibrations.

GARLIC *(Allium sativum)*
Folk Names: *Ajo* (Spanish), Poor Man's Treacle, Stinkweed
Gender: Masculine
Planet: Mars
Element: Fire
Deity: Hecate
Powers: Protection, Healing, Exorcism, Lust, Anti-Theft
Ritual Uses:

Garlic was eaten on festival days to Hecate, and was left at a crossroads as a sacrifice in Her name.
Magical Uses:

Garlic was once worn to guard against the plague. It is still used to absorb diseases. Simply rub fresh, peeled cloves of garlic onto the afflicted part of the body, then throw into running water. An old spell utilized garlic in protecting against hepatitis. To do this, simply wear thirteen cloves of garlic at the end of a cord around the neck for thirteen days. On the last day, in the middle of the night, walk to a corner of an intersection of two streets, remove the necklace, throw it behind you and run home without looking back.

Garlic is also extremely protective. Sailors carry some while on board ship to protect against its wreckage. Soldiers wore garlic as a defense in the middle ages, while Roman soldiers ate it to give them courage. It is placed in the home to guard against the intrusion of evil, to keep out robbers and thieves, and is hung over the door to repel envious people. Garlic is especially protective in new homes.

Worn, garlic guards against foul weather (mountaineers wear it) as well as monsters, and it also shields you from the blows of your enemies.

When evil spirits are about, bite into garlic to send them away, or sprinkle powdered garlic on the floor (if you don't mind smelling it for some time). Garlic is also placed beneath children's pillows to protect them while asleep, and brides once carried a clove of garlic in the pocket for good luck and to keep evil far from her on her big day. Rubbed onto pots and pans before cooking in them garlic removes negative vibrations which might otherwise contaminate the food.

When eaten, garlic acts as a lust-inducer, and when a magnet or lodestone is rubbed with garlic it loses its magical powers.

GENTIAN *(Gentiana lutea)*
Folk Names: Bitter Root, Yellow Gentian
Gender: Masculine
Planet: Mars
Element: Fire

Powers: Love, Power
Magical Uses:

Gentian is added to love baths and sachets. When used in any incense or sachet gentian adds a great deal of extra power. It is also used to break hexes and curses.

GERANIUM *(Pelargonium* spp.)
Gender: Feminine
Planet: Venus
Element: Water
Powers: Fertility, Health, Love, Protection
Magical Uses:

Geraniums of all types are protective when grown in the garden or brought into the home freshly-cut and placed into water.

The geranium protects against snakes, for:

> *Snakes will not go*
> *Where geraniums grow*

A plot of red geraniums, planted near the Witch's cottage, told of coming visitors by their movements. The flowers were magically charged to point to the direction of the approaching strangers and thus warn the Witch of their impending arrival.

Banks or pots of red geraniums are quite protective, and strengthen health.

Pink-flowered geraniums are used in love spells, while the white varieties increase fertility.

Curanderos in contemporary Mexico cleanse and heal patients by brushing them with red geraniums, together with fresh rue and pepper tree branches.

The rose geranium *(Pelargonium graveolens)* with its highly scented leaves, is used in protection sachets, or the fresh leaves are rubbed onto doorknobs and windows to protect them.

All of the scented geraniums have various magical properties, most of which can be deduced from the scent (nutmeg, lemon, peppermint, etc.) Nutmeg-scented geraniums possess much the same powers as nutmeg, and so on.

GINGER *(Zingiber officinalis)*
Folk Names: African Ginger
Gender: Masculine
Planet: Mars
Element: Fire
Powers: Love, Money, Success, Power
Magical Uses:

Eating ginger before performing spells will lend them power, since you have been 'heated up' by the ginger. This is especially true of love spells, in which ginger is much-used.

Whole ginger roots are planted and grown to attract money, or the powdered root is sprinkled into pockets or onto money for this purpose.

Ginger is also used in success spells, or to ensure the success of a magical operation.

In the Pacific the Dobu islanders make much use of ginger in their magic. They chew it and spit it at the 'seat' of an illness to cure it, and also spit chewed ginger at an oncoming storm, while at sea, to halt it.

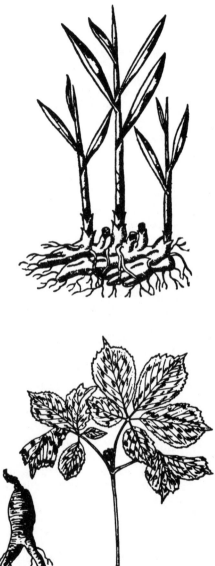

GINSENG *(Panax quinquefolius)*
Folk Names: Sang, Wonder of the World
　Root
Gender: Masculine
Planet: Sun
Element: Fire
Powers: Love, Wishes, Healing, Beauty,
　Protection, Lust
Magical Uses:

The root is carried to attract love, as well as to guard one's health, to draw money, and to ensure sexual potency. Ginseng will also bring beauty to all who carry it.

Burn ginseng to ward off evil spirits

and to break hexes and curses.

A tea of ginseng is used as a power-ful lust-inducing drink, whether alone or mixed with other like herbs.

Hold a ginseng root in your hands, visualize your wish into the root, and throw it into running water. Or, carve your wish onto a root and toss into the water.

Ginseng can be a substitute for the mandrake.

GOAT'S RUE *(Galega officinalis)*
Gender: Masculine
Planet: Mercury
Element: Air
Powers: Healing, Health
Magical Uses: Goat's rue is used in heal-ing rituals. Placing goat's rue leaves into the shoe cures and prevents rheumatism.

GOLDENROD *(Solidago odora)*
Folk Names: Aaron's Rod, Blue Mountain Tea, Goldruthe, Gonea Tea, Sweet Scented Goldenrod, Solidago, Verg d' Or, Wound Weed, Woundwort
Gender: Feminine
Planet: Venus
Element: Air
Powers: Money, Divination
Magical Uses:

To see your future love, wear a piece of goldenrod. He or she will appear on the morrow.

When held in the hand, the flower nods in the direction of hidden or lost objects, or where buried treasure lies.

If goldenrod springs up suddenly near the house door, unexpected good fortune will soon rain upon the family living there.

Goldenrod is also used in money spells.

GOLDEN SEAL *(Hydrastis canadensis)*
Folk Names: Eye Balm, Eye Root,

Ground Raspberry, Indian Dye, Indian
Paint, Jaundice Root, Orange Root,
Tumeric Root, Warnera, Wild Curcur-
ma, Yellow Puccoon, Yellow Root
Gender: Masculine
Planet: Sun
Element: Fire
Powers: Healing, Money
Magical Uses:

Golden seal is used in money spells
as well as healing rituals.

GORSE *(Ulex europaeus)*
Folk Names: Broom, Frey, Furze, *Fyrs*,
Gorst, Goss, Prickly Broom, Ruffet,
Whin
Gender: Masculine
Planet: Mars
Element: Fire
Deities: Jupiter, Thor
Powers: Protection, Money
Magical Uses:

Gorse is a good protectant against
evil. In Wales hedges of the prickly gorse
are used to protect the home against
fairies, who cannot penetrate the hedge.

Gorse is also used in money spells;
it attracts gold.

GOTU KOLA *(Hydrocotyl asiatica)*
Powers: Meditation
Magical Uses:

Use in meditation incenses. Burn a
small amount prior to (but not during)
meditation.

GOURD *(Curcurbita* spp.)
Gender: Feminine
Planet: Moon
Element: Water
Powers: Protection
Magical Uses:

Gourds hung at the front door are a
protection against fascination. Pieces of
gourds carried in the pocket or purse
ward off evil.

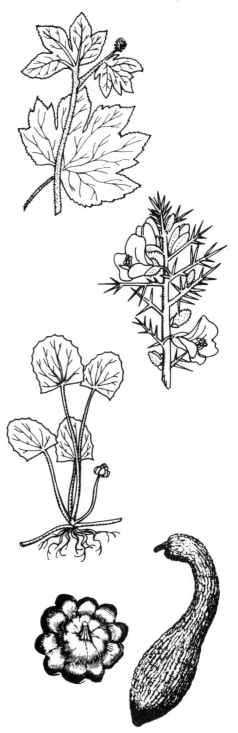

Gourds are used to make rattles (place dried beans inside) which scare evil spirits, and a dried gourd, it's top cut off, is filled with water and used as a scrying bowl.

GRAIN
Powers: Protection
Magical Uses:

To protect yourself against evil, scatter grain all around your bedroom. To protect children when they are away from you (such as at school) throw a handful of grain after them as they leave. Be sure they do not see you do this.

GRAINS OF PARADISE *(Aframomum melequeta)*
Folk Names: African Pepper, Guinea Grains, Mallaquetta Pepper, Melequeta
Gender: Masculine
Planet: Mars
Element: Fire
Powers: Lust, Luck, Love, Money, Wishes
Magical Uses:

Grains of paradise are used in love, lust, luck and money spells and sachets. It is also one of the herbs used for wishing. Hold some in your hands, make a wish and then throw a little of the herb to each direction, beginning in the North and ending in the West.

GRAPE *(Vitis vinifera)*
Gender: Feminine
Planet: Moon
Element: Water
Deities: Dionysus, Bacchus, Hathor
Powers: Fertility, Garden Magic, Mental Powers, Money
Magical Uses:

Pictures of grapes can be painted onto garden walls to ensure fertility, as was done in ancient Rome.

Eating grapes or raisins increases fertility, as well as strengthens mental

powers.

Place grapes on the altar during money spells.

GRASS
Powers: Psychic Powers, Protection
Magical Uses:

Suspend a ball of green grass in the front window of the home to drive out evil and to protect it. Tie knots in grass around the home for the same purpose.

Blades of grass, carried, help psychic powers.

Use green grass to mark a wish on a stone, or simply rub the grass against it to make a greenish spot. Visualize your need and then bury the stone or throw it into running water.

GROUND IVY *(Nepeta glechoma)*
Folk Names: Alehoof, Cat's Foot, Gill-Go-Over-The-Ground, Haymaids, Hedge-maids, Lizzy-Run-Up-The-Hedge, Rob-in-Run-In-The-Hedge, Tunhoof
Powers: Divination
Magical Uses:

Use ground ivy to discover who is working negative magic against you. Place the herb around the base of a yellow candle and burn on a Tuesday. The person will become known to you.

GROUNDSEL *(Senecio* spp.)
Folk Names: Groundeswelge (Anglo-Saxon, 'Ground-Swallower'), Ground Glutton, Grundy Swallow, Séntion, Simson
Gender: Feminine
Planet: Venus
Element: Water
Powers: Health, Healing
Magical Uses:

Groundsel is carried as an amulet against toothache, as well as to stop the pain if it starts. It is also carried to keep the teeth in good health generally.

HAWTHORN (*Crataegus oxacantha*)

Folk Names: Bread and Cheese Tree, Gaxels, Hagthorn, Halves, Haw, Hazels, Huath, Ladies' Meat, May, Mayblossom, May Bush, Mayflower, Quick, Thorn, Tree of Chastity

Gender: Masculine

Planet: Mars

Element: Fire

Deities: Cardea, Flora, Hymen

Powers: Fertility, Chastity, Fishing Magic, Happiness

Ritual Uses:

Hawthorn was once used to decorate May poles. At one time Hawthorns were believed to be Witches who had transformed themselves into trees. Witches have long danced and performed their rites beneath the thorn.

Magical Uses:

Hawthorn has long been used to increase fertility. Because of this power it is incorporated into weddings, especially those performed in the spring.

The leaves, curiously enough, are also used to enforce or maintain chastity or celibacy. The leaves are placed beneath the mattress or around the bedroom for this purpose.

Carried in a sachet on a fishing trip hawthorn ensures a good catch, and worn or carried it promotes happiness in the troubled, depressed, or sad.

Hawthorn protects against lightning, and in the house in which it resides, no evil ghosts may enter. It is also powerful for protecting against damage to the house from storms. The Romans placed hawthorn in cradles to guard the child from evil spells.

In the past most Witch's gardens contained at least one hawthorn hedge.

The hawthorn is sacred to the fairies, and is part of the tree fairy triad of Britain: 'Oak, Ash and Thorn,' and where all three trees grow together it is said that one may see fairies.

HAZEL *(Corylus* spp.)
Folk Name: Coll
Gender: Masculine
Planet: Sun
Element: Air
Deities: Mercury, Thor, Artemis, Diana
Powers: Luck, Fertility, Anti-Lightning, Protection, Wishes
Magical Uses:

String the nuts and hang in the house for luck, or present a batch of them to a bride to wish her good fortune.

The nuts, eaten, give wisdom and increase fertility. They are often eaten prior to divination. One can be carried for increasing fertility.

To protect yourself (or your plants) while outdoors, draw a circle in the dirt with a hazel twig, around yourself or the plant concerned.

Weave hazel twigs into a crown. Put this on your head and wish very hard. Your wish may come true.

Hazel crowns were also worn to induce invisibility.

Twigs of hazel are placed in window frames to guard the house against lightning, and three pins of hazel wood driven into your house will protect it from fire.

Hazel wood can be used to make fine all-purpose magical wands. The forked branches are utilized by dowsers to divine hidden objects.

HEATHER *(Calluna* spp; *Erica* spp.)
Folk Names: Common Heather, Heath, Ling, Scottish Heather
Gender: Feminine
Planet: Venus
Element: Water
Deity: Isis
Powers: Protection, Rain-Making, Luck

Magical Uses:

Heather is carried as a guard against rape and other violent crimes, or just to bring good luck. White heather is the best for this purpose.

Heather when burned with fern outside attracts rain. Heather has also long been used to conjure ghosts.

HELIOTROPE *(Heliotropium europaeum* **POISON**
or *H. arborescens)*
Folk Names: Cherry Pie, Turnsole
Gender: Masculine
Planet: Sun
Element: Fire
Deity: Apollo
Powers: Exorcism, Prophetic Dreams, Healing, Wealth, Invisibility
Magical Uses:

Placed beneath the pillow heliotrope induces prophetic dreams. This is especially useful when you have been robbed—the thief will appear in a dream.

Heliotrope is used in exorcism incenses and mixtures, as well as healing sachets. When placed in the pocket or purse it attracts wealth and money. Also ring green candles and burn down to the socket.

To become invisible, fill a small horn with heliotrope. Wear or carry and your actions and movements shall not attract attention.

HELLEBORE, BLACK *(Helleborus niger)* **POISON**
Folk Names: Melampode
Gender: Feminine
Planet: Saturn
Element: Water
Magical Uses:

Scatter powdered hellebore before you as you move and you shall be invisible.

Hellebore was also used in exorcism rituals, and was at one time used in inducing astral projection. As with most poisonous herbs it is simply too dangerous to use.

HEMLOCK *(Conium maculatum)* **POISON**

Folk Names: Beaver Poison, Herb Bennet, Keckies, Kex, Musquash Root, Poison Hemlock, Poison Parsley, Spotted Corobane, Spotted Hemlock, Water Parsley

Gender: Feminine

Planet: Saturn

Element: Water

Deities: Hecate

Magical Uses:

Another poisonous plant, hemlock was once used in magic to induce astral protection, and in spells to destroy sexual drives. Its juice was rubbed onto magical knives and swords to empower and purify them before use.

HEMP *(Cannibis sativa)*

Folk Names: Chanvre, Gallowgrass, Ganeb, Ganja, Grass, Hanf, Kif, Marijuana, Neckweede, *Tekrouri*, Weed

Gender: Feminine

Planet: Saturn

Element: Water

Powers: Healing, Love, Visions, Meditation

Magical Uses:

Marijuana, or hemp as it was commonly named, was once widely used in magic. Due to laws enacted during the 1930's which restrict its use and sale, many of these practices are dying out. Here is a sampling of them.

Hemp has long been used in love spells and divinations, such as in the following infamous 'Hempseed Spell': Take a handful of hempseeds to a church at midnight, preferably just as Midsummer begins. Walk around the church nine times, sprinkling the hemp seed as you walk, and repeat the following words:

Hempseed I sow, hempseed I sow,
Who will come after me and mow?

You will see a vision of your future husband or wife—and you may also get the local church in trouble with the law!

Hemp was part of many vision and scrying incenses, the smoke of which opened the psychic senses. Mugwort and hemp were prescribed to be burned before a magic mirror to gain visions. It was also added to meditation incenses.

Scourges made of hemp were used in China as imitation snakes, which were beat against the beds of the sick to drive out the malicious, illness-causing demons.

HENBANE *(Hyosycamus niger)* POISON
Folk Names: Black Nightshade, Cassilago, Cassilata, *Deus Caballinus*, Devil's Eye, Hebenon, Henbells, Hogsbean, Isana, Jupiter's Bean, *Jusquiame* (French), Poison Tobacco, Symphonica
Gender: Feminine
Planet: Saturn
Element: Water
Magical Uses:

Another poisonous plant largely ignored in herb magic today due to its toxicity, henbane is still sometimes utilized as a love-bringing herb in the following manner: to bring love, a man should gather henbane naked, early in the morning, while standing on one foot. Worn it will bring love.

Burned out of doors, it attracts rain, but the fumes would be poisonous (substitute fern in this usage).

HENNA *(Lawsonia inermis)*
Powers: Healing
Magical Uses:

Place on forehead to relieve headache. Attracts love if worn near the heart. Protects from illness and the evil eye.

HIBISCUS *(Hibiscus* spp.)
Folk Names: *Kharkady* (Arabic)
Gender: Feminine
Planet: Venus
Element: Water

Powers: Lust, Love, Divination
Magical Uses:

The flowers of a red hibiscus are brewed into a strong red tea which is drunk for its lust-inducing powers. This drink is forbidden to women in Egypt for this very reason.

The blossoms have also been used in love incenses and sachets. They are placed in wreaths in marriage ceremonies in the tropics.

Sorcerers in Dobu in the Western Pacific divine in a wooden bowl of water onto which are placed a few hibiscus flowers.

HICKORY *(Carya* spp.)

Powers: Legal Matters
Magical Uses:

Burn a piece of hickory root to ashes. Mix with cinquefoil and place this mixture in a box. Hang over the door to ensure that you do not have trouble with the law.

HIGH JOHN THE CONQUEROR *(Ipo-* **POISON**
moea Purga or *I. jalapa)*

Gender: Masculine
Planet: Mars
Element: Fire
Powers: Money, Love, Success, Happiness
Magical Uses:

Anoint one of the roots with mint oil and tie up in a green sachet. Carry to attract money.

John the conqueror is also carried to stop depression, bring love and success, protect from all hexes and curses, and to break and destroy spells and hexes.

To make a simple anointing oil suitable for all purposes, take three high John the conqueror roots, make small cuts into them with a sharp knife, and place these in a bottle of vegetable, olive, or mineral oil. Let the roots soak in the oil for several

weeks. Leave the roots in the oil and use as desired; to anoint candles, sachets, and so on.

HOLLY *(Ilex aquifolium* or *I. opaca)*
Folk Names: Aquifolius, Bat's Wings, Christ's Thorn, Holy Tree, Holm Chaste, Hulm, Hulver Bush, Tinne
Gender: Masculine
Planet: Mars
Element: Fire
Powers: Protection, Anti-Lightning, Luck, Dream Magic
Magical Uses:

A *par excellence* protective herb, holly guards against lightning, poison and evil spirits. Planted around the home it protects it and its inhabitants from mischievious sorcerers. When thrown at wild animals, holly makes them lie down quietly and leave you alone, even if you don't hit them with the plant. Holly water (infused or distilled) is sprinkled on newborn babies to protect them.

Holly is also carried to promote good luck, especially by men, since the holly is a 'male' plant. (Ivy is the corresponding plant for women.) It is also hung around the house for good luck at Yule.

After midnight on a Friday, without making a sound, gather nine holly leaves, preferably from a non-spiny plant (one that has smooth leaves). Wrap these up in a white cloth using nine knots to tie the ends together. Place this beneath your pillow, and your dreams will come true.

HONESTY *(Lunaria* spp.)
Folk Names: Lunary, Money Plant, Silver Dollar
Gender: Feminine
Planet: Moon
Element: Earth
Powers: Money, Repelling Monsters

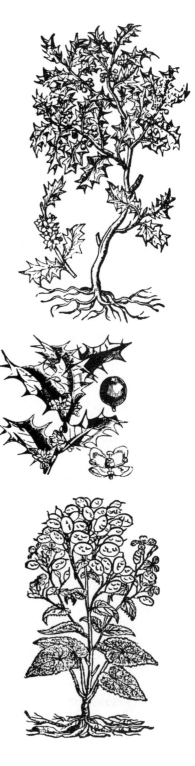

Magical Uses:

Honesty, when carried or scattered about a place, will put all monsters to flight.

The honesty is used in money spells, since the seed pods resemble silver coins. Place one of these beneath a green candle and burn down to the socket, or place it in the purse or pocket to draw money.

HONEYSUCKLE *(Lonicera caprifolium)*
Folk Names: Dutch Honeysuckle, Goat's Leaf, Woodbine
Gender: Masculine
Planet: Jupiter
Element: Earth
Powers: Money, Psychic Powers, Protection
Magical Uses:

Ring green candles with honeysuckle flowers to attract money, or place them in a vase in the house for the same purpose.

Lightly crush the fresh flowers and then rub on the forehead to heighten psychic powers.

If a honeysuckle plant grows outside near your home it will bring good luck, and if it grows over the door it will keep fevers at bay for the household.

HOPS *(Humulus lupulus)*
Folk Names: Beer Flower, *Flores de Cerveza*
Gender: Masculine
Planet: Mars
Element: Air
Powers: Healing, Sleep
Magical Uses:

A pillow stuffed with dried hops brings on sleep and rest.

Hops are also used in healing sachets and incenses.

HOREHOUND *(Marrubium vulgare)*
Folk Names: Bull's Blood, Eye of the

Star, Haran, Hoarhound, Huran, *Llwyd y cwn* (Welsh), Marrubium, Maruil, Seed of Horus, Soldier's Tea, White Horehound

Gender: Masculine
Planet: Mercury
Element: Air
Deity: Horus
Powers: Protection, Mental Powers, Exorcism, Healing
Ritual Uses:

Burn to Horus, the ancient Egyptian God, after which the plant was named.

Magical Uses:

Horehound is used in protective sachets, and is carried to guard against sorcery and fascination. Horehound is also scattered as an exorcism herb.

Drink an infusion of the herb and it will clear your mind and promote quick thinking, as well as strengthen the mental powers.

Horehound, when mixed with ash leaves and placed in a bowl of water, releases healing vibrations, and should be placed in a sickroom.

HORSE CHESTNUT *(Aesculus* spp.) **POISON**
Folk Name: Buckeye
Gender: Masculine
Planet: Jupiter
Element: Fire
Powers: Money, Healing
Magical Uses:

Carry to ward off rheumatism, backaches, arthritis and chills. Carry three to guard against giddiness.

Wrap a dollar bill around a buckeye, place into a sachet, and carry to attract money. Also carry for success in all things.

HORSERADISH *(Cochlearia armoracia)*
Gender: Masculine
Planet: Mars
Element: Fire

Powers: Purification, Exorcism
Magical Uses:

Horseradish root (dried and grated or ground) should be sprinkled around the house, in corners, on the steps outside, and on doorsills. This will make all evil powers clear out, and will difuse any spells that may have been sent against you.

HORSETAIL *(Equisetum* spp.)
Folk Names: Bottle Brush, Dutch Rushes, Paddock Pipes, Pewterwort, Shave-Grass
Gender: Feminine
Planet: Saturn
Element: Earth
Powers: Snake Charming, Fertility
Magical Uses:

Whistles made of the stems of the horsetail, when played, will call snakes to the musician.

Horsetail is also used in fertility mixtures, or placed in the bedroom for this purpose.

HOUNDSTONGUE *(Cynoglossum officinale)*
Folk Names: Dog-Bur, Dog's Tongue, Gypsy Flower, Sheep Lice, Tongue of Dog, Woolmat
Gender: Masculine
Planet: Mars
Element: Fire
Powers: Tying Dog's Tongues
Magical Uses:

If placed in the shoe, this herb will prevent dogs from barking at you; in effect 'tying' their tongues.

HOUSELEEK *(Sempervivum tectorum)*
Folk Names: Hen and Chickens, Sengren, Welcome-Home-Husband-Though-Never-So-Drunk, Welcome-Home-Husband-Though-Never-So-Late
Gender: Masculine

Planet: Jupiter
Element: Air
Powers: Luck, Protection, Love
Magical Uses:

Gives good luck and protects a building from lightning if grown on the roof.

Houseleek has also been used as a love-inducing herb, worn fresh and renewed every few days.

HUCKLEBERRY *(Gaylussacia* spp.)
Gender: Feminine
Planet: Venus
Element: Water
Powers: Luck, Protection, Dream Magic, Hex-Breaking
Magical Uses:

Placed in sachets and carried, the leaves are luck-inducing. They also keep away evil and break hexes and curses.

To make all your dreams come true, burn the leaves in your bedroom directly before going to sleep. In seven days you should see results.

HYACINTH *(Hyacinthus orientalis)*
Gender: Feminine
Planet: Venus
Element: Water
Powers: Love, Protection, Happiness
Magical Uses:

Use in sachets to ease the pain of childbirth. The plant grown in the bedroom guards against nightmares.

Sniffing the fresh flowers of the hyacinth relieves grief and depression, and also cures fascination.

The dried flowers are used in love mixtures.

HYDRANGEA *(Hydrangea arborescens)*
Folk Names: Seven Barks
Powers: Hex-Breaking
Magical Uses:

Use the bark of the hydrangea to

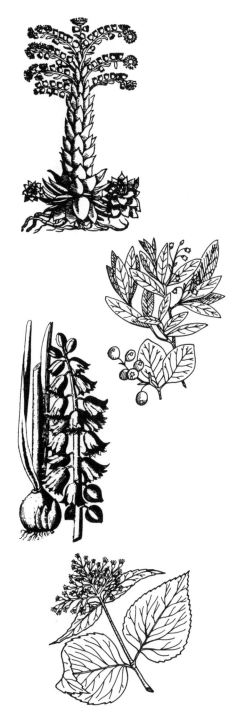

unhex by carrying, scattering around the home, or burning.

HYSSOP *(Hyssopus officinalis)*
Folk Names: Hyssop Herb, Isopo, Ysopo, Yssop
Gender: Masculine
Planet: Jupiter
Element: Fire
Powers: Purification, Protection
Magical Uses:

Hyssop is the most widely used purification herb in magic. It is added to baths in sachets, infused and sprinkled on objects or persons to cleanse them, and hung up in the home to purge it of evil and negativity.

INDIAN PAINT BRUSH *(Castilleja* spp.)
Folk Names: Snake's Friend, Snake's Matches
Gender: Feminine
Planet: Venus
Element: Water
Powers: Love
Magical Uses:

Flowers of the Indian paint brush contain a strong love-attracting power. They should be carried in sachets to find a love.

IRIS *(Iris* spp.)
Gender: Feminine
Planet: Venus
Element: Water
Deities: Iris, Juno
Powers: Purification, Wisdom
Magical Uses:

The iris, one of the loveliest flowers, has been used for purification since Roman times. The fresh flowers are placed in the area to be cleansed.

The three points of its flower symbolize faith, wisdom and valour, and so can be used to induce these qualities.

IRISH MOSS *(Chondrus crispus)*
Folk Names: Carrageen, Pearl Moss
Gender: Feminine
Planet: Moon
Element: Water
Powers: Money, Luck, Protection
Magical Uses:

Irish moss is carried or placed beneath rugs to increase luck and to ensure a steady flow of money into the house or pockets of the person.

Irish moss is also carried while on trips for protection and safety, and is used to stuff luck or money poppets.

IVY *(Hedera* spp.)
Folk Name: Gort
Gender: Feminine
Planet: Saturn
Element: Water
Deities: Bacchus, Dionysus, Osiris
Powers: Protection, Healing
Ritual Uses:

The thyrsus, used in worshipping Bacchus, was often wound round with ivy.
Magical Uses:

Ivy is carried by women for good luck in general, and is worn by brides for this same reason.

Where ivy grows or is strewn, it guards against negativity and disaster.

Ivy is also used in fidelity and love charms. It is magically 'paired' to holly.

JASMINE *(Jasminum officinale* or *J. odoratissimum)*
Folk Names: Jessamin, Moonlight on the Grove
Gender: Feminine
Planet: Moon
Element: Water
Deity: Vishnu
Powers: Love, Money, Prophetic Dreams
Magical Uses:

Dried jasmine flowers are added to

sachets and other love mixtures. They will attract a spiritual (as opposed to a 'physical') love.

The flowers will also draw wealth and money if carried, burned or worn. Jasmine will also cause prophetic dreams if burned in the bedroom, and the flowers are smelled to induce sleep.

JOB'S TEARS *(Coix lachryma)*
Folk Name: Tear Grass
Powers: Healing, Wishes, Luck
Magical Uses:

The seeds are strung onto a necklace and placed around a child's neck to aid in teething, and are also worn by adults in the same manner for sore throats and colds. The seeds absorb the pain or illness.

Three seeds can be carried for good luck. For wishing magic, make a wish holding seven seeds (or 'tears,' as they are known) and then throw into running water. Alternately, count out seven seeds, concentrating on your wish. Carry these seeds for a week, and your wish should come true.

JOE-PYE WEED *(Eupatorium* spp.)
Folk Names: Gravelroot, Hempweed, Joe-Pie, Jopi Weed, Trumpet Weed
Powers: Love, Respect
Magical Uses:

Place a few leaves in the mouth when making love advances and you shall not fail.

Carry a few leaves of Joe-Pye so that you will be looked upon with respect and favor by everyone you meet.

JUNIPER *(Juniperus communis)*
Folk Names: Enebro, *Gemeiner Wachholder* (German), Geneva, Gin Berry, Ginepro, Gin Plant
Gender: Masculine
Planet: Sun
Element: Fire

Powers: Protection, Anti-Theft, Love, Exorcism, Health

Magical Uses:

Used throughout Europe as a protective herb, Juniper also guards against theft. It was probably one of the earliest incenses used by Mediterranean Witches. Juniper hung at the door protects against evil forces and persons, and it is burned in exorcism rites. A sprig of the plant protects its wearer against accidents and attacks by wild animals. It also guards against ghosts and sickness.

Juniper is added to love mixtures, and the berries are carried to increase male potency.

When carried or burned, juniper helps the psychic powers and breaks hexes and curses, and drives off snakes.

KAVA-KAVA *(Piper methysticum)*

Folk Names: Ava, Ava Pepper, Ava Root, Awa Root, Intoxicating Pepper

Gender: Feminine

Planet: Saturn

Element: Water

Deities: Lono, Kane, Kanaloa

Powers: Visions, Protection, Luck

Ritual Uses:

Long used in rites in Hawaii and Polynesia.

Magical Uses:

This Polynesian plant's root is infused and the resulting tea is drunk to offer protection against evil and to invite in good luck.

Infused and left to steep overnight in the refrigerator, it is then drunk to enhance psychic powers and to induce visions. Too much of the infusion, however, is damaging to the kidneys.

KNOTWEED *(Polygonum aviculare)*

Folk Names: Armstrong, Centinode, Cowgrass, Hogweed, Knotgrass, Nine Joints, Ninety Knot, Pigrush, Pigweed,

Red Robin, Sparrow's Tongue, Swynel
Grass
Gender: Feminine.
Planet: Saturn
Element: Earth
Powers: Binding, Health
Magical Uses:
To 'bind' woes and miseries, hold
some knotweed in your hand. Pour your
problems into the herb; see it absorbing
them and then burn it.
When carried knotweed strengthens
and protects the eyes.

LADY'S MANTLE *(Alchemilla vulgaris)*
Folk Names: Bear's Foot, Leontopodium,
Lion's Foot, Nine Hooks, Stellaria
Gender: Feminine
Planet: Venus
Element: Water
Powers: Love
Magical Uses:
Use the herb in love spells and
sachets.

LADY'S SLIPPER *(Cypripedium pubes-
cens)*
Gender: Feminine
Planet: Saturn
Element: Water
Powers: Protection
Magical Uses:
Lady's slipper is used in protective
sachets as it guards against all manner of
hexes, curses, spells and the evil eye.

LARCH *(Larix europaea)*
Gender: Masculine
Powers: Protection, Anti-Fire
Magical Uses:
Since larch wood cannot be pene-
trated by fire according to long magical
tradition, it is used in sachets designed to
prevent conflagrations.
Larch is also carried or worn to pre-
vent enchantment and protects against

the evil eye.

LARKSPUR *(Delphinium* spp.)
Folk Names: Delphinium
Gender: Feminine
Planet: Venus
Element: Water
Powers: Health, Protection
Magical Uses:

The larkspur keeps away ghosts. If you look through a bunch of larkspur at a Midsummer fire your eyes will be preserved for the next year, until another Midsummer.

The flowers frighten off scorpions and other venemous creatures.

LAVENDAR *(Lavendula officinale* or *L. vera)*
Folk Names: Elf Leaf, Nard, Nardus, Spike
Gender: Masculine
Planet: Mercury
Element: Air
Powers: Love, Protection, Sleep, Chastity, Longevity, Purification, Happiness, Peace
Magical Uses:

Lavendar has long been used in love spells and sachets. Clothing rubbed with the fragrant flowers (or lavendar placed in drawers with clothes) attracts love. A piece of paper on which you've rubbed lavendar is excellent for writing love notes. The scent of lavendar particularly attracts men, and lavendar water or the essential oil was worn by prostitutes several centuries ago to both advertise their profession as well as to attract (through magic) customers. Lavendar also protects against cruel treatment at the hands of a spouse if worn.

These flowers are also burned or smouldered to induce sleep and rest, and are scattered about the home to maintain its peacefulness. The plant is so powerful that, if when depressed, one gazes upon

the plant all sorrow will depart and a joyous feeling will settle upon the observer.

Indeed, the odor of lavendar is conducive to long life, and so should be smelled as often as possible if this is a concern.

Lavendar is also used in healing mixtures, carried to see ghosts, and worn to protect against the evil eye. It is added to purification baths.

Despite lavendar's love associations, in the Renaissance it was believed that lavendar together with rosemary, if worn, would preserve a woman's chastity.

A wish divination: Place lavendar under your pillow while thinking of your wish. Do this just prior to retiring for the night. In the morning, if you have dreamt of anything relating to your wish, it will come true. However, if you did not dream, or if they were unconnected with your wish, it will not manifest.

LEEK *(Allium* spp.)
Gender: Masculine
Planet: Mars
Element: Fire
Powers: Love, Protection, Exorcism
Magical Uses:

When two people eat leeks they will fall in love with each other.

Leeks are also carried as protective amulets, and are bitten to break hexes and drive away evil.

LEMON *(Citrus limon)*
Gender: Feminine
Planet: Moon
Element: Water
Powers: Longevity, Purification, Love, Friendship
Magical Uses:

Lemon juice is mixed with water and the resultant mixture is used to wash amulets, jewelry and other magical objects which have been obtained second-hand.

This wash ensures that all negative vibrations are cleansed from the object in question. The juice is also added to bath water at the time of the full Moon for its purificatory powers.

The dried flowers and peel are added to love sachets and mixtures, and the leaves are used in lust teas. A lemon tree grown from a seed which was taken from a lemon that you have consumed is a highly appropriate gift to a loved one, although admittedly this is a long process. Lemon pie, served to a spouse, will help strengthen fidelity, and a slice of fresh lemon placed beneath a visitor's chair ensures that your friendship will last.

Obtain a green (unripe) lemon from a tree. It should be no larger than 1½ inches in diameter. Next, obtain some color-headed pins. Every color except black is fine; if any black-headed pins are present remove them. Now stick the pins, one at a time, into the lemon, until it is fairly bristling with them. Attach a piece of yarn or ribbon to the lemon and hang up in the home to bring blessings and luck, or give to a friend. These 'lemon and pins' charms are easy to make and are quite effective, too.

A lemon may serve as a poppet.

LEMONGRASS *(Cymbopogon citratus)*
Gender: Masculine
Planet: Mercury
Element: Air
Powers: Repel Snakes, Lust, Psychic Powers
Magical Uses:

(Not Shown)

Lemongrass planted around the home and in the garden will repel snakes.

It is also used in some lust potions, as well as in an infusion to aid in developing psychic powers.

LEMON VERBENA *(Lippia citriodora)*
Folk Names: Cedron, Yerba Louisa
Gender: Masculine
Planet: Mercury
Element: Air
Powers: Purification, Love
Magical Uses:

If this plant is hung around the neck, or a bit of its juice is drunk, it will preserve you from dreaming.

Lemon verbena is also worn to make oneself attractive to the opposite sex, and is used in love spells and mixtures.

The herb is added to other mixtures to increase their strength, and is sometimes utilized to purify an area, or is added to bathwater for purificatory purposes.

LETTUCE *(Lactuca sativa)*
Folk Names: Garden Lettuce, Lattouce, Sleep Wort
Gender: Feminine
Planet: Moon
Element: Water
Powers: Chastity, Protection, Love Divination, Sleep
Magical Uses:

Rub lettuce juice onto the forehead or eat the leaves to have no trouble falling asleep.

Lettuce when grown in the garden is protective, but some say that if too many are raised, sterility will result in the household.

If you wish to preserve yourself against temptations of the flesh, eat lettuce. When eaten, lettuce also prevents seasickness.

Plant lettuce or cress seeds in the form of a name of someone you love. If the seeds sprout well, so too will love between you.

LICORICE *(Glycyrrhiza glabra)*
Folk Names: *Lacris* (Welsh), Licourice,

Lycorys, *Reglisse* (Welsh), Sweet Root
Gender: Feminine
Planet: Venus
Element: Water
Powers: Lust, Love, Fidelity
Magical Uses:

Chewing on a licorice stick (the root, not a piece of candy) will make you passionate. It is also a good practice to use while quitting smoking.

Licorice is added to love and lust sachets, carried to attract love, and used in spells to ensure fidelity.

Licorice sticks make useful wands.

LIFE-EVERLASTING *(Anaphalis* spp; *Gnaphalium uliginosum)*
Folk Names: Chafe Weed, Everlasting, Field Balsam, Indian Posy, Old Field Balsam, Sweet Scented Life Everlasting, White Balsam
Powers: Longevity, Health, Healing
Magical Uses:

Use in spells of longevity, as well as for restoring youth. It is also kept in the home or carried to prevent sickness and ill-health.

Drink an infusion of life-everlasting every morning, before eating or drinking anything else, while saying:
Chills and ills, pains and banes,
Do your fasting with life everlasting.
This will ensure a long life comparatively free of illness.

LILAC *(Syringa vulgaris)*
Folk Names: Common Lilac
Gender: Feminine
Planet: Venus
Element: Water
Powers: Exorcism, Protection
Magical Uses:

Lilac drives away evil where it is planted or strewn, and indeed in New England lilacs were originally planted to keep evil from the property.

The flowers, fresh, can be placed in a haunted house to help clear it.

LILY *(Lilium* spp.)
Gender: Feminine
Planet: Moon
Element: Water
Deities: Venus, Juno, Nepthys, Kwan Yin
Powers: Protection, Breaking Love Spells
Magical Uses:

Plant lillies in the garden to keep away ghosts and evil, protect against the evil eye, and to keep unwanted visitors from your home.

Lillies are also good antidotes to love spells; for this purpose a fresh lily should be worn or carried. This breaks love spells which have been cast involving a specific person.

To bring clues in solving a crime committed in the past year, bury an old piece of leather in a bed of lillies.

The first white lily of the season will bring strength to he or she who finds it.

LILY OF THE VALLEY *(Convallaria magalis)* POISON
Folk Names: Convallaria, Jacob's Ladder, Ladder to Heaven, Lily Constancy, Male Lily, May Lily, Our Lady's Tears
Gender: Masculine
Planet: Mercury
Element: Air
Deities: Apollo, Aesculapius
Powers: Mental Powers, Happiness
Magical Uses:

Use to improve the memory and mind. When placed in a room, these flowers cheer the heart and lift the spirits of those present.

LIME *(Citrus aurantifolia* or *L. Limetta)*
Gender: Masculine
Planet: Sun

Element: Fire
Powers: Healing, Love, Protection
Magical Uses:

Take a fresh lime, pierce it with old iron nails, spikes, pins and needles, and throw it into a deep hole in the ground. This will rid you of all ills, hexes, and so on.

Wear a necklace of limes to cure a sore throat. Lime peel is used in love mixtures and incenses. To cure a toothache, drive a nail into the trunk of a lime tree (but thank the lime tree first before you do so).

Twigs of the lime tree protect against the evil eye when carried.

LINDEN *(Tilia europaea)*
Folk Names: Lime, Lime Tree
Gender: Masculine
Planet: Jupiter
Element: Air
Deities: Venus, Lada
Powers: Protection, Immortality, Luck, Love, Sleep
Ritual Uses:

Lithuanian women once made sacrifices to linden trees as part of religious rites.

Magical Uses:

Linden is extensively used in Europe as a protective tree. The branches are hung over the door for this purpose, or the tree itself is grown in the garden.

The bark of the linden carried prevents intoxication, while the leaves and flowers are used in love spells. Since it is a tree of immortality its leaves are used in spells of this nature.

Linden and lavendar equally mixed make excellent pillows which hasten sleep in the insomniac, and good luck charms are carved from the wood and carried.

LIQUIDAMBER *(Liquidambar* spp.)
Folk Names: Styrax, Sweet Gum, Voodoo

Witch Burr, Witch Burr
Gender: Masculine
Planet: Sun
Element: Fire
Powers: Protection
Magical Uses:

The seed pods are placed on the altar or held during magical rites for protection against evil forces.

Liquidamber bark is substituted for storax bark.

LIVERWORT *(Anemone hepatica*—American; *Peltigera canina*—English)
Folk Names: Edellebere, Heart Leaf, Herb Trinity, Liverleaf, Liverweed, Trefoil
Gender: Masculine
Planet: Jupiter
Element: Fire
Powers: Love
Magical Uses:

A woman may secure the love of a man by carrying liverwort in a sachet at all times.

LOBELIA *(Lobelia inflata)* **POISON**
Folk Names: Asthma Weed, Bladderpod, Gagroot, Indian Tobacco, Pukeweed
Gender: Feminine
Planet: Saturn
Element: Water
Powers: Halting Storms, Love
Magical Uses:

Throw some powdered lobelia at an oncoming storm to stop its approach.

Lobelia is also used to attract a love.

LOOSESTRIFE *(Lythrum salicaria)*
Folk Names: Blooming Sally, Lythrum, Partyke, Purple Willow Herb, Rainbow Weed, Sage Willow, Salicaire
Gender: Feminine
Planet: Moon
Element: Earth
Powers: Peace, Protection

Magical Uses:

To settle an argument you've had with a friend, give some of this herb to him or her.

Strewn about the home loosestrife disperses peaceful vibrations and keeps evil forces at bay.

LOTUS *(Nymphaea lotus)*
Gender: Feminine
Planet: Moon
Element: Water
Powers: Protection, Lock-Opening
Ritual Uses:

The lotus has long been revered in the East as a mystical symbol of life, spirituality, and the center of the universe. The ancient Egyptians considered the plant to be sacred and the lotus was used as an offering to the gods.

Magical Uses:

Anyone who breathes the scent of the lotus will receive its protection.

Place the root of a lotus under the tongue, and say the words "SIGN, ARG-GIS' toward a locked door. It will miraculously open.

Lotus seeds and pods are used as antidotes to love spells, and any part of the lotus carried or worn ensures blessings by the Gods and good luck.

LOVAGE *(Levisticum officinale)*
Folk Names: Chinese Lovage, Cornish Lovage, Italian Lovage, Italian Parsley, Lavose, Love Herbs, Love Rod, Love Root, Loving Herbs, Lubestico, Sea Parsley
Gender: Masculine
Planet: Sun
Element: Fire
Powers: Love
Magical Uses:

Place lovage in the bath water (in a sachet). This will make you more attractive and love-inspiring. Such baths are best

taken directly before going out to meet
new people.

LOVE SEED *(Lomatium foeniculaceum)*
Gender: Feminine
Planet: Venus
Element: Water
Powers: Love, Friendship
Magical Uses:

Pawnee Indians used this herb in
magic. The seeds are carried to attract
love and new friendships.

LUCKY HAND *(Orchis* spp.)
Folk Names: Hand of Power, Hand Root,
    Helping Hand, Salap
Gender: Feminine
Planet: Venus
Element: Water
Powers: Employment, Luck, Protection,
    Money, Travel
Magical Uses:

This root of an orchid plant is one
of the most famous New Orleans magical
botanicals. It has long been placed in
sachets and conjure bags for luck and general success, carried to obtain and maintain
employment, and to secure protection
from all ills.

Fill a jar with rose oil. Place several
lucky hands into the oil and let them
soak there. When you need something
take out one of the roots and wear it. If
you need love, wear it near your heart; if
you wish to travel, place it in your shoe;
if you need money carry one in your
wallet or purse, and so on.

MACE *(Myristica fragrans)*
Gender: Masculine
Planet: Mercury
Element: Air
Powers: Psychic Powers, Mental Powers
Magical Uses:

Mace, the outer covering of the nutmeg, is burned to increase psychic powers

and is carried to improve the intellect.

MAGUEY *(Agave* spp.)
Folk Name: Agave
Gender: Masculine
Planet: Mars
Element: Fire
Powers: Lust
Magical Uses:
The juice of the maguey has long been used in lust potions.

MAGNOLIA *(Magnolia grandifolia)*
Folk Names: Blue Magnolia, Cucumber Tree, Swamp Sassafras
Gender: Feminine
Planet: Venus
Element: Earth
Powers: Fidelity
Magical Uses:
Place some magnolia near or beneath the bed to maintain a faithful relationship.

MAHOGANY, MOUNTAIN *(Cercocarpus ledifolius)*
Gender: Masculine
Element: Fire
Powers: Anti-Lightning
Magical Uses:
Long used to protect against lightning, especially by mountain climbers. Mountain mahogany lives at high elevations where lightning and thunder live too, according to ancient American Indian tradition. Thus the tree gives protection from lightning strikes. Wear a piece of the bark in your hat or somewhere on your person while mountain climbing.

MAIDENHAIR *(Adiantum pedatim)*
Folk Names: Maidenhair Fern
Gender: Feminine
Planet: Venus
Element: Water

Deity: Venus
Powers: Beauty, Love
Magical Uses:

Immerse some maidenhair in water, then remove. If worn on the person or kept in the bedroom after this process it will grant you grace, beauty and love.

MALE FERN *(Dryopteris felix-mas)*
Gender: Masculine
Planet: Mercury
Element: Air
Powers: Luck, Love
Magical Uses:

Male fern is carried as a potent luck attractant, and it also draws women.

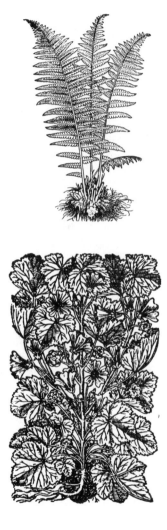

MALLOW *(Malva* spp.)
Gender: Feminine
Planet: Moon
Element: Water
Powers: Love, Protection, Exorcism
Magical Uses:

If your love has left you, gather a boquet of mallow and place in a vase outside your door (or in a window). This will cause him or her to think of you, and after that they may return. Mallow is also carried to attract love.

To make an effective protective magical ointment, steep mallow leaves and stems in vegetable shortening, then strain. This ointment rubbed onto the skin casts out devils as well as protects against the harmful effects of black magic.

MANDRAKE *(Mandragora officinale)* **POISON**
Folk Names: Alraun, Anthropomorphon, Baaras, Brain Thief, Circeium, Circoea, **Galgenmannchen**, Gallows, Herb of Circe, Hexenmannchen (German: Witches' Mannikin), Ladykins, Mandragen, Mandragor, Mannikin, Racoon Berry, Semihomo, Wild Lemon, Womandrake, *Zauberwurzel* (German: Sorcerer's Root)

Gender: Masculine
Planet: Mercury
Element: Fire
Deities: Hecate, Hathor
Powers: Protection, Fertility, Money, Love, Health
Magical Uses:

A whole mandrake root, placed on the mantel in the home, will give the house protection, fertility, and prosperity. Mandrake is also hung on the headboard for protection during sleep, carried to attract love, and worn to prevent contraction of illnesses.

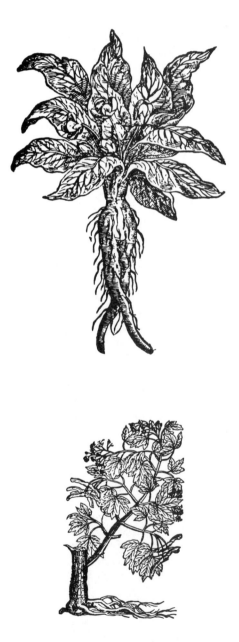

Where there is mandrake, demons cannot reside, and so the root is used in exorcism.

To 'activate' a dried mandrake root (i.e., to bring its powers out of hibernation), place it in some prominent location in the house and leave it there undisturbed for three days. Then place it in warm water and leave overnight. Afterwards, the root is activated and may be used in any magical practice. The water in which the root has bathed can be sprinkled at the windows and doors of the house to protect it, or onto people to purify them.

The mandrake has also long served as a poppet in image magic, but its extreme scarcity and high cost usually forces the magician and Witch to look for substitutes; ash roots, apples, the root of the briony, the American may-apple and many others have been used.

Money placed beside a mandrake root (especially silver coins) is said to double, and the scent of the mandrake causes sleep.

MAPLE *(Acer* spp.*)*
Gender: Masculine
Planet: Jupiter
Element: Air
Powers: Love, Longevity, Money

Magical Uses:

Maple leaves are used in love spells and money rituals, and branches of the maple have long served as magical wands.

A child passed through the branches of a maple tree will have a long life.

MARIGOLD *(Calendula officinalis)*

Folk Names: Bride of the Sun, Calendula, Drunkard, Goldes, Holigolde, Husband-man's Dial, Marybud, Marygold, Mary Gowles, Ruddes, Ruddles, *Spousa Solis,* Summer's Bride

Gender: Masculine

Planet: Sun

Element: Fire

Powers: Protection, Prophetic Dreams, Legal Matters, Psychic Powers

Magical Uses:

Marigolds, picked at noon when the Sun is at its hottest and strongest, will strengthen and comfort the heart.

Garlands of marigolds strung on the doorposts stop evil from entering the house, and scattered under the bed they protect you while asleep and make your dreams come true, i.e. give you prophetic dreams. Especially effective in discovering a thief who has robbed you.

Marigolds added to the bath water help win the respect and admiration of everyone you meet.

Looking at the bright flowers strengthens the sight, and carried in the pocket, marigold helps justice to smile favorably upon you while in court.

If a girl touches the petals of the marigold with her bare feet, she will understand the languages of the birds.

MARJORAM *(Origanum majorana* or *O. vulgare)*

Folk Names: Joy of the Mountain, Knotted Marjorane, Marjorlaine, Mountain Mint, Pot Marjoram, Sweet Marjoram, Wintersweet

Gender: Masculine
Planet: Mercury
Element: Air
Deities: Venus, Aphrodite
Powers: Protection, Love, Happiness, Health, Money
Magical Uses:

Marjoram is used in love spells, and is also added to food to strengthen love.

Carried it is protective, as it is when placed around the house, a bit in each room, and renewed each month. Grown in the garden it offers shielding powers against evil.

Violets and marjoram, mixed together, are worn during the winter months as an amulet against colds.

Given to a depressed person marjoram brings happiness. It is also used in money mixtures and sachets.

MASTERWORT *(Imperatoria ostruthium)*
Gender: Masculine
Planet: Mars
Element: Fire
Powers: Strength, Courage, Protection
Magical Uses:

Masterwort grants physical strength if worn, and so may be used by laborers and athletes to reinforce the body. It is also carried to aid the will and calm emotions, and as an amulet against evil. Sprinkle it about to make spirits appear.

MASTIC *(Pistacia lentiscus)*
Folk Names: Gum Mastic, Masticke
Gender: Masculine
Planet: Sun
Element: Air
Powers: Psychic Powers, Manifestations, Lust
Magical Uses:

Mastic is burned in magical operations wherein a manifestation of a spirit is desired.

It is also used as an incense to aid

the psychic powers and has long been dissolved and used in lust potions by magicians and Witches in the Middle East.

Added to any incense mastic lends potency and power.

MAY APPLE *(Podophyllum peltaltum)* **POISON**
Folk Names: American Mandrake, Duck's Foot, Hog Apple, Mandrake, Racoon Berry, Wild Lemon
Gender: Masculine
Planet: Mercury
Element: Fire
Powers: Money
Magical Uses:

American mandrake, or may apple, is generally used as a substitute for the European (true) mandrake. Its uses are practically identical.

The may apple is not related to the true mandrake.

MEADOW RUE *(Thalictrum* spp.*)*
Folk Names: Flute Plant
Powers: Love, Divination
Magical Uses:

Worn around the neck by American Indians as an all-around protective amulet, and also carried to attract love.

MEADOWSWEET *(Spiraea filipendula)*
Folk Names: Bride of the Meadow, Bridewort, Dollor, Gravel Root, Lady of the Meadow, Little Queen, Meadowwort, Meadowsweet, Queen of the meadow, Steeplebush, Trumpet Weed
Gender: Masculine
Planet: Jupiter
Element: Air
Powers: Love, Divination, Peace, Happiness
Magical Uses:

Fresh meadowsweet is placed on the altar for love spells, or dried is used in various love mixtures.

Also strewn about the house to

keep peace. The scent of meadowsweet cheers the heart.

If gathered on Midsummer, meadowsweet will give you information regarding thieves: if you have been robbed, place meadowsweet on water. If it sinks, the thief is a man. If it floats, a woman.

MESQUITE *(Prosopis juliflora)*
Folk Names: Mizquitl (Aztec)
Gender: Feminine
Planet: Moon
Element: Water
Powers: Healing
Magical Uses:

Add to healing incenses and mixtures. Mesquite is also used to fuel magical fires.

MIMOSA *(Acacia dealbata)*
Gender: Feminine
Planet: Saturn
Element: Water
Powers: Protection, Love, Prophetic Dreams, Purification
Magical Uses:

Mimosa is used in spells involving purification (scatter around the area), love, healing, and prophetic dreaming—the latter use, of course, entailing its placement beneath the pillow and subsequently sleeping on it.

A bath of mimosa (or an infusion of the plant sponged onto the body) destroys hexes and curses, and guards against future problems.

MINT *(Mentha* spp.)
Folk Names: Garden Mint
Gender: Masculine
Planet: Mercury
Element: Air
Deities: Pluto, Hecate
Powers: Money, Lust, Healing, Travel, Exorcism, Protection

Magical Uses:

Mint has long been used in healing potions and mixtures, and the fresh leaves rubbed against the head are said to relieve headaches. Mint worn at the wrist assures that you will not be ill. Stomach problems can be alleviated by stuffing a green poppet with mint and anointing it with healing oils.

Mint is also used in travel spells and to provoke lust. Its bright green leaves and crisp scent led to its use in money and prosperity spells; the easiest of which is to place a few leaves in the wallet or purse, or rub where your money is kept.

To rid a place of evil, sprinkle salt water with a sprinkler made of fresh sprigs of mint, marjoram and rosemary.

Fresh mint laid on the altar will call good spirits to be present and aid you in magic.

Mint is also kept in the home for protection.

'Mint' is a general term for any of the *Mentha* family.

MISTLETOE *(Viscum album*—European **POISON** Mistletoe; *Phoradendron flavescens*—American Mistletoe)

Folk Names: All Heal, Birdlime, Devil's Fuge, *Donnerbesen*, European Mistletoe, Golden Bough, Holy Wood, *Lignam sanctae crucis*, Misseltoe, Thunderbesem, Witches Broom, Wood of the Cross

Gender: Masculine

Planet: Sun

Element: Air

Deities: Apollo, Freya, Frigga, Venus, Odin

Powers: Protection, Love, Hunting, Fertility, Health, Exorcism

Ritual Uses:

As is well known, the Druids revered the mistletoe, especially when found growing on an oak. It was (and still is) cut on Midsummer's day, or else when the Moon is six days old. One stroke of a gold sickle was used to cut the herb, and it wasn't allowed to touch the ground.

Magical Uses:

Long used for protection against lightning, disease, misfortune of every kind, fires and so on, it is carried or placed in an appropriate spot for these uses. The leaves and berries are used. Mistletoe is placed in cradles to protect children from being stolen by fairies and replaced with changelings.

A ring carved of mistletoe wood will ward off sicknesses when worn and the plant will cure fresh wounds quickly when carried (do not apply to the wound).

Mistletoe is also carried or worn for good luck in hunting, and women carry the herb to aid in conception. It has also been utilized in spells designed to capture that elusive state of immortality, and to open locks.

Laid near the bedroom door, mistletoe gives restful sleep and beautiful dreams, as it does when placed beneath the pillow or hung at the headboard.

Kiss your love beneath mistletoe and you'll stay in love. Burned, mistletoe banishes evil. Wear it around your neck to attain invisibility. Mistletoe is an all-purpose herb.

MOLUKKA

Folk Names: Fairy's Eggs, Virgin Mary's Nut

(Not Shown)

Powers: Protection

Magical Uses:

The white molukka nuts are hung around the neck to indicate, as well as to banish, hexes and curses. If the nuts turn black they have averted an evil spell.

MOONWORT *(Botrychium* spp.)

Folk Name: Unshoe-Horse

Gender: Feminine

Planet: Moon
Element: Water
Powers: Money, Love
Magical Uses:

Moonwort placed in boxes and bags supposedly produces silver. It has long been used in money spells of all types.

This fern is also used in opening locks (by placing it in the keyhole) and breaking chains (by simply touching them).

Horses as well as humans who accidentally step on it lose their shoes, according to ancient tradition.

Moonwort is also utilized in love spells.

MORNING GLORY *(Ipomoea* spp.) **POISON**
Folk Names: Bindweed
Gender: Masculine
Planet: Saturn
Element: Water
Powers: Happiness, Peace
Magical Uses:

Place the seeds beneath the pillow to stop all nightmares. Grown in the garden, blue morning glories bring peace and happiness.

The root of the morning glory may be used as a substitute for high John the conqueror root.

MOSS
Powers: Luck, Money
Magical Uses:

To carry moss (any type) taken from a gravestone in your pocket, is a good ensurer of luck, especially financial luck.

Moss is used to stuff general-purpose poppets.

MUGWORT *(Artemisia vulgaris)*
Folk Names: Artemis Herb, Artemisia, Felon Herb, Muggons, Naughty Man,

Old Man, Old Uncle Henry, Sailor's Tobacco, St. John's Plant

Gender: Feminine

Planet: Venus

Element: Earth

Deities: Artemis, Diana

Powers: Strength, Psychic Powers, Protection, Prophetic Dreams, Healing, Astral Projection

Magical Uses:

Place mugwort in the shoes to gain strength during long walks or runs. For this purpose pick mugwort before sunrise, saying:

Tollam te artemesia, ne lassus sim in via.

A pillow stuffed with mugwort and slept upon will produce prophetic dreams. Mugwort is also burned with sandalwood or wormwood during scrying rituals, and a mugwort infusion is drunk (sweetened with honey) before divination.

The infusion is also used to wash crystal balls and magic mirrors, and mugwort leaves are placed around the base of the ball (or beneath it) to aid in psychic workings.

When carrying mugwort you cannot be harmed by poison, wild beasts or sunstroke, according to ancient tradition. In a building, mugwort prevents elves and 'evil thynges' from entering, and bunches of mugwort are used in Japan by the Ainus to exorcise spirits of disease who are thought to hate the odor. In China, it is hung over doors to keep evil spirits from buildings.

Mugwort is also carried to increase lust and fertility, to prevent backache, and to cure disease and madness. Placed next to the bed it aids in achieving astral projection.

MULBERRY *(Morus rubra)*

Gender: Masculine

Planet: Mercury

Element: Air

Deities: Minerva, San Ku Fu Jen, Diana
Powers: Protection, Strength
Magical Uses:

Mulberry protects the garden from lightning. It is also an aid when working on the will, and the wood is a powerful protectant against evil. Wands are made of mulberry.

MULLEIN *(Verbascum thapus)*
Folk Names: Aaron's Rod, Blanket Leaf, Candlewick Plant, Clot, Doffle, Felt-wort, Flannel Plant, Graveyard Dust, Hag's Tapers, Hedge Taper, Jupiter's Staff, Lady's Foxglove, Old Man's Fennel, Peter's Staff, Shepherd's Club, Shepherd's Herb, Torches, Velvetback, Velvet Plant
Gender: Feminine
Planet: Saturn
Element: Fire
Deity: Jupiter
Powers: Courage, Protection, Health, Love Divination, Exorcism
Magical Uses:

Mullein is worn to keep wild animals from you while hiking in untamed areas. It also instills courage in the bearer, and a few leaves placed in the shoe keeps one from catching a cold. Mullein is also carried to obtain love from the opposite sex.

Stuffed into a small pillow or placed beneath your pillow mullein guard against nightmares.

In India, mullein is regarded as the most potent safeguard against evil spirits and magic, and is hung over doors, in windows, and carried in sachets. It is also used to banish demons and negativity.

In the Ozarks, men performed a simple love divination. The man went to a clearing where a mullein grew and bent it down so that it pointed toward his love's house. If she loved him the mullein would grow upright again; if she loved another it would die.

Graveyard dust—an infrequent ingredient in spells—can be substituted with powdered mullein leaves.

At one time Witches and magicians used oil lamps to illuminate their spells and rites, and the downy leaves and stems of the mullein often provided the wicks.

MUSTARD *(Brassica* spp.)
Gender: Masculine
Planet: Mars
Element: Fire
Deity: Aesculapius
Powers: Fertility, Protection, Mental Powers
Magical Uses:

The Hindus used mustard seed to travel through the air. A more down-to-Earth use is carrying mustard seed in a red cloth sachet to guard against colds and to increase mental powers.

Italian peasants sprinkle mustard seed on the doorsill for protective reasons, and mustard seed buried under your doorstep will keep all manner of supernatural beings from your home.

When eaten mustard seed increases fertility in women.

MYRRH *(Commiphora myrrha)*
Folk Names: Gum Myrrh Tree, Karan, *Mirra Balsom Odendron*
Gender: Feminine
Planet: Moon
Element: Water
Deities: Isis, Adonis, Ra, Marian
Powers: Protection, Exorcism, Healing, Spirituality
Ritual Uses: Myrrh was burned to Ra at noon in ancient Egypt, and was also fumed in the temples of Isis.
Magical Uses:

Burned as an incense myrrh purifies the area, lifts the vibrations and creates peace. However, it is rarely burned alone; usually in conjunction with frankincense or other resins. Myrrh increases the power of any incense to which it is added.

Myrrh is also included in healing incenses and sachets, and its smoke is used to consecrate, purify and bless objects such as amulets, talismans, charms and magical tools.

Myrrh also aids meditation and contemplation. It is often added to sachets, usually with frankincense.

MYRTLE *(Myrtus communis)*
Gender: Feminine
Planet: Venus
Element: Water
Deities: Venus, Artemis, Aphrodite, Hathor, Astarte, Ashtoreth, Marian
Powers: Love, Fertility, Youth, Peace, Money
Magical Uses:

Myrtle has long been considered a 'love' herb. A chaplet of fresh leaves and flowers worn on the head while performing love spells is highly appropriate. Myrtle is added to all love sachets and spells, especially those designed to keep love alive and exciting.

Myrtle is also worn to increase fertility, but interestingly enough it is also worn at weddings by brides to ensure that they do not quickly become pregnant!

Myrtle wood, when carried, preserves youthfulness. A cup of myrtle tea, drunk every three days, will do the same, but it must be drunk every three days without fail.

When carried, myrtle preserves love. If grown on each side of the house love and peace will reside within, and it is a lucky plant to grow in window-boxes, *if* it is planted there by a woman. Myrtle is also used in money spells.

NETTLE *(Urtica dioica)*
Folk Names: *Ortiga ancha*, Stinging Nettle

Gender: Masculine
Planet: Mars
Element: Fire
Deity: Thor
Powers: Exorcism, Protection, Healing, Lust
Magical Uses:

The protective powers of the nettle have long been used in magic. To remove a curse and send it back, stuff a poppet with nettle, or carry some in a sachet.

Also, sprinkle nettle around the house to keep evil out and to send it back. Nettle is also thrown onto a fire to avert danger, held in the hand to ward off ghosts, carried with yarrow to allay fear, and worn as an amulet to keep negativity far away.

A pot of freshly cut nettles placed beneath a sickbed will aid in the person's recovery.

Nettle has sometimes been used as a lust-inducing herb, and contemporary Mexican spiritualists recommend its use in purification baths because it is 'more carnivorous' than other herbs, and so will work more efficiently.

NORFOLK ISLAND PINE *(Auricaria excelsa)*
Gender: Masculine
Planet: Mars
Element: Fire
Powers: Protection, Anti-Hunger
Magical Uses:

The Norfolk Island pine offers protection against hunger and evil spirits when grown in the home or near it.

NUTMEG *(Myristica fragrans)*
Gender: Masculine
Planet: Jupiter
Element: Fire
Powers: Luck, Money, Health, Fidelity

Magical Uses:

Nutmegs have long been carried as good luck charms, and are strung with star anise and tonka beans for a potent herbal necklace. Specifically, nutmegs are carried to ward off rheumatism, cold sores, neuraligis, boils and sties. A nutmeg hung from a string around a baby's neck will aid in its teething.

Nutmeg is included in many money/prosperity mixtures, and (ground) is sprinkled onto green candles for this purpose as well.

To ensure your lover's fidelity, cut a nutmeg into exactly four pieces. Bury one part in the Earth; throw one off a cliff into the air; burn the third part, and boil the last in water. Drink a sip of the water and take this last piece of nutmeg with you everywhere; sleep with it under your pillow at night. No one will tempt your mate.

NUTS
Powers: Fertility, Prosperity, Love, Luck
Magical Uses:

All nuts are potent fertility-inducers, and are carried for such uses.

They are also included in many prosperity and money mixtures. Heart-shaped nuts are carried to promote love, while double-nuts are very lucky charms indeed.

OAK *(Quercus alba)*
Folk Names: Duir, Jove's Nuts, *Juglans* (Latin)
Gender: Masculine
Planet: Sun
Element: Fire
Deities: Dagda, Dianus, Jupiter, Thor, Zeus, Herne, Janus, Rhea, Cybele, Hecate, Pan, Erato
Powers: Protection, Health, Money, Healing, Potency, Fertility, Luck
Ritual Uses:

Since the oak was a source of food

for early settlers in Britain as well as Europe, it came to be revered and worshipped far back into pre-history. The Druids (traditionally) would not meet for rituals unless an oak was present, and the very words 'oak' and 'Druid,' some say, are related. Religious idols were fashioned from oak wood, and Witches often danced beneath the tree.

Magical Uses:

A tree as long-lived and strong as the oak naturally offers magical protection. Two twigs of oak, bound with red thread so that they form an equal-armed cross, makes a potent safeguard against evil. It should be hung in the house.

Acorns placed in windows guard against the entrance of lightning, and a piece of oak wood, carried, protects its bearer from all harm.

If you can catch a falling oak leaf you shall have no colds all winter. When a sick person is in the house make a fire of oakwood and warm the house with it to 'draw off' the illness. (Do this only if you have a fireplace, of course!). Carry an acorn against illnesses and pains, for immortality or longevity, and to preserve youthfulness.

Planting an acorn in the dark of the Moon ensures that you shall receive money in the near future. Carrying an acorn increases fertility and strengthens sexual potency.

Carrying any piece of the oak draws good luck.

OATS *(Avena sativa)*
Folk Names: Groats, Oatmeal
Gender: Feminine
Planet: Venus
Element: Earth
Powers: Money
Magical Uses:

Use in prosperity and money spells.

OLEANDER *(Nerium oleander)* **POISON**
Gender: Feminine
Planet: Saturn
Element: Earth
Powers: Love
Magical Uses:

Although Italian magical thought says that keeping any part of an oleander in the house brings sickness, disgrace and misfortune of every kind to its inhabitants, oleander is occasionally used in love spells —but *never internally*.

OLIVE *(Olea europaea)*
Folk Names: Olivier
Gender: Masculine
Planet: Sun
Element: Fire
Deities: Athena, Apollo, Irene, Minerva, Ra
Powers: Healing, Peace, Fertility, Potency, Protection, Lust
Ritual Uses:

The oil was burned in lamps to light temples in ancient times.

Magical Uses:

On an olive leaf write Athena's name. Press this against the head or wear on the body and it will cure a headache. Olive oil has long been used as an anointing oil to aid in healing.

Olive leaves scattered or placed in a room spread a peaceful vibration throughout the area.

When eaten, olives ensure fertility as well as sexual potency in men, and are also lust-inducing. Athenian brides wore crowns of olive leaves to ensure their fertility.

A branch of olive hung over the door guards the house against all evils, and on the chimney wards off lightning. Olive leaves, worn, bring luck.

ONION *(Allium cepa)*
Folk Names: Oingnum, Onyoun, Un-

youn, Yn-leac
Gender: Masculine
Planet: Mars
Element: Fire
Deity: Isis
Powers: Protection, Exorcism, Healing, Money, Prophetic Dreams, Lust
Ritual Uses:

According to some ancient authorities, the onion was worshipped in some cities in ancient Egypt, and was sometimes invoked while taking oaths.

Magical Uses:

Take a small white onion, stick it full of black-headed pins, and place in a window. This will guard against the intrusion of evil into the home. The flowers are decorative and protective, and can be dried and placed in the home for an unusual and attractive protective amulet. Carried, the onion gives protection against venemous beasts. Grown in pots or in the garden they also shield against evil.

Halved or quartered onions, placed in the house, will absorb negativity and evil, as well as disease.

For healing, rub the cut edge of an onion against the afflicted part of the body, visualizing the disease going into the onion. Then destroy the onion (burn or smash to pieces and bury). Settlers in New England hung strings of onions over doorways to guard against infections, and a cut onion placed beneath the kitchen sink has long been used for the same purpose. To cure warts, rub them with a piece of onion and throw over your right shoulder. Walk away without looking back. A large red onion tied to the bedpost protects its occupants against sickness, and aids in recuperation.

Never throw onion skins and peelings onto the ground; if you do, you throw away your prosperity. Instead, burn them in the fireplace or cookstove to attract riches.

An onion placed beneath the pillow can produce prophetic dreams. If you are faced with making a decision, scratch your options on onions, one to each onion. Place them in the dark. The first one that sprouts answers you.

Some ancient authorities state that when eaten, the onion 'provokes to venery', i.e. produces lust.

Magical knives and swords are purified by rubbing their blades with cut fresh onions, and if you throw an onion after a bride you'll throw away her tears.

ORANGE *(Citrus sinesis)*

Folk Name: Love Fruit
Gender: Masculine
Planet: Sun
Element: Fire
Powers: Love, Divination, Luck, Money
Magical Uses:

The dried peel and seeds are added to love sachets, and the flowers to those sachets designed to lead to wedded bliss. The fresh or dried blossoms added to the bath make the bather more attractive.

When you eat an orange, think of a question you want answered; it must be a yes/no question. Count the seeds in the orange: if they are of an even number, the answer is no. If odd, yes.

Orange peel is added to prosperity powders, incenses and mixtures, and the Chinese have long considered oranges symbols of luck and good fortune.

Orange juice is drunk in rituals in place of wine. An infusion of orange peels, drunk, will guard against later drunkeness, while the water distilled from orange flowers is added to love and lust potions and baths.

ORCHID *(Orchis spp.)*

Folk Names: Levant Salap, *Sahlab* (Arabic), Sahleb, Salep, Saloop, Satyrion

Gender: Feminine
Planet: Venus
Element: Water
Powers: Love
Magical Uses:

Orchids have long been used in love spells, especially the root, which is carried in a sachet.

Of course, the flower is currently one of the commoner floral symbols of love in the West, and when given, clearly conveys its message.

Some types of orchids are used in creating visions, trance-states and inducing psychic powers.

OREGON GRAPE *(Berberis aquifolium)*
Folk Names: California Barberry, Oregon Grape Root, Rocky Mountain Grape, Trailing Grape, Wild Oregon Grape
Gender: Feminine
Planet: Earth
Powers: Money, Popularity
Magical Uses:

Carry this root to draw money and financial security and to gain popularity.

ORRIS *(Iris florentina)*
Folk Names: Florentine Iris, Queen Elizabeth Root
Gender: Feminine
Planet: Venus
Element: Water
Deities: Aphrodite, Isis, Osiris, Hera, Iris
Powers: Love, Protection, Divination
Magical Uses:

The orris root has long been used to find and hold love. The whole orris root is carried, the powder added to sachets, sprinkled on sheets, clothing and the body, as well as around the house. Orris root powder is sometimes known as 'Love Drawing Powder'.

In Japan the orris was used as a protectant against evil spirits; the roots and leaves were hung from the eaves of the house and added to the bath water for personal protection.

Suspend a whole root from a small length of cord or yarn and with this pendulum find answers to your questions.

PALM, DATE *(Phoenix dactylifera)*
Gender: Masculine
Planet: Sun
Element: Air
Deities: Taht, Apollo, Artemis, Hecate, Isis, Ras
Powers: Fertility, Potency
Magical Uses:

The date palm is a celebrated fertility tree, owing to the tremendous amount of fruits produced by it. Thusly, dates or pieces of palm leaves are worn or carried for this purpose; dates are eaten to increase fertility, and the pits are carried by men who wish to regain sexual potency.

Where the palm grows, it protects the area from inclement weather, and a leaf of the palm kept near the entrance of the home keeps evil and uncanny creatures from entering.

PANSY *(Viola tricolor)*
Folk Names: Banewort, *Banwort* (Anglo-Saxon), Bird's Eye, *Bonewort* (Anglo-Saxon), Bouncing Bet, Garden Violet, Heart's Ease, Horse Violet, Johnny Jumper, Johnny Jump-Ups, Kiss-Me-At-The-Garden-Gate, Little Stepmother, Love Idol, Love-In-Idleness, Love-Lies Bleeding, Loving Idol, Meet-Me-In-The-Entry, *Pensee* (French), Stepmother, Tittle-My-Fancy
Gender: Feminine
Planet: Saturn
Element: Water
Powers: Love, Rain Magic, Love Divination
Magical Uses:

Worn or carried the pansy draws love. It is also potent for love divinations:

plant pansies in the shape of a heart; if they prosper, so too will your love.

A woman whose sailor-love goes to sea, can ensure that he thinks of her by burying sea sand in the pansy bed and watering the flowers before sunrise.

If pansies are picked when dew is still on them, it will soon rain.

PAPAYA *(Carica papaya)*
Folk Name: Paw-Paw
Gender: Feminine
Planet: Moon
Element: Water
Powers: Love, Protection
Magical Uses:

The papaya has long been used in magical rites. One of the simplest of these is to tie a rag around a limb of a papaya tree while visualizing your need.

Hang several twigs of papaya wood over the doorsill; this will keep evil from entering the house.

Eat the fruit and serve to a loved one; it will intensify feelings of love.

PAPYRUS *(Cyperus papyrus)*
Gender: Masculine
Planet: Mercury
Element: Air
Powers: Protection
Magical Uses:

Place in boats to protect against attacks by crocodiles.

PAROSELA *(Parosela* spp.; *Dalea* spp.)
Folk Names: Citrus Plant, Desert Rue
Powers: Hunting
Magical Uses:

Parosela was worn by American Indians as a magical aid to hunting.

PARSLEY *(Petroselinum sativum)*
Folk Names: Devil's Oatmeal, Percely, Persil, Petersilie, Petroselinum, Rock Parsley

Gender: Masculine
Planet: Mercury
Element: Air
Deity: Persephone
Powers: Lust, Protection, Purification
Magical Uses:

When eaten, parsley provokes lust and promotes fertility, but if you are in love don't cut parsley—you'll cut your love as well.

Though the plant has associations with death and is often regarded as evil, the Romans tucked a sprig of parsley into their togas every morning for protection. It is also placed on plates of food to guard it from contamination.

Parsley is also used in purification baths, and those to stop all misfortune. A wreath of parsley worn on the head prevents (or delays) inebriation.

PASSION FLOWER *(Passiflora incarnata)*
Folk Names: Grandilla, Maracoc, May-
    pops, Passion Vine
Gender: Feminine
Planet: Venus
Element: Water
Powers: Peace, Sleep, Friendships
Magical Uses:

Contrary to its name, the passion flower is placed in the house to calm problems and troubles, and to bring peace.

Carried, it attracts friends and great popularity. Placed below the pillow it aids in sleep.

PATCHOULY *(Pogostemon cablin* or *P. patchouli)*
Folk Names: Pucha-Pot
Gender: Feminine
Planet: Saturn
Element: Earth
Powers: Money, Fertility, Lust
Magical Uses:

Patchouly smells like rich earth,

and so has been used in money and prosperity mixtures and spells. It is sprinkled onto money, added to purses and wallets, and placed around the base of green candles.

Also, owing to its earthiness, patchouly is used in fertility talismans, and is also substituted for 'graveyard dust' where it is called for.

Patchouly is added to love sachets and baths. Although in contemporary American voodoo-based herbal magic patchouly is used for 'separation', this is a modern concept and has no long tradition. In point of fact, patchouly is actually used to attract people and to promote lust. This points to differences in herb magic practices.

PEA *(Pisum sativum)*
Gender: Feminine
Planet: Venus
Element: Earth
Powers: Money, Love
Magical Uses:

Shelling peas brings fortune and profits in business, and the dried peas are used in monetary mixtures.

If a woman finds a pod containing exactly nine peas, she should hang it over the door. The first eligible man to walk under the pod will be her future husband (if she is unmarried).

PEACH *(Prunus persica)*
Gender: Feminine
Planet: Venus
Element: Water
Powers: Love, Exorcism, Longevity, Fertility, Wishes
Magical Uses:

The fruit, when eaten, induces love, and so a peach or peach pie served to a desired one may help to win his or her heart. The fruit is also eaten to gain wisdom.

Branches of the peach tree are used to drive off evil spirits in China, and also to root out illnesses. Children in China wear a peach pit suspended about the neck to keep demons away.

Carrying a bit of peach wood will increase one's life span and may even lead to immortality.

The Japanese use the peach to increase fertility, and branches of the tree are utilized as divining and magical wands.

PEAR *(Pyrus communis)*
Gender: Feminine
Planet: Venus
Element: Water
Powers: Lust, Love
Magical Uses:

The fruit is used in love spells, and also is eaten to induce sexual arousal. Pear wood makes fine magical wands, and it is said that Witches once danced beneath pear trees.

PECAN *(Carya illinoensis)*
Gender: Masculine
Planet: Mercury
Element: Air
Powers: Money, Employment
Magical Uses:

Pecans are added to all money and prosperity spells.

To ensure that you do not lose your job, obtain a small amount of pecans. Shell them, eat them slowly while visualizing yourself working and enjoying your job. Take the shells, wrap them in a bag and place them somewhere at work where they won't be found or removed.

PENNYROYAL *(Mentha pulegium)*
Folk Names: Lurk-In-The-Ditch, Mosquito Plant, Organ Broth, Organs, Organ Tea, Piliolerian, Pudding Grass, Run-By-The-Ground, Squaw Mint, Tickweed

Gender: Masculine
Planet: Mars
Element: Fire
Deity: Demeter
Powers: Strength, Protection, Peace
Magical Uses:

Pennyroyal placed in the shoe prevents weariness during travel and strengthens the body in general.

When worn it acts against the evil eye and aids in making business deals.

When given to quarreling couples it will cause them to cease their fighting, and so pennyroyal is an herb of peace. It is also carried on board ships to prevent seasickness.

PEONY *(Paeonia officinalis)*
Folk Name: Paeony
Gender: Masculine
Planet: Sun
Element: Fire
Powers: Protection, Exorcism
Magical Uses:

The peony has long been revered for its protective powers. Worn, it guards the body, spirit and soul; placed in the home it wards off evil spirits, and planted in the garden it protects it against evil and storms. The seeds or roots are hung around a child's neck to guard it from mischievious fairies and imps. A variation of this entails carving peony roots into small beads (called 'piney beads') and then stringing them. These are also worn for protection. Peony roots worn with coral and flint keeps away the incubus.

Additionally, the peony is used in exorcisms and the root is carried to cure lunacy. It should only be gathered at night, when its seeds are said to shine with an eerie light. Its root is sometimes substituted for the mandrake.

PEPPER *(Piper nigrum)*
Folk Names: Black Pepper

Gender: Masculine
Planet: Mars
Element: Fire
Powers: Protection, Exorcism
Magical Uses:

Pepper is added to amulets as a protectant against the evil eye, and when worn it frees the mind of envious thoughts. Mixed with salt and scattered about the property it dispels evil.

PEPPERMINT *(Mentha piperita)*
Folk Names: Brandy Mint, Lammint
Gender: Masculine
Planet: Mercury
Element: Fire
Deity: Pluto
Powers: Purification, Sleep, Love, Healing, Psychic Powers
Magical Uses:

Peppermint has long been used in healing and purification spells. Its presence raises the vibrations of an area. Smelled, it compels one toward sleep, and placed beneath the pillow it sometimes offers one glimpses of the future in dreams.

It is rubbed against furniture, walls and floorboards to cleanse them of evil and negativity. Pliny stated that peppermint excites love, and so can be added to this type of mixture.

PEPPER TREE *(Schinus molle)*
Folk Names: California Pepper Tree, Peruvian Mastic Tree, *Piru* (Spanish)
Gender: Masculine
Planet: Mars
Element: Fire
Powers: Purification, Healing, Protection
Magical Uses:

Branches of the pepper tree have long been used by Mexican *curanderos* in healing rituals. The sick person is brushed with pepper tree branches to absorb the disease, and then the branches are buried to destroy the illness. Rue is sometimes used with the pepper tree.

The leaves are added to purification baths by Mexican spiritualists and *brujas*, and the bright red berries are carried for protection.

PERIWINKLE *(Vinca minor)* **POISON**
Folk Names: Blue Buttons, *Centocchiio* (Italian: Hundred Eyes), Devil's Eye, Joy on the Ground, Sorcerer's Violet
Gender: Feminine
Planet: Venus
Element: Water
Powers: Love, Lust, Mental Powers, Money, Protection
Magical Uses:

A powerful magical herb (as noted in the folk name 'Sorcerer's Violet'), periwinkle should be gathered according to strict procedures before it is of any efficacy in magic (or so said the Pseudo-Apuleius).

It is to be gathered when one is 'clean of every uncleanness' when the Moon is one night old, nine nights old, eleven nights old or thirteen nights old, and the following incantation should be uttered while plucking the plant:

> *I pray thee, vinca pervinca, thee that art to be had for thy many useful qualities, that thou come to me glad blossoming with thy mainfulness, that thou outfit me so that I be shielded and prosperous and undamaged by poisons and water.*

After this the plant is carried to obtain grace, to attract money, and to protect against snakes, poison, wild beasts, terror, the evil eye and spirits. It is also placed over the door to protect the home.

Periwinkle is utilized in love spells and is thought to increase one's passions

when carried or sprinkled under the bed. When gazed upon it restores lost memories.

PERSIMMON *(Diospyros virginiana)*
Gender: Feminine
Planet: Venus
Element: Water
Powers: Changing Sex, Healing, Luck
Magical Uses:

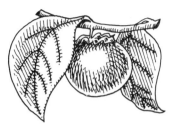

Until recently, in Alabama, it was supposedly believed that if a girl wished to become a boy all she had to do was to eat nine unripe persimmons. She would surely change her sex within two weeks!

If you are plagued with chills, tie a knot in a piece of string (one for each chill you've had) and tie the string to a persimmon tree. This should halt them.

If you wish to have good luck, bury green persimmons.

PILOT WEED *(Silphium laciniatum)*
Folk Names: Bumweed, Compass Point
Powers: Protection
Magical Uses:

The dried root of the pilot weed is burned during electrical storms to avert a lightning strike.

PIMENTO *(Pimenta dioica)*
Gender: Masculine
Planet: Mars
Element: Fire
Powers: Love
Magical Uses:

Pimento has been used in love spells and sachets for centuries, especially among the continental Gypsies. Eaten it has the same effect.

PIMPERNEL *(Pimpinella* spp.)
Folk Names: Blessed Herb, Greater Pimpernel, Herb of Mary, *Luib na muc,* Pimpinella, Poorman's Weatherglass, Shepherd's Weatherglass
Gender: Masculine

Planet: Mercury
Element: Air
Powers: Protection, Health
Magical Uses:

The pimpernel is carried for protection and to keep people from deceiving you. When placed in the home it wards off illnesses and prevents accidents.

Its power is supposed to be so great that when dropped into running water it will move against the current.

Magical knife blades are rubbed with pimpernel juice to purify and empower them.

PINE *(Pinus* spp.)
Gender: Masculine
Planet: Mars
Element: Air
Deities: Cybele, Pan, Venus, Attis, Dionysus, Astarte, Sylvanus
Powers: Healing, Fertility, Protection, Exorcism, Money
Magical Uses:

Cones from pine trees are carried to increase fertility and to have vigorous old age. A pine cone gathered on Midsummer (still retaining its seeds) is an awesome magical object, for if its possessor eats one pine nut from it every day, it will make him or her immune to gunshots.

Pine needles are burned during the winter months to purify and cleanse the house. Scattered on the floor they drive away evil, and when burned, exorcise the area of negativity. They are also used in cleansing baths. Pine needles are burned to reverse and send back spells.

Branches of the pine placed above or over the bed keeps sickness far away (or, if they weren't placed in time, aid the ill). In Japan it was customary to place a pine branch over the door of the house to ensure continual joy within, for the leaves are evergreen.

A cross made of pine needles placed before the fireplace keeps evil from entering through it. Pine is also used in money spells, and its sawdust is a base for incenses.

PINEAPPLE *(Ananas comusus)*
Gender: Masculine
Planet: Sun
Element: Fire
Powers: Luck, Money, Chastity
Magical Uses:

Dried pineapple is placed in bags and added to baths to draw good luck to the bather. The juice is added as well. Pineapple juice is drunk to hinder lust, and the dried peel or flesh is added to money mixtures.

PIPSISSEWA *(Chimaphila umbellata)*
Folk Names: False Wintergreen, Ground Holly, Price's Pine, Princess Pine
Powers: Money, Spirit Calling
Magical Uses:

Crush pipsissewa, blend with rose hips and violet flowers, and burn to draw good spirits for magical aid. Also carry to attract money.

PISTACHIO *(Pistachia vera)*
Gender: Masculine
Planet: Mercury
Element: Air
Powers: Breaking Love-Spells
Magical Uses:

The Arabs believe that pistachio nuts, when eaten, act as an antidote to love spells. The nuts are also given to zombies to bring them out of their trances and to give them the rest of death. Curiously enough, the pistachios which have been artificially dyed red are said to be the best for this purpose.

PLAINTAIN *(Plantago* spp.)
Folk Names: Cuckoo's Bread, English-

man's Foot, The Leaf of Patrick, Patrick's Dock, Ripple Grass, St. Patrick's Leaf, Slan-lus, Snakebite, Snakeweed, Waybread, Waybroad, *Weybroed* (Anglo-Saxon), White Man's Foot

Gender: Feminine
Planet: Venus
Element: Earth
Powers: Healing, Strength, Protection, Snake Repelling
Magical Uses:

Bind the plantain with red wool to the head to cure headaches, and place beneath the feet to remove weariness.

Plaintain is also hung in the car to guard against the intrusion of evil spirits. A piece of the root in the pocket protects its bearer from snakebites.

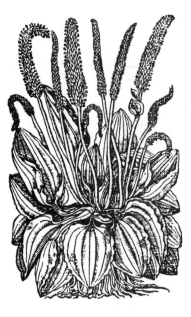

PLUM *(Prunus domestica)*
Gender: Feminine
Planet: Venus
Element: Water
Powers: Love, Protection
Magical Uses:

Plum branches placed over doors and windows guard the home against evil intrusions.

The fruit is eaten to inspire or maintain love.

PLUM, WILD *(Prunus americana)*
Gender: Feminine
Planet: Venus
Element: Water
Powers: Healing
Magical Uses:

The Dakota Indians of North America used wild plum sprouts in fashioning prayer sticks. The sprouts were peeled and painted and an offering (usually a small amount of tobacco) was fastened near the top of the stick. These were made for sick persons and were set up around the altar or stuck into the ground outside for the gods.

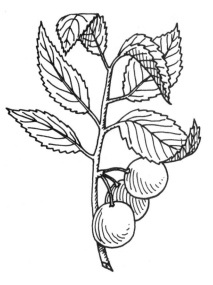

This same idea can be adapted by anyone with a little imagination.

PLUMERIA *(Plumeria acutifolia)* **POISON**   (Not Shown)
Folk Names: Frangipangi, Graveyard Flowers, *Melia* (Hawaiian), Temple Tree
Gender: Feminine
Planet: Venus
Element: Water
Deity: Buddha
Powers: Love
Magical Uses:

Plumeria flowers are used in love spells.

POKE *(Phytolacca americana)* **POISON**
Folk Names: Coakum, Cocan, Crowberry, Garget, Inkberry, Pigeon Berry, Pocan, Pokeberry Root, Poke Root, Polk Root, Scoke, Virginian Poke
Gender: Masculine
Planet: Mars
Element: Fire
Powers: Courage, Hex-Breaking
Magical Uses:

Poke is used at the new Moon to break hexes and curses. Make an infusion and sprinkle around the home. Add a bit to the bath water as well. (Note: Do not drink!)

When carried, poke gives courage. To find a lost object, mix poke with hydrangea, violet and galangal. Sprinkle this around the area where the article was last seen.

The berries are crushed and the resulting juice is used as a magical ink.

POMEGRANATE *(Punica granatum)*
Folk Names: Carthage Apple, Grenadier, Malicorio, *Malum Punicum*, Pound Garnet
Gender: Masculine
Planet: Mercury
Element: Fire

Deities: Persephone, Ceres
Powers: Divination, Luck, Wishes, Wealth, Fertility
Magical Uses:

The seeds have long been eaten to increase fertility, and the skin carried for the same reason.

The pomegranate is a lucky, magical fruit. Always make a wish before eating one and your wish may come true.

A branch of pomegranate discovers concealed wealth, or will attract money to its possessor. The skin, dried, is added to wealth and money incenses.

Women who wish to know how many children they will have should throw a pomegranates hard on the ground. The number of seeds which fall out indicate the number of their offspring.

Branches of pomegranate hung over doorways guard against evil, and the juice is used as a blood substitute or a magical ink.

POPLAR *(Populus tremuloides)*
Gender: Feminine
Planet: Saturn
Element: Water
Powers: Money, Flying
Magical Uses:

The poplar buds and leaves are carried to attract money or are added to money incenses.

They have also been added to flying ointments, which are used to facilitate astral projection, and so are sometimes placed upon the body or made into an ointment when working with this procedure.

POPPY *(Papaver* spp.)
Folk Names: Blind Buff, Blindeyes, Headaches, Head Waak
Gender: Feminine
Planet: Moon

Element: Water
Deities: Hypnos, Demeter
Powers: Fertility, Love, Sleep, Money, Luck, Invisibility
Magical Uses:

Poppy seeds and flowers are used in mixtures designed to aid sleep. They are also eaten or carried to promote fertility and to attract luck and money. At one time poppy seed heads were gilded and worn as talismans to draw wealth.

The seeds are also added to food to induce love, or are used in love sachets.

If you wish to know the answer to a question, write it in blue ink on a piece of white paper. Place this inside a poppy seed pod and put this beneath your pillow. The answer will appear in a dream.

Soak poppy seeds in wine for fifteen days. Then drink the wine each day for five days while fasting. According to tradition you will be able to make yourself invisible at will.

POTATO *(Solanum tuberosum)*
Folk Names: Blye Eyes, Flukes, Lapstones, Leather Jackets, Murphies, No Eyes, Pinks, Red Eyes, Rocks, Taters, Tatties
Gender: Feminine
Planet: Moon
Element: Earth
Powers: Image Magic, Healing
Magical Uses:

Potatoes are often used as poppets, and the 'eyes' can be used as eyes in fashioning other kinds of poppets.

A potato carried in the pocket cures toothaches and guards against rheumatism, warts and gout. To protect against contracting a cold, a potato should be carried in the pocket or purse all winter—the same potato.

PRICKLY ASH *(Zanthoxylum americanum)*

Gender: Masculine
Planet: Mars
Element: Fire
Powers: Love
Magical Uses:

Use the fruits of the prickly ash as a perfume to attract love.

PRIMROSE *(Primula vulgaris)*
Folk Names: Butter Rose, English Cowslip, Password
Gender: Feminine
Planet: Venus
Element: Earth
Deity: Freya
Powers: Protection, Love
Magical Uses:

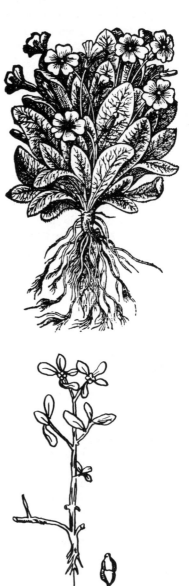

Blue and red primroses growing in the garden protect it from all adversities, and they also attract fairies.

Though primroses, to some, represent wantoness, women carry them to attract love.

They are also worn to cure madness and sewn into children's pillows to gain their undying respect and loyalty.

PURSLANE *(Portulaca sativa)*
Folk Names: Garden Purslane, Golden Purslane, Pigweed
Gender: Feminine
Planet: Moon
Element: Water
Powers: Sleep, Love, Luck, Protection, Happiness
Magical Uses:

If purslane is laid on the bed no nightmares will disturb its occupants during the night.

Carried, purslane draws love and luck and also keeps evil afar. Soldiers carried purslane to protect themselves in battle. Purslane sprinkled around the home spreads happiness throughout.

QUASSIA *(Picraena excelsa)*
Powers: Love
Magical Uses:

Quassia is used in love mixtures, both to draw and to maintain love. The powdered wood is used in incense bases.

QUINCE *(Cydonia* spp.)
Gender: Feminine
Planet: Saturn
Element: Earth
Deity: Venus
Powers: Protection, Love, Happiness
Ritual Uses:

Legends connect the quince to various deities and it was used in worship, especially to Venus. In Pompeiian art quinces are seen in the paws of bears, probably in reference to some mythological association.

Magical Uses:

Quince seed, carried, protects against evil, physical harm, and accidents.

In Roman times a quince was shared by a bridal couple to ensure their future happiness. Pregnant women who eat quinces often will cause their child to be 'ingenious'. Serve quinces to loved ones to ensure fidelity.

RADISH *(Raphanus sativus)*
Folk Names: Rapuns
Gender: Masculine
Planet: Mars
Element: Fire
Powers: Protection, Lust
Magical Uses:

When carried, the radish protects against the evil eye. It increases lust when eaten.

A type of wild radish was carried in Germany to determine the whereabouts of sorcerers.

RAGWEED *(Ambrosia* spp.)
Powers: Courage

Magical Uses:

Chew the root of the ragweed at night to drive away all fear.

RAGWORT *(Senecio* spp.)

Folk Names: Cankerwort, Dog Standard, Fairies' Horses, Ragweed, St. James' Wort, Staggerwort, Stammerwort, stinking Nanny, Stinking Willie

Gender: Feminine

Planet: Venus

Element: Water

Powers: Protection

Magical Uses:

The Greeks used the ragwort as an amulet against charms and spells, and Witches were said to ride upon ragwort stalks at midnight in the bad old days of the persecutions.

RASPBERRY *(Rubus idaeus)*

Folk Names: European Raspberry, Red Raspberry

Gender: Feminine

Planet: Venus

Element: Water

Powers: Protection, Love

Magical Uses:

The brambles (branches) of the raspberry are hung up at doors and windows for protection. This is also done when a death has occured, so that the spirit won't re-enter the house once it has left.

Raspberry is served as a love-inducing food, and the leaves are carried by pregnant women to alleviate the pains of pregnancy and childbirth.

RATTLESNAKE ROOT *(Polygala senega)*

Powers: Protection, Money

Magical Uses:

An infusion of rattlesnake root added to the bath and used in the rinse water for clothing, offers protection from others trying to harm you.

The root was carried by some American Indians to guard against rattlesnake bites, and the infusion is rubbed onto the hands or feet to lead the anointer to money.

RHUBARB *(Rheum* spp.)
Gender: Feminine
Planet: Venus
Element: Earth
Powers: Protection, Fidelity
Magical Uses:
Wear a piece of rhubarb root around the neck on a string to protect against pains in the stomach.

Rhubarb pie served to a mate helps to maintain his or her fidelity.

RICE *(Oryza sativa)*
Folk Names: Bras, Dhan, Nirvara, Paddy
Gender: Masculine
Planet: Sun
Element: Air
Powers: Protection, Rain, Money, Fertility
Magical Uses:
When placed on the roof, rice guards against all misfortunes. Brahmins carried rice as an amulet against evil, and a small jar of rice placed near the entrance of the house also guards it.

Throwing rice into the air can cause rain.

Rice is also added to money spells, and is thrown after wedded couples to increase their fertility.

ROOTS
Powers: Protection, Power Divination
Magical Uses:
If you must sleep outside without protection wear any root around your neck and you will be guarded from wild animals.

An old superstition has it that roots dug from a churchyard (or any old sacred site) will avert death so long

as the collector wears or carries them.

According to Southern magical lore, a person planning to study magic should go to a field at night. There he or she should pull up a weed, roots and all. The amount of soil which adheres to the roots indicates the amount of power and skill the student will achieve in the magical arts. This is sometimes done by the prospective teacher, to get a glimpse of the future success of their novices.

ROSE *(Rosa* spp.)
Gender: Feminine
Planet: Venus
Element: Water
Deities: Hathor, Hulda, Eros, Cupid, Demeter, Isis, Adonis, Harpocrates, Aurora
Powers: Love, Psychic Powers, Healing, Love Divination, Luck, Protection
Magical Uses:

Roses have long been used in love mixtures, owing to the flower's associations with the emotions. A chaplet of roses worn when performing love spells (remove the thorns), or a single rose in a vase on the altar, are powerful love-magic aids. Rose water distilled from the petals is added to love baths. Rose hips (the fruit of the rose) are strung and worn as love-attracting beads.

A tea of rosebuds drunk before sleep induces prophetic dreams. To discover their romantic future, women used to take three green rose leaves and name each for one of her lovers. The one that stayed green the longest answered the question of 'which one?'

Rose petals and hips are also used in healing spells and mixtures, and a rosewater saturated cloth laid to the temples will relieve headache pain.

Roses are also added to fast-luck mixtures and, when carried, act as personal protectants.

Rose petals sprinkled around the house calm personal stress and household upheavals.

Rose planted in the garden attract fairies, and are said to grow best when stolen.

ROSEMARY *(Rosemarinus officinalis)*
Folk Names: Compass Weed, Dew of the Sea, Elf Leaf, Guardrobe, Incensier, *Libanotis* (Greek), Polar Plant, Sea Dew
Gender: Masculine
Planet: Sun
Element: Fire
Powers: Protection, Love, Lust, Mental Powers, Exorcism, Purification, Healing, Sleep, Youth
Magical Uses:

Rosemary, when burned, emits powerful cleansing and purifying vibrations, and so is smouldered to rid a place of negativity, especially prior to performing magic. It is one of the oldest incenses.

When placed beneath the pillow rosemary ensures a good sleep and drives away nightmares. Laid under the bed it protects the sleeper from all harm. Rosemary is also hung on the porch and door-posts to keep thieves from the house and is carried to remain healthy. Placed in the bath it purifies.

A chaplet of rosemary, worn, aids the memory, while the wood, smelled often, preserves youthfulness. To ensure the latter add a rosemary infusion to the bath water.

Rosemary has long been used in love and lust incenses and other mixtures, and healing poppets are stuffed with rosemary to take advantage of its curative vibrations. Rosemary infusion is used to wash the hands before healing work, and the leaves mixed with juniper berries are burned in sickrooms to promote healing.

If you wish to receive knowledge or

the answer to a question, burn rosemary on charcoal and smell its smoke. Rosemary is also grown to attract elves, and the powdered leaves wrapped in linen cloth and bound to the right arm dispel depression and make the emotions light and merry.

Rosemary is generally used as a substitute for frankincense.

ROWAN *(Sorbus acuparia)*

Folk Names: Delight of the Eye, Mountain Ash, Quickbane, Ran Tree, Roden-Quicken, Roden-Quicken-Royan, Roynetree, Sorb Apple, Thor's Helper, Whitty, Wicken-Tree, Wiggin, Wiggy, Wiky, Wild Ash, Witchbane, Witchen, Witchwood

Gender: Masculine

Planet: Sun

Element: Fire

Deity: Thor

Powers: Psychic Powers, Healing, Power, Success, Protection

Magical Uses:

Rowan wood, carried, increases psychic powers, and the branches are often used in fashioning dowsing rods and magical wands. Add the leaves and berries to divination incenses as well as those designed to increase psychic powers.

Carrying rowan berries (or the bark) aids in recuperation, and are added to healing and health sachets and mixtures, as well as all power, success and luck sachets.

For centuries rowan has been used for protective purposes in Europe. Two twigs tied together with red thread to make a cross is an age-old protective amulet. Cornish peasants carried these in their pockets, and Scottish Highlanders inserted them into the lining of their clothing.

Walking sticks made of rowan wood are excellent tools for the person who roams woods and fields by night. Rowan carried on board ship will prevent its involvement in storms; kept in the house it guards against lightning strikes, and when planted on a grave Rowan keeps the deceased one from haunting the place.

The rowan tree planted near the house protects it and its occupants, and those rowans growing near stone circles are the most potent.

RUE *(Ruta graveolens)*
Folk Names: *Bashoush* (Coptic), Garden Rue, German Rue, Herb of Grace, Herbygrass, Hreow, Mother of the Herbs, Rewe, Ruta
Gender: Masculine
Planet: Mars
Element: Fire
Deities: Diana, Aradia
Powers: Healing, Health, Mental Powers, Exorcism, Love
Magical Uses:

Rue leaves placed on the forehead relieve headaches. Worn around the neck rue aids in recuperation from illnesses and also wards off future health problems. Rue is added to healing incenses and poppets.

Fresh rue, sniffed, clears the head in love matters and also improves mental processes.

Rue added to baths breaks all hexes and curses that may have been cast against you, and it is also added to exorcism incenses and mixtures. It is protective when hung up at the door or placed in sachets, and the fresh leaves rubbed on the floorboards sends back any ill spells sent against you. The Romans ate rue as a preservative against the evil eye, and the plant was also carried to guard the bearer from poisons, werewolves, and all manner of ills. A sprig of fresh rue is used as a sprinkler to distribute salt water throughout the house. This clears it of negativity.

Mix fresh rue juice with morning dew and sprinkle in a circle around you while performing magical acts for protection, if desired or needed.

Rue is another plant said to grow best when stolen, and indeed its presence in the garden beautifies and protects it. For some reason toads have an aversion to rue, however.

RYE *(Secale* spp.)
Gender: Feminine
Planet: Venus
Element: Earth
Powers: Love, Fidelity
Magical Uses:

The Romany Gypsies use rye in love spells. Rye bread served to loved ones ensures their love.

SAFFRON *(Crocus sativa)*
Folk Names: Autumn Crocus, Crocus, Karcom, Krokos, *Kunkuma* (Sanskrit), *Saffer* (Arabic), Spanish Saffron
Gender: Masculine
Planet: Sun
Element: Fire
Deities: Eos, Ashtoreth
Powers: Love, Healing, Happiness, Wind Raising, Lust, Strength, Psychic Powers
Ritual Uses:

The Phoenecians baked saffron into crescent-shaped cakes, which they ate in honor of the Moon and fertility Goddess, Ashtoreth.
Magical Uses:

Saffron is added to love sachets as well as those aimed at raising lustful feelings. It is used in healing spells, and the infusion is used as wash water for the hands prior to healing rituals.

At one time in Persia (Iran) pregnant women wore a ball of saffron at the pit of

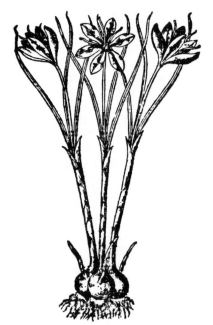

the stomach to ensure a speedy delivery.

The infusion, drunk, enables you to foresee the future, and simply ingesting saffron dispels melancholy. In fact, one early author warns against eating too much saffron lest one should 'die of excessive joy'!

Saffron in the home keeps lizards from venturing in, and wearing a chaplet of saffron will protect you from inebriation (and will probably be the subject of a few comments from your friends).

Sheets were rinsed with a saffron infusion in Ireland so that the arms and legs would be strengthened during sleep, and the ancient Persians utilized saffron to raise the wind.

SAGE *(Salvia officinalis)*

Folk Names: Garden Sage, Red Sage, Sawge

Gender: Masculine

Planet: Jupiter

Element: Air

Powers: Immortality, Longevity, Wisdom, Protection, Wishes

Magical Uses:

Sage has been utilized to ensure a long life—sometimes even immortality. This is done by eating some of the plant every day, or at least in May, for:

> He who would live for aye
> Must eat sage in May.

Sage is carried to promote wisdom, and the leaves are used in countless healing and money spells.

To guard yourself against contracting the dreaded evil eye wear a small horn filled with sage.

There are a few curious gardening tips concerning sage: first, it is bad luck to plant sage in your own garden; a stranger should be found to do the work. Second, a full bed of sage brings ill luck, so ensure that some other plant shares the plot. Incidentally, toads love sage.

If you desire to make a wish come true, write it on a sage leaf and hide it beneath your pillow. For three nights sleep upon it. If once you dream of what you desire your wish will be materialized; if not, bury the sage in the ground so that you do not come to harm.

SAGEBRUSH *(Artemisia* spp.)

Gender: Feminine
Planet: Venus
Element: Earth
Powers: Purification, Exorcism
Ritual Uses:

Sagebrush has long been burned in American Indian ceremonies.

Magical Uses:

Bathe with sagebrush to purify yourself of all past evils and negative deeds.

Burning sagebrush drives away malevolent forces and is also useful in healing.

ST. JOHN'S WORT *(Hypericum* **POISON** *perforatum)*

Folk Names: Amber, *Fuga daemonum* (Latin: Scare-Devil), Goat Weed, Herba John, John's Wort, Klamath Weed, Sol Terrestis, Tipton Weed
Gender: Masculine
Planet: Sun
Element: Fire
Deity: Baldur
Powers: Health, Protection, Strength, Love Divination, Happiness
Magical Uses:

Worn, St. John's Wort wards off fevers and colds, makes soldiers invincible, and attracts love. If it is gathered on Midsummer or on a Friday and worn it will keep mental illness at bay and will also cure melancholy.

When placed in a jar and hung by a window, St. John's wort protects against thunderbolts, fire and evil spirits. Both flowers and leaves are used for this pur-

pose. It is also dried over the Midsummer fires and hung near the window to keep ghosts, necromancers and other evil doers from the house, and is burned to banish spirits and demons.

Any part of the herb placed beneath the pillow allows unmarried women to dream of their future husbands. Use in rituals or carry to detect other magicians; at one time it was held to the mouth of accused Witches to attempt to force them to confess.

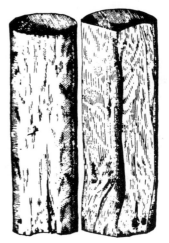

SANDALWOOD *(Santalum album)*
Folk Names: Sandal, Santal, White Sandalwood, White Saunders, Yellow Sandalwood
Gender: Feminine
Planet: Moon
Element: Water
Powers: Protection, Wishes, Healing, Exorcism, Spirituality
Magical Uses:

Sandalwood powder is burned during protection, healing and exorcism spells. When mixed with lavendar it makes an incense designed to conjure spirits.

This fragrant wood possesses very high spiritual vibrations and is burned at seances and Full Moon rituals when mixed with frankincense.

Write your wish on a chip of sandalwood and burn in the censer or cauldron. As it burns it sets the magic flowing, but remember to visualize your wish at the same time.

Sandalwood beads are protective and promote a spiritual awareness when worn.

Powdered sandalwood can be scattered about a place to clear it of negativity, and it is also used as an incense base.

SARSAPARILLA *(Smilax aspera)*
Folk Name: Bamboo Briar
Gender: Masculine

Planet: Jupiter
Element: Fire
Powers: Love, Money
Magical Uses:

Sarsaparilla is mixed with cinnamon and sandalwood powder and sprinkled around the premises to draw money. It is also utilized in love spells.

SASSAFRAS *(Sassafras albidum)*
Gender: Masculine
Planet: Jupiter
Element: Fire
Powers: Health, Money
Magical Uses:

Sassafras is placed in the purse or wallet to attract money, or is burned for this purpose. It is also added to sachets and spells designed to aid healing.

SAVORY, SUMMER *(Satureja hortensis)*
Gender: Masculine
Planet: Mercury
Element: Air
Powers: Mental Powers
Magical Uses:

Summer savory strengthens the mind when carried or worn.

SCULLCAP *(Scutellaria galericulata)*
Folk Names: Greater Scullcap, Helmet
    Flower, Hoodwort, Madweed
Gender: Feminine
Planet: Saturn
Element: Water
Powers: Love, Fidelity, Peace
Magical Uses:

Scullcap is used in spells of relaxation and peace. A woman who wears scullcap protects her husband against the charms of other women.

SENNA *(Cassia marilandica* or *C. acuti-*
    folia)
Gender: Masculine
Planet: Mercury

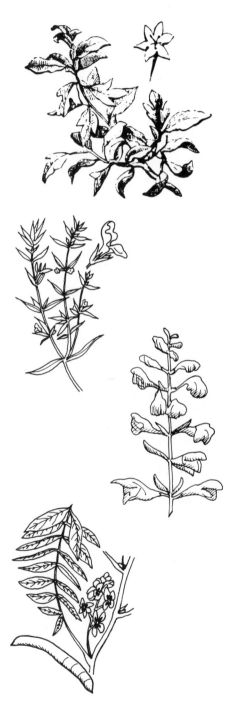

Element: Air
Powers: Love
Magical Uses:

Use senna in love spells.

SESAME *(Sesamum orientale)*
Gender: Masculine
Planet: Sun
Element: Fire
Deity: Ganesha
Powers: Money, Lust
Magical Uses:

Sesame seeds, when eaten, are lust-inducing.

A jar of sesame seeds left open in the house draws cash to it. Change the seeds every month.

The infamous magical command 'open sesame!' refers to the plant's legendary powers to discover hidden treasures, reveal secret passageways, and open locked doors.

SHALLOT *(Allium* spp.)
Gender: Masculine
Planet: Mars
Element: Fire
Powers: Purification
Magical Uses:

Add shallots to a bath to cure misfortunes.

SKUNK CABBAGE *(Symplocarpus fo- etidus)*
Folk Names: Meadow Cabbage, Pole Cat Weed, Skunk Weed, Suntull, Swamp Cabbage
Gender: Feminine
Planet: Saturn
Element: Water
Powers: Legal Matters
Magical Uses:

A small amount of skunk cabbage wrapped in a bay leaf on a Sunday forms a talisman which draws good fortune to the bearer. It is also of efficacy in court

cases.

SLIPPERY ELM *(Ulmus fulva)*
Folk Names: Indian Elm, Moose Elm,
    Red Elm
Gender: Feminine
Planet: Saturn
Element: Air
Powers: Halts Gossip
Magical Uses:

Burn slippery elm and throw
into the fire a knotted yellow cord
or thread. Any gossip against you will
stop.

Slippery elm bark worn about a
child's neck will give it a persuasive
tongue when fully grown.

SLOE *(Prunus spinosa)*
Folk Names: Blackthorn, Mother of the
    Wood, Wishing Thorn
Gender: Masculine
Planet: Mars
Element: Fire
Powers: Exorcism, Protection
Magical Uses:

Hung over doorways or carried, the
sloe wards off evil and calamity, banishes
demons and negative vibrations.

The wood is sometimes used to
make divining rods and wishing rods.
These 'wishing rods' are used in spells of
all types and are actually all-purpose magical wands.

SNAKEROOT *(Aristolochia serpentaria)*
Folk Names: Pelican Flower, Radix
    Viperina, Serpentary Radix, Ser-
    pentary Rhizome, Snagree, Snagrel,
    Snakeweed, Virginian Snakeroot
Powers: Luck, Money
Magical Uses:

This root is carried as a good luck
talisman and also to break hexes and
curses. It is also said to lead its bearer to
money.

SNAKEROOT, BLACK *(Sanicula maril-andica)*
Gender: Masculine
Planet: Mars
Element: Fire
Powers: Love, Lust, Money
Magical Uses:

Black snakeroot is worn to attract lovers and is also placed in the bedroom and added to baths. Carried, it attracts money.

SNAPDRAGON *(Antirrhinum majus)*
Folk Name: Calf's Snout
Gender: Masculine
Planet: Mars
Element: Fire
Powers: Protection
Magical Uses:

Any part of the snapdragon worn on your body prevents people from deceiving you. The seed worn around the neck ensures that you will never be bewitched.

If you are outside and feel evil nearby, step on a snapdragon or hold one of its flowers in your hand until the evil passes. Place a vase of fresh snapdragons on the altar while performing protective rituals.

If someone has sent negative energy to you (hexes, curses, etc.) place some snapdragons on the altar with a mirror behind them. This will send the curses back.

SOLOMON'S SEAL *(Polygonatum officianle* or *P. multiflorum)*
Folk Names: Dropberry, Lady's Seal, St. Mary's Seal, Sealroot, Sealwort, Solomon Seal
Gender: Feminine
Planet: Saturn
Element: Water
Powers: Protection, Exorcism
Magical Uses:

The root is placed in the four quarters of the house to guard it; it is used in exorcism and protection spells of all kinds, and an infusion of the roots sprinkled about clears the area of evil.

Solomon's seal is also used in offeratory incenses.

SORREL, WOOD *(Oxalis acetosella)*
Folk Names: Cuckowe's Meat, Fairy Bells, Sourgrass, Sour Trefoil, Stickwort, Stubwort, Surelle, Three-Leaved Grass, Wood Sour
Gender: Feminine
Planet: Venus
Element: Earth
Powers: Healing, Health
Magical Uses:

If the leaves of the wood sorrel (dried) are carried they preserve the heart against disease.

Fresh wood sorrel placed in sickrooms aids in recuperation from illnesses and wounds.

SOUTHERNWOOD *(Artemisia abrotanum)*
Folk Names: Appleringie, Boy's Love, Garde Robe, Lad's Love, Maid's Ruin, Old Man
Gender: Masculine
Planet: Mercury
Element: Air
Powers: Love, Lust, Protection
Magical Uses:

Southernwood is used in love spells, either carried or placed in the bedroom. Sometimes southernwood is placed beneath the bed to rouse lust in its occupants.

Burned as an incense southernwood guards against trouble of all kinds, and the smoke drives away snakes.

SPANISH MOSS
Powers: Protection
Magical Uses:

Grown on or in the home, spanish moss is protective. Use to stuff protection poppets and add to protective sachets.

SPEARMINT *(Mentha spicata)*
Folk Names: Brown Mint, Garden Mint, Green Mint, Green Spine, Lamb Mint, Mackerel Mint, *Mismin* (Irish Gaelic), Our Lady's Mint, Spire Mint, *Yerba Buena* (Spanish)
Gender: Feminine
Planet: Venus
Element: Water
Powers: Healing, Love, Mental Powers
Magical Uses:
Spearmint is used in all healing applications, especially in aiding lung diseases. Smelled, spearmint increases and sharpens mental powers.

For protection while asleep, stuff a pillow or mattress with spearmint.

SPIDERWORT *(Tradescantia Virginia)*
Folk Name: Spider Lily
Powers: Love
Magical Uses:
The Dakota Indians carried the spiderwort to attract love.

SPIKENARD *(Inula conyza)*
Folk Name: Nard
Gender: Feminine
Planet: Venus
Element: Water
Powers: Fidelity, Health
Magical Uses:
Spikenard worn around the neck brings good luck and wards off disease. It is also used to remain fidelitous.

SQUILL *(Urginea scilla)*
Folk Names: Red Squill, Sea Onion, White Squill
Gender: Masculine
Planet: Mars
Element: Fire

Powers: Money, Protection, Hex-Breaking
Magical Uses:

The squill, or sea onion, has been used in magic since classical times. To protect your home, hang a squill over the window. To draw money, place one in a jar or box and add silver coins. If you feel you have been hexed carry a squill with you and it will break the spell.

STAR ANISE *(Illicum verum)*
Folk Name: Chinese Anise
Gender: Masculine
Planet: Jupiter
Element: Air
Powers: Psychic Powers, Luck
Magical Uses:

The seeds are burned as incense to increase psychic powers, and are also worn as beads for the same purpose.

Sometimes star anise is placed on the altar to give it power; one is placed to each of the four directions. It is also carried as a general luck-bringer, and the seeds make excellent pendulums.

STILLENGIA *(Stillingia sylvatica)*
Folk Names: Queen's Delight, Queen's Root, Silver Leaf, Stillingia, Yaw Root
Powers: Psychic Powers
Magical Uses:

Burn the root to develop psychic powers. If you have lost something, burn stillengia and follow the smoke to its hiding place.

STRAW
Powers: Luck, Image Magic
Magical Uses:

Straw is lucky; hence it is often carried in small bags. For a home luck talisman, take a used horseshoe and some straw, sew up into a small bag, and place it above or below the bed.

Small magical images may be made of straw and these can then be used as poppets.

Straw attracts fairies (some say that fairies live inside straws).

STRAWBERRY *(Fragaria vesca)*
Gender: Feminine
Planet: Venus
Element: Water
Deity: Freya
Powers: Love, Luck
Magical Uses:

Strawberries are served as a love food, and the leaves are carried for luck.

Pregnant women may wish to carry a small packet of strawberry leaves to ease their pregnancy pains.

SUGAR CANE *(Saccharum officinarum)*
Folk Name: *Ko* (Hawaiian)
Gender: Feminine
Planet: Venus
Element: Water
Powers: Love, Lust
Magical Uses:

Sugar has long been used in love and lust potions. Chew a piece of the cane while thinking of your loved one.

Sugar is also scattered to dispel evil and to cleanse and purify areas before rituals and spells.

SUMBUL *(Ferula sumbul)*
Folk Names: Euryangium Musk Root, Jatamansi, Ofnokgi, Ouchi
Powers: Love, Psychic Powers, Health, Luck

(Not Shown)

Magical Uses:

To attract love, carry, burn as incense, or add the infusion to the bath. All three of the above procedures can be done to ensure results.

Sumbul is burned to increase psychic powers, and worn around the neck, it offers good luck and keeps disease at bay.

SUNFLOWER *(Helianthus annuus)*
Folk Names: *Corona Solis*, Marigold of
    Peru, *Solo Indianus*
Gender: Masculine
Planet: Sun
Element: Fire
Powers: Fertility, Wishes, Health, Wis-
    dom
Magical Uses:

    Sunflower seeds are eaten by women who wish to conceive. To protect yourself against smallpox wear sunflower seeds around the neck, either in a bag or strung like beads.

    If you cut a sunflower at sunset while making a wish, the wish will come true before another sunset—as long as the wish isn't too grand.

    Sleeping with a sunflower under the bed allows you to know the truth in any matter.

    If you wish to become virtuous anoint yourself with juice pressed from the stems of the sunflower.

    Sunflowers growing in the garden guard it against pests and grant the best of luck to the gardener.

SWEETGRASS *(Hierochloe odorata)*
Powers: Calling Spirits
Magical Uses:

    Burn sweetgrass to attract good spirits, or beings, before performing spells.

SWEETPEA *(Lathyrus odoratus)*
Gender: Feminine
Planet: Venus
Element: Water
Powers: Friendship, Chastity, Courage,
    Strength
Magical Uses:

    Wearing fresh sweetpea flowers attracts people and causes friendships to develop.

When carried or held in the hand, sweetpea causes all to tell you the truth.

Sweetpea also preserves your chastity if placed in the bedroom, and gives courage and strength when worn.

TAMARIND *(Tamarindus indica)*
Folk Names: *Tamarindo* (Spanish)
Gender: Feminine
Planet: Saturn
Element: Water
Powers: Love
Magical Uses:

Carry tamarind to attract love.

TAMARISK *(Tamarix* spp.)
Gender: Feminine
Planet: Saturn
Element: Water
Deity: Anu
Powers: Exorcism, Protection
Magical Uses:

The tamarisk has an ancient history of use in exorcisms, dating back at least 4,000 years. During exorcism rites a branch of the tree is held in the hand and the leaves are scattered about to drive out demons and evil. For best results the tamarisk should be cut with a gold axe and a pruning knife fashioned of silver.

The smoke of burning tamarisk drives away snakes, and tamarisk sticks were used for divining by the Chaldeans.

TANSY *(Tanacetum vulgare)*
Folk Names: Buttons
Gender: Feminine
Planet: Venus
Element: Water
Powers: Health, Longevity
Magical Uses:

A bit of tansy placed in the shoes helps cure persistent fevers. Since this plant was given to Ganymede to make him immortal, tansy is carried to lengthen the life-span. Ants don't like tansy.

TEA *(Camellia* spp.)
Folk Names: Black Tea, China Tea
Gender: Masculine
Planet: Sun
Element: Fire
Powers: Riches, Courage, Strength
Magical Uses:

Burn the leaves of the tea plant to ensure future riches, and add to all money mixtures and sachets.

Tea is also included in talismans designed to give their bearer courage and strength.

The infusion is used as a base for mixing lust drinks.

THISTLE *(Carduus* spp.)
Folk Names: Lady's Thistle, Thrissles
Gender: Masculine
Planet: Mars
Element: Fire
Deities: Thor, Minerva
Powers: Strength, Protection, Healing,
　　　　　Exorcism, Hex-Breaking
Magical Uses:

A bowl of thistles placed in a room strengthens the spirits and renews the vitality of all within it. Carry a thistle (or part of a thistle) for energy and strength.

Grown in the garden, thistles ward off thieves, grown in a pot and on the doorstep they protect against evil. A thistle blossom   carried in the pocket guards its bearer. Thrown onto a fire, thistles deflect lightning away from the house.

If you have had a spell cast against you, wear a shirt made of fibers spun and woven from the thistle to break it and any other spells. Stuff hex-breaking poppets with thistles. Thistles are strewn in homes and other buildings to exorcise evil.

Thistles are also used in healing spells, and when men carry it they become better lovers. Thistles also drive

out melancholy when worn or carried.

Wizards in England used to select the tallest thistle in the patch to use as a magical wand or walking stick.

To call spirits, place some thistle in boiling water. Remove from heat and lie or sit beside it. As the steam rises call the spirits and listen carefully; they may answer your questions.

THISTLE, HOLY *(Centaurea benedicta)*
Folk Names: Blessed Thistle
Gender: Masculine
Planet: Mars
Element: Fire
Powers: Purification, Hex-Breaking
Magical Uses:

Wear the holy thistle to protect yourself from evil, and add to purificatory baths, holy thistle is also used in hex-breaking spells.

THISTLE, MILK *(Carduus Marianus)*
Folk Names: Marian Thistle
Gender: Masculine
Planet: Mars
Element: Fire
Powers: Snake-Enraging
Magical Uses:

The Anglo-Saxons recorded the fact that if the milk thistle was hung around a man's neck, all snakes in his presence would begin fighting.

THYME *(Thymus vulgaris)*
Folk Names: Common Thyme, Garden
Thyme
Gender: Feminine
Planet: Venus
Element: Water
Powers: Health, Healing, Sleep, Psychic
Powers, Love, Purification, Courage
Magical Uses:

Thyme is burned to attract good health and is also worn for this purpose. It is also used in healing spells.

Placed beneath the pillow, it ensures restful sleep and a pleasant lack of nightmares. Worn, thyme aids in developing psychic powers, and women who wear a sprig of thyme in the hair make themselves irresistible.

Thyme is also a purificatory herb; the Greeks burned it in their temples to purify them and so thyme is often burned prior to magical rituals to cleanse the area. In spring a magical cleansing bath composed of marjoram and thyme is taken to ensure all the sorrows and ills of the past are removed from the person.

Thyme is also carried and smelled to give courage and energy. If you wear it you will be able to see fairies.

TI *(Cordyline terminalis)*
Folk Names: Good Luck Plant, *Ki* (Hawaiian)
Gender: Masculine
Planet: Jupiter
Element: Fire
Deities: Kane, Lono, Pele
Powers: Protection, Healing
Magical Uses:

Ti leaves, when carried on board ship, keep storms away, and when worn ensures that the bearer won't drown.

Planted around the house the ti creates a type of protective barrier. The green ti should be used for this, not the red variety; though the latter is sacred to Pele, it traditionally gives bad luck to homeowners when planted.

A bit of ti placed beneath the bed protects the sleeper, and a ti leaf rubbed on the head relieves headaches.

TOADFLAX *(Linaria vulgaris)*
Folk Names: Churnstaff, Doggies, Dragon Bushes, Flax Weed, Fluellin, Gallwort, Pattens and Clogs, Rabbits, Ramsted, Toad
Gender: Masculine

Planet: Mars
Element: Fire
Powers: Protection, Hex-Breaking
Magical Uses:

The toadflax is used as an amulet to keep evil from the wearer, and is also used to break hexes.

TOADSTOOL
Powers: Rain Making
Magical Uses:

Accidentally breaking down toadstools will cause rain to fall, but I don't know if showers occur when this is deliberately done.

TOBACCO *(Nicotiana* spp.) POISON
Folk Names: Tabacca
Gender: Masculine
Planet: Mars
Element: Fire
Powers: Healing, Purification
Ritual Uses:

Candidates for some shamanic systems must drink tobacco juice to induce visions as part of their training. Tobacco has long been used in religious ceremonies by some of the American Indians. Indeed, many peoples still regard the plant as sacred.

Magical Uses:

South American Indians smoke tobacco to allow them to converse with spirits. Tobacco is also thrown into the river when beginning a journey by boat to propitiate the river gods.

Burning tobacco as an incense purifies the area of all negativity and spirits (both good and bad), and to cure earaches tobacco smoke is blown into the ear.

If you have nightmares they may cause sickness. To prevent this, immediately upon waking, wash in a running stream and throw tobacco into the water as an offering to the Water Spirit who has cleansed you of the evil.

Tobacco is a magical substitute for sulphur, as well as for datura and nightshade, both of which are related to tobacco. Although it is regularly smoked by millions, tobacco is a very poisonous plant and can kill.

TOMATO *(Lycopersicon* spp.)
Folk Name: Love Apples
Gender: Feminine
Planet: Venus
Element: Water
Powers: Prosperity, Protection, Love
Magical Uses:

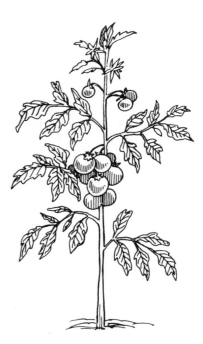

Place a large red tomato on the mantle to bring prosperity to the home. Replace every three days.

When a tomato is placed on the windowsill or any other household entrance it repels evil from entering. The plants in the garden are protective, since the yellow flowers and bright red fruits scare off evil.

The tomato, when eaten, has the power of inspiring love.

TONKA *(Coumarouna odorata;*   **POISON** *Dipteryx odorata)*
Folk Names: Coumaria Nut, Tonqua, Tonquin Bean
Gender: Feminine
Planet: Venus
Element: Water
Powers: Love, Money, Courage, Wishes
Magical Uses:

These fragrant beans are used in love sachets and mixtures, and are also carried to attract love.

Tonka beans are worn or carried to attract money, bring luck, grant courage and ward off illnesses.

To make wishes come true, hold a tonka bean in your hand, visualize your wish, and then toss the bean into running water.

TORMENTIL *(Potentilla tormentilla)*
Folk Names: Biscuits, Bloodroot, Earth-bank, Ewe Daisy, Five Fingers, Flesh and Blood, Septfoil, Shepherd's Knot, Thormantle
Gender: Masculine
Planet: Sun
Element: Fire
Deity: Thor
Powers: Protection, Love
Magical Uses:

The infusion is drunk to give protection, or is served to a loved one to keep their love. Mediums drink the infusion to guard themselves against permanent possession by spirits.

The plant is hung up in the home to drive away evil and is carried to attract love.

TRILLIUM *(Trillium spp.)*
Folk Names: Beth, Beth Root, Indian Root, True Love
Gender: Feminine
Planet: Venus
Element: Water
Powers: Money, Luck, Love
Magical Uses:

Carrying trillium attracts money and luck to its bearer. The root of the trillium is also rubbed onto the body to attract love.

TULIP *(Tulipa spp.)*
Gender: Feminine
Planet: Venus
Element: Earth
Powers: Prosperity, Love, Protection
Magical Uses:

The tulip is worn to safeguard against poverty and bad luck in general.

'Tulip' means 'turban' and the flower is often worn in the turban in Middle Eastern countries for protection.

Tulips are placed on the altar during love spells.

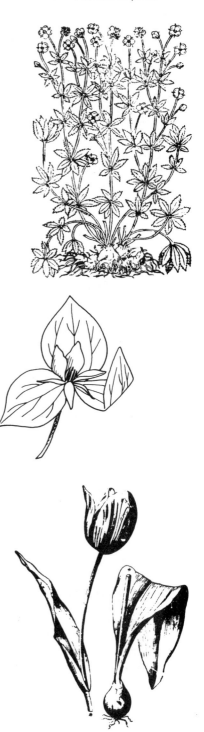

TURMERIC *(Cucurma longa)*
Folk Names: *Olena* (Hawaiian)
Powers: Purification
Magical Uses:

Turmeric has long been used in Hawaiian magic for purification; salt water and turmeric are mixed together and then sprinkled in the area to be purified, sometimes with a ti leaf.

Turmeric is also sometimes scattered on the floor or about the magic circle for protection.

TURNIP *(Brassica rapa)*
Gender: Feminine
Planet: Moon
Element: Earth
Powers: Protection, Ending Relationships
Ritual Uses:

On Samhain (October 31) large turnips were once hollowed out and candles lit within. These were carried or placed in windows to scare off evil spirits.
Magical Uses:

If you have an admirer you simply can't convince to leave you alone, place a dish of turnips in front of him or her. They'll get the idea.

Turnips placed in the home ward off every form of negativity.

UVA URSA *(Arctostaphylos uva-ursi)* **POISON**
Folk Names: Arberry, Bearberry, Bear's
    Grape, Kinnikinnick, Mealberry,
    Mountain Box, Mountain Cranberry,
    Mountain Cranberry, Red Bearberry,
    Sagackhomi, Sandberry
Powers: Psychic Workings
Ritual Uses:

American Indians used the uva ursa in religious ceremonies.
Magical Uses:

Add to sachets designed to increase psychic powers.

VALERIAN *(Valeriana officinalis)*
Folk Names: All-Heal, Amantilla, Bloody Butcher, Capon's Trailer, Cat's Valerian, English Valerian, Fragrant Valerian, Garden Heliotrope, Phu, Red Valerian, St. George's Herb, Sete Wale, Set Well, Vandal Root
Gender: Feminine
Planet: Venus
Element: Water
Powers: Love, Sleep, Purification, Protection

Magical Uses:

The rather ill-smelling root, powdered, is used in protective sachets, hung in the home to guard it against lightning, and placed in pillows to aid in falling asleep.

A sprig of the plant pinned to a woman's clothing will cause men to 'follow her like children'. Valerian root is also added to love sachets.

If a couple is quarreling introduce some of this herb into the area and all will soon be calm.

The Greeks hung a sprig of valerian under a window to charm away evil.

Valerian root, powdered, is sometimes used as 'graveyard dust'.

VANILLA *(Vanilla aromatica* or *V. planifolia)*
Gender: Feminine
Planet: Venus
Element: Water
Powers: Love, Lust, Mental Powers
Magical Uses:

Vanilla, a type of fermented orchid, is used in love sachets; the scent and taste are considered to be lust-inducing. A vanilla bean placed in a bowl of sugar will infuse it with loving vibrations; the sugar can then be used to sweeten love infusions.

A vanilla bean, carried, will restore lost energy and improve the mind.

VENUS' FLYTRAP *(Dionaea muscipula)*
Gender: Masculine
Planet: Mars
Element: Fire
Powers: Protection, Love
Magical Uses:

These fascinating insect-eating plants are now readily available at nurseries and through the mail. Though it may seem strange that such a plant would be dedicated to a goddess of love, such is the case, and so Venus' flytraps can be grown as a love attractant.

More commonly, though, this plant is grown in the home for its protective qualities, and also in order to 'trap' something.

VERVAIN *(Verbena officinalis)*
Folk Names: Brittanica, Enchanter's Plant, Herba Sacra, Herb of Enchantment, Herb of Grace, Herb of the Cross, Holy Herb, Juno's Tears, Pigeon's Grass, Pigeonwood, Simpler's Joy, Van-Van, Verbena, Vervan
Gender: Feminine
Planet: Venus
Element: Earth
Deities: Kerridwen, Mars, Venus, Aradia, Isis, Jupiter, Thor, Juno
Powers: Love, Protection, Purification, Peace, Money, Youth, Chastity, Sleep, Healing
Ritual Uses:

Priests in ancient Rome used vervain to cleanse the altars of Jupiter. Small bundles of vervain were fashioned and the altars were swept with these. According to tradition, daughters of Druids who were initiated were crowned with vervain; this was a sign of the attained rank. (As with anything 'Druidic,' this has to be looked upon as poetic, rather than historic fact.)
Magical Uses:

Vervain is traditionally gathered at

Midsummer or at the rising of the Dog Star when neither Sun nor Moon is out, but this is not necessary.

Vervain is a common ingredient in love mixtures and protective spells. A crown of vervain on the head protects the magician while invoking spirits. Any part of the plant may be carried as a personal amulet. Vervain placed in the home protects it from lightning and storms.

The infusion sprinkled around the premises chases off evil spirits and malignant forces. Vervain is also added to exorcism incenses and sprinkling mixtures. It is also a common ingredient in purification bath sachets.

The dried herb is scattered around the home as a peace-bringer and is also worn to calm the emotions.

Vervain is used in money and prosperity spells. If the herb is buried in the garden or placed in the house, wealth will flow and plants will thrive.

To remain chaste for long periods of time, rise before the Sun on the first day of the New Moon. Gather vervain (still before Sunrise), press out its juice, and drink it down. According to ancient instructions, it will cause you to lose all desire for sex for seven years.

Vervain carried may offer everlasting youth, and when placed in the bed, hung around the neck, or made into an infusion and drunk prior to sleep, no dreams will haunt you.

Vervain is also a fine healing herb. The undiluted juice of the vervain smeared on the body cures diseases and guards against future health problems. To aid in recuperation the root tied with a yard of white yarn is placed around the patient's neck. It should remain there until recovery.

To discover if someone lying sick will live or die, place vervain in your hand and press it against the patient, so

that the herb is undetected. Ask them how they feel; if they are hopeful they shall live; if not they might not.

If someone you know has taken something from you, wear vervain and confront the person. You shall surely regain possession of the stolen articles.

If vervain is placed in a baby's cradle the child will grow up with a happy disposition and a love of learning.

The juice of the vervain, smeared on the body, will allow the person to see the future, have every wish fulfilled, turn enemies into friends, attract lovers and be protected against all enchantments. Burnt, it dispels unrequited love.

VETCH, GIANT *(Vicia* spp.)
Powers: Fidelity
Magical Uses:

If your loved one has gone astray, rub the root of the giant vetch on your body, then wrap it up in cloth and place under your pillow. This will remind him or her that you're still around, waiting.

VETIVERT *(Vetiveria zizanioides)*
Folk Names: Khus-Khus, Vetiver
Gender: Feminine
Planet: Venus
Element: Earth
Powers: Love, Hex-Breaking, Luck, Money, Anti-Theft
Magical Uses:

Vetivert root is burned to overcome evil spells. It is also used in love powders, sachets and incenses and is added to the bathwater in a sachet to make yourself attractive to the opposite sex.

Vetivert is also used in money spells and mixtures, placed in the cash register to increase business, carried to attract luck and burned in anti-theft incenses.

(Not Shown)

VIOLET *(Viola odorata)*
Folk Names: Blue Violet, Sweet Violet
Gender: Feminine
Planet: Venus
Element: Water
Deity: Venus
Powers: Protection, Luck, Love, Lust,
  Wishes, Peace, Healing
Magical Uses:

When the flowers are carried they offer protection against 'wykked sperytis' and bring changes in luck and fortune. Mixed with lavendar, they are a powerful love stimulant and also arouse lust.

If you gather the first violet in the spring your dearest wish will be granted.

Ancient Greeks wore the violet to calm tempers and to induce sleep.

Violets fashioned into a chaplet and placed on the head cures headaches and dizziness, and the leaves worn in a green sachet help wounds to heal and prevent evil spirits from making the wounds worse.

WAHOO *(Euonymus atropurpuraea)*   **POISON**
Folk Names: Burning Bush, Indian Arrow Wood, Spindle Tree
Powers: Hex-Breaking, Courage, Success
Magical Uses:

Make an infusion of the bark. Let cool. Rub on a hexed person's forehead (or your own) saying 'Wahoo!' seven times. (Some people say you should trace a cross with the infusion.) This will break any hexes cast against the person.

When carried, it brings success in all undertakings and imparts courage.

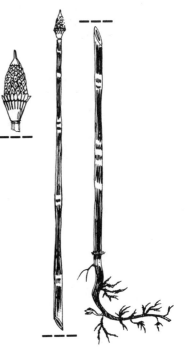

WALNUT *(Juglans regia)*
Folk Names: Carya, Caucasian Walnut, English Walnut, Tree of Evil, Walnoot
Gender: Masculine
Planet: Sun
Element: Fire

Powers: Health, Mental Powers, Infertility, Wishes

Ritual Uses:

Witches were supposed to dance beneath walnut trees in Italy during their secret rites.

Magical Uses:

When carried, walnuts strengthen the heart and ward off rheumatism pains. They also attract lightning, so don't carry one in an electrical storm.

If anyone gives you a bag of walnuts, you will see all your wishes fulfilled.

When placed in a hat or around the head, walnut leaves prevent headaches and sunstroke.

If a woman about to be married wishes to delay any 'blessed events' she should place in her bodice as many roasted walnuts as correspond to the number of years she wishes to remain childless. She must do this on her wedding day.

WAX PLANT *(Hoya carnosa)*

Folk Names: Pentagram Flowers, Pentagram Plant

Gender: Masculine

Planet: Mercury

Element: Air

Powers: Protection

Magical Uses:

The wax plant is grown in bedrooms and throughout the house for protection. The star-shaped flowers are dried and kept as protective amulets, and are also placed on the altar to give spells extra power.

WHEAT *(Triticum* spp.)

Gender: Feminine

Planet: Venus

Element: Earth

Deities: Ceres, Demeter, Ishtar

Powers: Fertility, Money

Magical Uses:

Her yellow hair was braided
    in a tress,
Behind her back, a full yard
    long, I guess,
And in the garden, as the sun
    uprose,
She walketh up and down,
    and, as she chose,
She gathered flowers—partly
    white and red—
To make a fine woven garland
    for her head;
And, as an Angel's, heavenly
    was her song;

Wheat, a symbol of fruitfulness, is sometimes carried or eaten to induce fertility and conception. Sheaves of wheat are placed in the home to attract money, and grains are carried in sachets for the same reason.

WILLOW *(Salix alba)*

Folk Names: Osier, Pussy Willow, Saille, Salicyn Willow, Saugh Tree, Tree of Enchantment, White Willow, Witches' Aspirin, Withe, Withy

Gender: Feminine

Planet: Moon

Element: Water

Deities: Artemis, Ceres, Hecate, Persephone, Hera, Mercury, Belili, Belinus

Powers: Love, Love Divination, Protection, Healing

Ritual Uses:

Burial mounds in Britain which are sited near marshes and lakes were often lined with willows, probably for symbolic associations with death.

Magical Uses:

Willow leaves are carried or used in mixtures to attract love, and the wood is used to fashion magical wands dedicated to Moon Magic. If you wish to know if you will be married in the new year, on New Year's Eve throw your shoe or boot into a willow tree. If it doesn't catch and stay in the branches the first time, you have eight more tries. If you succeed in trapping your shoe in the tree you will be wed within 12 months—but you'll also have to shake or climb the tree to retrieve your shoe.

All parts of the willow guard against evil and can be carried or placed in the home for this purpose. Knock on a willow tree ('knock on wood') to avert evil.

The leaves, bark and wood of the willow are also utilized in healing spells.

If you wish to conjure spirits, mix

crushed willow bark with sandalwood and burn at the waning Moon outdoors.

Magical brooms, especially Witch's brooms, are traditionally bound with a willow branch.

WINTERGREEN *(Gaultheria procumbens)*
Folk Names: Checkerberry, Mountain Tea, Teaberry
Gender: Feminine
Planet: Moon
Element: Water
Powers: Protection, Healing, Hex-Breaking
Magical Uses:

Wintergreen is placed in children's pillows to protect them and grant them good fortune throughout their lives.

When sprinkled in the home it removes hexes and cures, especially when mixed with mint.

Wintergreen is also utilized in healing spells, and when fresh sprigs are placed on the altar they call good spirits to witness and aid your magic.

WINTER'S BARK *(Drimys winteri)*
Folk Names: True Winter's Bark, Wintera, *Wintera aromatica*, Winter's Cinnamon
Powers: Success
Magical Uses:

Carry or burn winter's bark to ensure success in all your undertakings.

WITCH GRASS *(Agropyron repens)*
Folk Names: Couch Grass, Dog Grass, Quick Grass, Witches Grass
Gender: Masculine
Planet: Jupiter
Powers: Happiness, Lust, Love, Exorcism
Magical Uses:

Witch grass carried or sprinkled under the bed attracts new lovers. Witch grass is also used in all manner of unhexing and uncrossing rituals, the infusion is sprinkled around the premises to disperse entities, and when worn it dispels depression.

WITCH HAZEL *(Hamamelis virginica)*
Folk Names: Snapping Hazelnut, Spotted Alder, Winterbloom
Gender: Masculine
Planet: Sun
Element: Fire
Powers: Protection, Chastity
Magical Uses:

Witch hazel has long been used to fashion divining rods, hence the common name. The bark and twigs are also used to protect against evil influences. If carried, witch hazel helps to mend a broken heart and cool the passions.

WOLF'S BANE *(Aconitum napellus)* **POISON**
Folk Names: Aconite, Cupid's Car, Dumbledore's Delight, Leapord's Bane, Monkshood, Storm Hat, Thor's Hat, Wolf's Hat
Gender: Feminine
Planet: Saturn
Element: Water
Deity: Hecate
Powers: Protection, Invisibility
Magical Uses:

Wolf's bane is added to protection sachets, especially to guard against vampires and werewolves. This is quite fitting, since wolf's bane is also used by werewolves to cure themselves. The seed, wrapped in a lizard's skin and carried, allows you to become invisible at will.

Do not eat or rub any part of this plant on the skin; it is virulently poisonous.

WOOD ROSE *(Ipomoea tuberosa)*
Folk Names: Ceylon Morning Glory, Frozen Roses, Spanish Arbor Vine
Powers: Luck
Magical Uses:

Carry a wood rose to attract good

luck and fortune. Also place some in the home to ensure it is lucky as well.

WOODRUFF *(Asperula odorata)*
Folk Names: Herb Walter, Master of the Woods, Sweet Woodruff, Wood Rove, Wuderove
Gender: Masculine
Planet: Mars
Element: Fire
Powers: Victory, Protection, Money
Magical Uses:

Woodruff is carried to attract money and prosperity, to bring victory to athletes and warriors, and when placed in a sachet of leather it guards against all harm.

WORMWOOD *(Artemisia absinthium)* **POISON**
Folk Names: Absinthe, Old Woman, Crown for a King
Gender: Masculine
Planet: Mars
Element: Fire
Deities: Iris, Diana, Artemis
Powers: Psychic Powers, Protection, Love, Calling Spirits
Magical Uses:

Wormwood is burned in incenses designed to aid in developing psychic powers, and is also worn for this purpose.

Carried, wormwood protects not only against bewitchment, but also from the bite of sea serpents. Also, according to ancient traditions, it counteracts the effects of poisoning by hemlock and toadstools, but I wouldn't bet my life on its effectiveness in this area. Hung from the rear-view mirror wormwood protects the vehicle from accidents on treacherous roads.

Wormwood is also sometimes used in love infusions, probably because it was once made into an alcoholic beverage called absinthe. This highly-addictive and dangerous liqueur is now outlawed or banned in many countries, but the repu-

tation lingers and wormwood is still used in love mixtures. One such use is to place it under the bed to draw a loved one.

Wormwood is also burned to summon spirits. It is sometimes mixed with sandalwood for this purpose. If burned in graveyards the spirits of the dead will rise and speak, according to old grimoires.

YARROW *(Achillea millefolium)*

Folk Names: Achillea, Arrowroot, Bad Man's Plaything, Carpenter's Weed, Death Flower, Devil's Nettle, Eerie, Field Hops, Gearwe, Hundred Leaved Grass, Knight's Milfoil, Knyghten, Lady's Mantle, Milfoil, Militaris, Military Herb, Millefolium, Noble Yarrow, Nosebleed, Old Man's Mustard, Old Man's Pepper, Sanguinary, Seven Year's Love, Snake's Grass, Soldier's Woundwort, Stanch Griss, Stanch Weed, Tansy, Thousand Seal, Wound Wort, Yarroway, *Yerw*

Gender: Feminine

Planet: Venus

Element: Water

Powers: Courage, Love, Psychic Powers, Exorcism

Magical Uses:

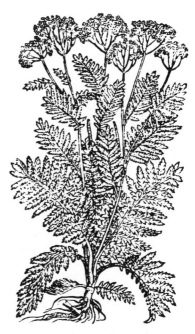

When worn, yarrow protects the wearer, and when held in the hand, it stops all fear and grants courage.

A bunch of dried yarrow hung over the bed or yarrow used in wedding decorations ensures a love lasting at least seven years. Yarrow is also used in love spells.

Carrying yarrow not only brings love but it also attracts friends and distant relations you wish to contact. It draws the attention of those you most want to see.

The flowers are made into an infusion and the resulting tea is drunk to improve psychic powers.

Washing the head with a yarrow infusion will prevent baldness but won't cure it if it has already begun.

Yarrow is also used to exorcise evil and negativity from a person, place or thing.

YELLOW EVENING PRIMROSE *(Oenothera biennis)*
Folk Name: War Poison
Powers: Hunting
Magical Uses:
American Indians rubbed this plant against their moccasins and body to ensure a good hunt, and to cause snakes to avoid them.

YERBA MATE *(Ilex paraguariensis)*
Folk Names: Mate, *Paraguay Tea*, Yerba
Gender: Masculine
Powers: Fidelity, Love, Lust
Magical Uses:
Wear to attract the opposite sex. The infusion is a fine 'lust' potion and if drunk with a loved one will ensure that you stay together. To break off the relationship spill some onto the ground.

YERBA SANTA *(Eriodictyon californicum)*
Folk Names: Bear Weed, Consumptive's Weed, Gum Bush, Holy Herb, Mountain Balm, Sacred Herb
Gender: Feminine
Powers: Beauty, Healing, Psychic Powers, Protection
Magical Uses:
Yerba santa is carried to improve or to attain beauty, and the infusion is added to baths for the same reason.

The leaves are added to healing incenses and are worn around the neck to ward off illnesses and wounds.

It is also carried for spiritual strength, to increase psychic powers and to protect the bearer.

YEW *(Taxus baccata)* **POISON**
Gender: Feminine
Planet: Saturn
Element: Water
Powers: Raising the Dead
Magical Uses:

This poisonous plant is sometimes used in spells to raise the spirits of the dead. Though it has a long mythic history it is little used in magic due to its high toxicity.

YOHIMBE *(Pausinystalia yohimbe)* **POISON**
Powers: Love, Lust
Magical Uses:

Yohimbe infusion is drunk as a 'lust' potion and the powdered herb is added to love mixtures.

Consume in small amounts only.

(Not Shown)

YUCCA *(Yucca* spp.)
Gender: Masculine
Planet: Mars
Element: Fire
Powers: Transmutation, Protection, Purification
Magical Uses:

A hoop or loop of twisted yucca fibers will transmutate a person into an animal if he or she jumps through it, according to American Indian magic. Another method instructs the magician to place a small wreath of yucca fibers on his or her head. This allows the person to assume any form desired.

A cross of yucca fibers twisted together and placed on the hearth protects the house from evil.

Suds made from the yucca plant are used in purifying the body before magic. If a spell to remove curses or illnesses is performed, repeat the yucca-suds bath afterward to ensure that all traces of the evil or sicknesses are removed.

The Tables

As explained earlier, these tables summarize part (but not all) of the information presented in Part II, and are to be used for reference. This part is divided into four sections: Gender, Planetary Rulers, Elemental Rulers, and Magical Intentions. For information not available here, check the indexes.

GENDER

MASCULINE HERBS

Acacia
Agaric
Agrimony
Alder
Allspice
Almond
Anemone
Angelica
Anise
Arabic, Gum
Arbutus
Asafoetida
Ash
Aspen
Avens
Bamboo
Banyan
Basil
Bay
Bean
Benzoin
Bergamot, Orange
Betony, Wood
Bistort
Bittersweet
Black Cohosh
Black Snakeroot
Bloodroot
Bodhi
Borage
Bracken
Brazil Nut
Briony
Bromeliad
Broom
Cactus
Caraway
Carnation
Carrot
Cashew
Cat Tail
Cedar

Celandine
Celery
Centaury
Chamomile
Chestnut
Chicory
Chili Pepper
Chrysanthemum
Cinnamon
Cinquefoil
Citron
Clove
Clover
Copal
Coriander
Cubeb
Cumin
Curry
Damiana
Dandelion
Deerstongue
Dill
Dock
Dragon's Blood
Elecampane
Endive
Eyebright
Fennel
Fenugreek
Fern
Fig
Filbert
Flax
Frankincense
Galangal
Garlic
Gentian
Ginger
Goat's Rue
Golden Seal
Gorse
Grains of Paradise

Hawthorn
Hazel
Heliotrope
High John
  the Conqueror
Holly
Honeysuckle
Hops
Horehound
Horse Chestnut
Horseradish
Houndstongue
Houseleek
Hyssop
Juniper
Larch
Lavendar
Leek
Lemongrass
Lemon Verbena
Lily of the
  Valley
Lime
Linden
Liquidamber
Liverwort
Lovage
Mace
Maquey
Mahogany,
  Mountain
Male Fern
Mandrake
Maple
Marigold
Marjoram
Masterwort
Mastic
May Apple
Meadowsweet
Mint
Mistletoe

Mulberry
Mushroom
Mustard
Nettle
Norfolk Island
  Pine
Nutmeg
Oak
Olive
Onion
Orange
Palm
Papyrus
Parsley
Pecan
Pennyroyal
Peony
Pepper
Peppermint
Pepper Tree
Pimento
Pimpernel
Pine
Pineapple

Pistachio
Poke Root
Pomegranate
Prickly Ash
Radish
Red Sandal-
  wood
Reed
Rice
Rosemary
Rowan
Rue
Saffron
Sage
St. John's
  Wort
Sarsaparilla
Sassafras
Savory, Summer
Senna
Sesame
Shallot
Sloe
Snapdragon

Southernwood
Squill
Star Anise
Sunflower
Tangerine
Tea, Oriental
Thistle
Thistle, Holy
Thistle, Milk
Ti
Toadflax
Tobacco
Tormentil
Venus' Flytrap
Walnut
Wax Plant
Witch Grass
Witch Hazel
Woodruff
Wormwood
Yerba Mate
Yucca

FEMININE HERBS

Adam & Eve
Adder's Tongue
African Violet
Alfalfa
Aloe
Aloes, Wood
Althea
Amaranth
Apple
Apricot
Asphodel
Aster
Avocado
Bachelor's Buttons

Balm, Lemon
Balm of Gilead
Banana
Barley
Bedstraw,
  Fragrant
Beech
Beet
Belladonna
Birch
Bistort
Blackberry
Bladderwrack
Bleeding Heart

Blue Flag
Boneset
Buchu
Buckthorn
Burdock
Cabbage
Calamus
Camellia
Camphor
Caper
Cardamom
Catnip
Cherry
Chickweed

Club Moss
Coconut
Coltsfoot
Columbine
Comfrey
Corn
Cotton
Cowslip
Crocus
Cuckoo-Flower
Cucumber
Cyclamen
Cypress
Daffodil
Daisy
Datura
Dittany of Crete
Dodder
Dulse
Elder
Elm
Eryngo
Eucalyptus
Euphorbia
Feverfew
Fleabane
Foxglove
Fumitory
Gardenia
Geranium
Goldenrod
Gourd
Grape
Groundsel
Heather
Hellebore
Hemlock
Hemp
Henbane
Hibiscus
Honesty
Horsetail
Huckleberry
Hyacinth
Indian Paint
  Brush

Iris
Irish Moss
Ivy
Jasmine
Kava-Kava
Knot Weed
Lady's Mantle
Lady's Slipper
Larkspur
Lemon
Lettuce
Licorice
Lilac
Lily
Lobelia
Loosestrife
Lotus
Love Seed
Lucky Hand
Magnolia
Maidenhair
Mallow
Mesquite
Mimosa
Moonwort
Morning Glory
Mugwort
Mullein
Myrrh
Myrtle
Oats
Oleander
Orchid
Orris
Pansy
Papaya
Passion Flower
Pea
Peach
Pear
Periwinkle
Persimmon
Plantain
Plum
Plum, Wild
Plumeria

Poplar
Poppy
Potato
Primrose
Purslane
Quince
Ragwort
Raspberry
Rhubarb
Rose
Rye
Sagebrush
Sandalwood
Scullcap
Skunk Cabbage
Slippery Elm
Solomon's Seal
Sorrel, Wood
Spearmint
Spikenard
Strawberry
Sugar Cane
Sweetpea
Tamarind
Tamarisk
Tansy
Thyme
Tomato
Tonka
Trillium
Tulip
Turnip
Valerian
Vanilla
Vervain
Veitvert
Violet
Wheat
Willow
Wintergreen
Wolf's Bane
Yarrow
Yerba Santa
Yew

PLANETARY RULERS

SUN

Acacia	Copal	Palm
Angelica	Eyebright	Peony
Arabic, Gum	Frankincense	Pineapple
Ash	Ginseng	Rice
Bay	Goldenseal	Rosemary
Benzoin	Hazel	Rowan
Bromeliad	Heliotrope	Rue
Carnation	Juniper	Saffron
Cashew	Lime	St. John's Wort
Cedar	Liquidamber	Sandalwood
Celandine	Lovage	Sesame
Centaury	Marigold	Sunflower
Chamomile	Mastic	Tangerine
Chicory	Mistletoe	Tea
Chrysanthemum	Oak	Tormentil
Cinnamon	Olive	Walnut
Citron	Orange	Witch Hazel

MOON

Adder's Tongue	Cucumber	Lotus
Aloe	Dulse	Mallow
Balm, Lemon	Eucalyptus	Mesquite
Bladderwrack	Gardenia	Moonwort
Buchu	Gourd	Myrrh
Cabbage	Grape	Papaya
Calamus	Honesty	Poppy
Camellia	Irish Moss	Potato
Camphor	Jasmine	Purslane
Chickweed	Lemon	Sandalwood
Club Moss	Lettuce	Turnip
Coconut	Lily	Willow
Cotton	Loosestrife	Wintergreen

MERCURY

Agaric	Fenugreek	May Apple
Almond	Fern	Mint
Aspen	Filbert	Mulberry
Bean	Flax	Papyrus
Bergamot, Orange	Goat's Rue	Parsley
Bittersweet	Horehound	Pecan
Bracken	Lavendar	Peppermint
Brazil Nut	Lemongrass	Pimpernel
Caraway	Lemon Verbena	Pistachio
Celery	Lily of the Valley	Pomegranate
Clover	Mace	Savory, Summer
Dill	Male Fern	Senna
Elecampane	Mandrake	Southernwood
Fennel	Marjoram	Wax Plant

VENUS

Adam and Eve
African Violet
Alder
Alfalfa
Aloes, Wood
Apple
Apricot
Aster
Avocado
Bachelor's Buttons
Balm of Gilead
Banana
Barley
Bedstraw, Fragrant
Birch
Blackberry
Bleeding Heart
Blue Flag
Buckwheat
Burdock
Caper
Cardamom
Catnip
Cherry
Coltsfoot
Columbine
Corn
Cowslip
Crocus
Cuckoo-Flower
Cyclamen
Daffodil

Daisy
Dittany of Crete
Elder
Eryngo
Feverfew
Foxglove
Geranium
Goldenrod
Groundsel
Heather
Hibiscus
Huckleberry
Hyacinth
Indian Paint Brush
Iris
Lady's Mantle
Larkspur
Licorice
Lilac
Lucky Hand
Magnolia
Maidenhair
Mugwort
Myrtle
Oats
Orchid
Orris
Passion Flower
Pea
Peach
Pear
Periwinkle

Persimmon
Plantain
Plum
Plum, Wild
Plumeria
Primrose
Ragwort
Raspberry
Rhubarb
Rose
Rye
Sagebrush
Sorrel, Wood
Spearmint
Spikenard
Strawberry
Sugar Cane
Sweetpea
Tansy
Thyme
Tomato
Tonka
Trillium
Tulip
Valerian
Vanilla
Vervain
Vetivert
Violet
Wheat
Willow

MARS

Allspice
Anemone
Asafoetida
Basil
Black Snakeroot
Blood Root
Briony
Broom
Cactus
Carrot
Chili Pepper
Coriander
Cubeb
Cumin
Curry Leaf
Damiana
Deerstongue
Dragon's Blood
Galangal
Garlic
Gentian

Ginger
Gorse
Grains of Paradise
Hawthorn
High John the
  Conqueror
Holly
Hops
Horseradish
Houndstongue
Leek
Maguey
Masterwort
Mustard
Nettle
Norfolk Island Pine
Onion
Pennyroyal
Pepper
Peppermint
Pepper Tree

Pimento
Pine
Poke Root
Prickly Ash
Radish
Reed
Shallot
Sloe
Snapdragon
Squill
Thistle
Thistle, Holy
Thistle, Milk
Toadflax
Tobacco
Venus' Flytrap
Woodruff
Wormwood
Yucca

JUPITER

Agrimony
Anise
Avens
Banyan
Betony, Wood
Bodhi
Borage
Chestnut
Cinquefoil
Clove

Dandelion
Dock
Endive
Fig
Honeysuckle
Horse Chestnut
Houseleek
Hyssop
Linden
Liverwort

Maple
Meadowsweet
Nutmeg
Sage
Sarsparilla
Sassafras
Star Anise
Ti
Witch Grass

SATURN

Amaranth
Asphodel
Beech
Beet
Belladonna
Bistort
Boneset
Buckthorn
Comfrey
Cypress
Datura
Dodder
Elm
Euphorbia

Fumitory
Hellebore
Hemlock
Hemp
Henbane
Horsetail
Ivy
Kava-Kava
Knot Weed
Lady's Slipper
Lobelia
Mimosa
Morning Glory
Mullein

Pansy
Patchouly
Poplar
Quince
Scullcap
Skunk Cabbage
Slippery Elm
Solomon's Seal
Tamarind
Tamarisk
Wolf's Bane
Yew

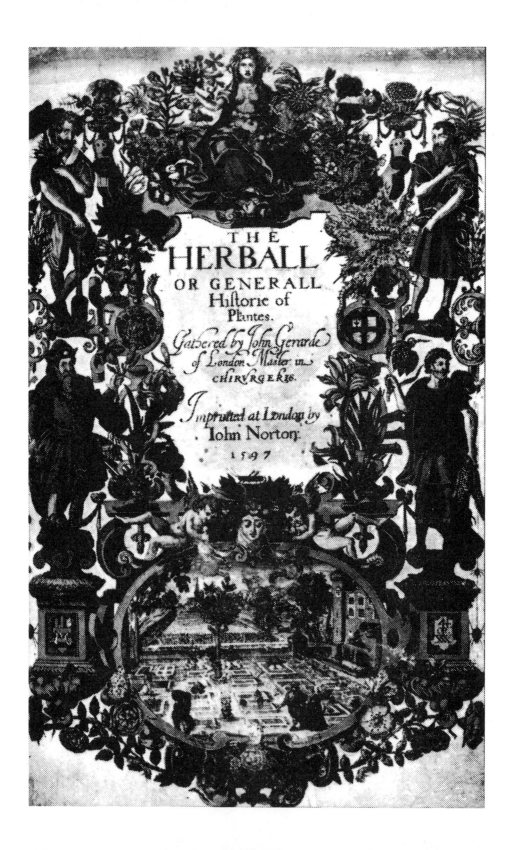

THE
HERBALL
OR GENERALL
Historie of
Plantes.

Gathered by John Gerarde
of London Master in
CHIRVRGERIE.

Imprinted at London by
Iohn Norton.
1597

ELEMENTAL RULERS

EARTH

Alfalfa
Asphodel
Barley
Beet
Bistort
Buckwheat
Corn
Cotton
Cypress
Fern
Fumitory
Honesty

Honeysuckle
Horehound
Horsetail
Knotweed
Loosestrife
Magnolia
Mugwort
Oats
Oleander
Patchouly
Pea
Potato

Primrose
Quince
Rhubarb
Rye
Sagebrush
Sorrel, Wood
Tulip
Turnip
Vervain
Vetivert
Wheat

AIR

Acacia
Agaric
Agrimony
Almond
Anise
Aspen
Banyan
Bean
Benzoin
Bergamot, Orange
Bistort
Bittersweet
Bodhi
Borage
Bracken
Brazil Nut
Bromeliad
Broom
Caraway
Chicory
Citron

Clover
Dandelion
Dock
Elecampane
Endive
Eyebright
Fenugreek
Filbert
Goat's Rue
Goldenrod
Hazel
Hops
Houseleek
Lavendar
Lemongrass
Lemon Verbena
Lily of the Valley
Linden
Mace
Male Fern
Maple

Marjoram
Mastic
Meadowsweet
Mint
Mistletoe
Mulberry
Palm
Papyrus
Parsley
Pecan
Pimpernel
Pine
Pistachio
Rice
Sage
Savory, Summer
Senna
Slipppery Elm
Southernwood
Star Anise
Wax Plant

FIRE

Alder
Allspice
Amaranth
Anemone
Angelica
Asafoetida
Ash
Avens
Basil
Bay
Betony, Wood
Black Snakeroot
Blood Root
Briony
Cactus
Carnation
Carrot
Cashew
Cat Tail
Cedar
Celandine
Celery
Centaury
Chestnut
Chili Pepper
Chrysanthemum
Cinnamon
Cinquefoil
Clove
Copal
Coriander
Cubeb
Cumin
Curry
Damiana
Deerstongue
Dill
Dragon's Blood
Fennel

Fig
Flax
Frankincense
Galangal
Garlic
Gentian
Ginger
Ginseng
Golden Seal
Gorse
Grains of Paradise
Hawthorn
Heliotrope
High John the Con-
    queror
Holly
Horse Chestnut
Houndstongue
Hyssop
Juniper
Leek
Lime
Liquidamber
Liverwort
Lovage
Maguey
Mahogany, Mountain
Mandrake
Marigold
Masterwort
May Apple
Mullein
Mustard
Norfolk Island
    Pine
Nutmeg
Oak
Olive
Onion

Orange
Pennyroyal
Pepper
Peppermint
Pepper Tree
Pimento
Pineapple
Poke Root
Pomegranate
Prickly Ash
Radish
Rosemary
Rowan
Rue
Saffron
St. John's Wort
Sarsaparilla
Sassafras
Sesame
Shallot
Sloe
Snapdragon
Squill
Sunflower
Tangerine
Tea
Thistle
Thistle, Holy
Thistle, Milk
Ti
Toadflax
Tobacco
Tormentil
Venus' Flytrap
Walnut
Witch Hazel
Woodruff
Wormwood
Yucca

WATER

Adam and Eve
African Violet
Aloe
Aloes, Wood
Althea
Apple
Apricot
Aster
Avocado
Bachelor's Buttons
Balm, Gilead
Balm, Lemon
Banana
Bedstraw, Fragrant
Belladonna
Birch
Blackberry
Bladderwrack
Bleeding Heart
Blue Flag
Boneset
Buchu
Buckthorn
Burdock
Cabbage
Calamus
Camellia
Camphor
Caper
Cardamom
Catnip
Chamomile
Cherry
Chickweed
Club Moss
Coconut
Coltsfoot
Columbine
Comfrey
Cowslip
Crocus
Cuckoo-Flower
Cucumber
Cyclamen
Daffodil
Daisy

Datura
Dittany of Crete
Dodder
Dulse
Elder
Elm
Eryngo
Eucalyptus
Euphorbia
Feverfew
Foxglove
Gardenia
Gourd
Grape
Groundsel
Heather
Hellebore
Hemlock
Hemp
Henbane
Hibiscus
Huckleberry
Hyacinth
Indian Paint Brush
Iris
Irish Moss
Jasmine
Kava-Kava
Lady's Mantle
Lady's Slipper
Larkspur
Lemon
Lettuce
Licorice
Lilac
Lily
Lobelia
Lotus
Love Seed
Lucky Hand
Maidenhair
Mallow
Mesquite
Mimosa
Moonwort
Morning Glory

Myrrh
Myrtle
Orchid
Orris
Pansy
Papaya
Passion Flower
Peach
Pear
Periwinkle
Persimmon
Plum
Plum, Wild
Plumeria
Poplar
Poppy
Purslane
Ragwort
Raspberry
Rose
Sandalwood
Scullcap
Skunk Cabbage
Solomon's Seal
Spearmint
Spikenard
Strawberry
Sugar Cane
Sweetpea
Tamarind
Tamarisk
Tansy
Thyme
Tomato
Tonka
Trillium
Valerian
Vanilla
Violet
Willow
Wintergreen
Wolf's Bane
Yarrow
Yew

MAGICAL INTENTIONS

ASTRAL PROTECTION, to aid:
Dittany of Crete
Mugwort
Poplar

BEAUTY, to attain:
Avocado
Catnip
Flax
Ginseng
Maidenhair
Yerba Santa

CHASTITY, to maintain:
Cactus
Camphor
Coconut
Cucumber
Fleabane
Hawthorn
Lavendar
Pineapple
Sweetpea
Vervain
Witch Hazel

COURAGE, to attain:
Borage
Cohosh, Black
Columbine
Masterwort
Mullein
Poke
Ragweed
Sweetpea
Tea
Thyme
Tonka
Wahoo
Yarrow

DEAD, raising the:
Yew

DIVINATION:
Broom
Camphor
Cherry
Dandelion
Fig
Goldenrod
Ground Ivy
Hibiscus
Meadowsweet
Orange
Orris
Pomegranate

EMPLOYMENT, to attain/maintain
Devil's Shoestring
Lucky Hand
Pecan

EXORCISM:
Angelica
Arbutus
Asafoetida
Avens
Basil
Beans
Birch
Boneset
Buckthorn
Clove
Clover
Cumin
Devil's Bit
Dragon's Blood
Elder
Fern
Fleabane
Frankincense
Fumitory
Garlic
Heliotrope
Horehound
Horseradish
Juniper
Leek
Lilac

Mallow
Mint
Mistletoe
Mullein
Myrrh
Nettle
Onion
Peach
Peony
Pepper
Pine
Rosemary
Rue
Sagebrush
Sandalwood
Sloe
Snapdragon
Tamarisk
Thistle
Witch Grass
Yarrow

FERTILITY, to increase:
Agaric
Banana
Bistort
Bodhi
Carrot
Cuckoo-Flower
Cucumber
Cyclamen
Daffodil
Dock
Fig
Geranium
Grape
Hawthorn
Hazel
Horsetail
Mandrake
Mistletoe
Mustard
Myrtle
Nuts
Oak
Olive

Palm, Date
Patchouly
Peach
Pine
Pomegranate
Poppy
Rice
Sunflower
Wheat

FIDELITY:
Chickweed
Chili Pepper
Clover
Cumin
Elder
Licorice
Magnolia
Nutmeg
Rhubarb
Rye
Scullcap
Spikenard
Vetch, Giant
Yerba Mate

FRIENDSHIPS, to promote:
Lemon
Love Seed
Passion Flower
Sweetpea

GOSSIP, to halt:
Clove
Slippery Elm

HAPPINESS, to promote
Catnip
Celandine
Cyclamen
Hawthorn
High John the Conqueror
Hyacinth
Lavender
Lily of the Valley
Marjoram

Meadowsweet
Morning Glory
Purslane
Quince
Saffron
St. John's Wort
Witch Grass

HEALING, to promote:
Adder's Tongue
Allspice
Amaranth
Angelica
Apple
Balm, Lemon
Balm of Gilead
Barley
Bay
Bittersweet
Blackberry
Bracken
Burdock
Calamus
Carnation
Cedar
Cinnamon
Citron
Cowslip
Cucumber
Dock
Elder
Eucalyptus
Fennel
Figwort
Flax
Gardenia
Garlic
Ginseng
Goat's Rue
Golden Seal
Groundsel
Heliotrope
Hemp
Henna
Hops
Horehound

Horse Chestnut
Ivy
Job's Tears
Life Everlasting
Lime
Mesquite
Mint
Mugwort
Myrrh
Nettle
Oak
Olive
Onion
Peppermint
Pepper Tree
Persimmon
Pine
Plaintain
Plum, Wild
Potato
Rose
Rosemary
Rowan
Rue
Saffron
Sandalwood
Sorrel, Wood
Spearmint
Thistle
Thyme
Ti
Tobacco
Vervain
Violet
Willow
Wintergreen
Yerba Santa

HEALTH, to maintain:
Anemone
Ash
Camphor
Caraway
Coriander
Fern
Galangal

Geranium
Groundsel
Juniper
Knotweed
Larkspur
Life-Everlasting
Mandrake
Marjoram
Mistletoe
Mullein
Nutmeg
Oak
Pimpernel
Rue
St. John's Wort
Sassafras
Sorrel, Wood
Spikenard
Sumbul
Tansy
Thyme
Walnut

HEXES, to break:
Bamboo
Chili Pepper
Datura
Galangal
Huckleberry
Hydrangea
Poke
Squill
Thistle
Thistle, Holy
Toadflax
Vetivert
Wahoo
Wintergreen

HUNTING, to aid:
Fuzzy Weed
Mistletoe
Parosela
Yellow Evening Primrose

IMAGE MAGIC, plants to use for:
Ash
Briony
Mandrake
Potato
Straw

IMMORTALITY, to attain:
Apple
Linden
Sage

INFERTILITY, to create:
Walnut

INVISIBILITY, to attain:
Amaranth
Chicory
Edelweiss
Fern
Heliotrope
Mistletoe
Poppy
Wolf's Bane

LEGAL MATTERS, to assist in:
Buckthorn
Cascara Sagrada
Celandine
Hickory
Marigold
Skunk Cabbage

LOCKS, to open
Chicory
Lotus
Mistletoe
Moonwort

LONGEVITY, to attain:
Cypress
Lavendar
Lemon
Life-Everlasting
Maple
Peach

Sage
Tansy

LOVE, to attract:
Adam and Eve
Aloes, Wood
Apple
Apricot
Aster
Avens
Avocado
Bachelor's Buttons
Balm, Lemon
Balm of Gilead
Barley
Basil
Beans
Bedstraw, Fragrant
Beet
Betony
Bleeding Heart
Bloodroot
Brazil Nut
Caper
Cardamom
Catnip
Chamomile
Cherry
Chestnut
Chickweed
Chili Pepper
Cinnamon
Clove
Clover
Cohosh, Black
Coltsfoot
Columbine
Copal
Coriander
Crocus
Cubeb
Cuckoo-Flower
Daffodil
Daisy
Damiana
Devil's Bit

Dill
Dogbane
Dragon's Blood
Dutchman's Breeches
Elecampane
Elm
Endive
Eryngo
Fig
Fuzzy Weed
Gardenia
Gentian
Geranium
Ginger
Ginseng
Grains of Paradise
Hemp
Hibiscus
High John The Conqueror
Houseleek
Hyacinth
Indian Paint Brush
Jasmine
Joe-Pye Weed
Juniper
Kava-Kava
Lady's Mantle
Lavendar
Leek
Lemon
Lemon Verbena
Licorice
Lime
Linden
Liverwort
Lobelia
Lotus
Lovage
Love Seed
Maidenhair
Male Fern
Mallow
Mandrake
Maple
Marjoram
Mastic

Meadow Rue
Meadowsweet
Mimosa
Mistletoe
Moonwort
Myrtle
Nuts
Oleander
Orange
Orchid
Pansy
Papaya
Pea
Peach
Pear
Peppermint
Periwinkle
Pimento
Plum
Plumeria
Poppy
Prickly Ash
Primrose
Purslane
Quassia
Quince
Raspberry
Rose
Rosemary
Rue
Rye
Saffron
Sarsaparilla
Scullcap
Senna
Snakeroot, Black
Southernwood
Spearmint
Spiderwort
Strawberry
Sugar Cane
Sumbul
Tamarind
Thyme
Tomato
Tonka

Tormentil
Trillium
Tulip
Valerian
Vanilla
Venus' Flytrap
Vervain
Vetivert
Violet
Willow
Witch Grass
Wormwood
Yarrow
Yerba Mate
Yohimbe

LOVE, divinations of:
Dodder
Lettuce
Mullein
Pansy
Rose
St. John's Wort
Willow

LOVE SPELLS, to break:
Lily
Lotus
Pistachio

LUCK, to obtain:
Allspice
Aloe
Bamboo
Banyan
Be-Still
Bluebell
Cabbage
Calamus
China Berry
Cinchona
Cotton
Daffodil
Devil's Bit
Fern
Grains of Paradise

Hazel
Heather
Holly
Houseleek
Huckleberry
Irish Moss
Job's Tears
Linden
Lucky Hand
Male Fern
Moss
Nutmeg
Oak
Orange
Persimmon
Pineapple
Pomegranate
Poppy
Purslane
Rose
Snakeroot
Star Anise
Straw
Strawberry
Sumbul
Vetivert
Violet
Wood Rose

LUST, to increase or create:
Avocado
Caper
Caraway
Carrot
Cat Tail
Celery
Cinnamon
Daisy
Damiana
Deerstongue
Dill
Dulse
Endive
Eryngo
Galangal
Garlic

Ginseng
Grains of Paradise
Hibiscus
Lemongrass
Licorice
Maguey
Mint
Nettle
Olive
Onion
Parsley
Patchouly
Radish
Rosemary
Saffron
Sesame
Snakeroot, Black
Southernwood
Vanilla
Violet
Witch Grass
Yerba Mate
Yohimbe

LUST, to decrease:
Camphor
Lettuce
Vervain
Witch Hazel

MANIFESTATIONS, to aid:
Balm of Gilead
Dittany of Crete
Mastic

MEDITATION, to aid:
Bodhi
Gotu Kola

MENTAL POWERS; to strengthen:
Caraway
Celery
Eyebright
Grape
Horehound
Lily of the Valley

Mace
Mustard
Periwinkle
Rosemary
Rue
Savory, Summer
Spearmint
Walnut

MONEY, RICHES, TREASURES,
 WEALTH, to obtain:
Alfalfa
Allspice
Almond
Basil
Bergamot, Orange
Blackberry
Bladderwrack
Blue Flag
Briony
Bromeliad
Buckwheat
Calamus
Camellia
Cascara Sagrada
Cashew
Cedar
Chamomile
Cinnamon
Cinquefoil
Clove
Clover
Comfrey
Cowslip
Dill
Dock
Elder
Fenugreek
Fern
Flax
Fumitory
Galangal
Ginger
Goldenrod
Golden Seal
Gorse

Grains of Paradise
Grape
Heliotrope
High John the Conqueror
Honesty
Honeysuckle
Horse Chestnut
Irish Moss
Jasmine
Lucky Hand
Mandrake
Maple
Marjoram
May Apple
Mint
Moonwort
Moss
Myrtle
Nutmeg
Oak
Oats
Onion
Orange
Oregon Grape
Parchouly
Pea
Pecan
Periwinkle
Pine
Pineapple
Pipsissewa
Pomegranate
Poplar
Poppy
Rattlesnake Root
Rice
Snapdragon
Sassafras
Sesame
Snakeroot
Snakeroot, Black
Squill
Tea
Tonka
Trillium
Vervain

Vetivert
Wheat
Woodruff

PEACE, HARMONY, to instill:
Dulse
Eryngo
Gardenia
Lavendar
Loosestrife
Meadowsweet
Morning Glory
Myrtle
Olive
Passion Flower
Pennyroyal
Scullcap
Vervain
Violet

POWER, to obtain:
Carnation
Club Moss
Devil's Shoestring
Ebony
Gentian
Ginger
Rowan

PROPHETIC DREAMS, to cause:
Bracken
Buchu
Cinquefoil
Heliotrope
Jasmine
Marigold
Mimosa
Mugwort
Onion
Rose

PROSPERITY, to obtain:
Alfalfa
Alkanet
Almond

Ash
Banana
Benzoin
Nuts
Oak
Tomato
Tulip

PROTECTION, to gain:
Acacia
African Violet
Agrimony
Ague Root
Aloe
Althea
Alyssum
Amaranth
Anemone
Angelica
Anise
Arbutus
Asafoetida
Ash
Balm of Gilead
Bamboo
Barley
Basil
Bay
Bean
Betony, Wood
Birch
Bittersweet
Blackberry
Bladderwrack
Bloodroot
Blueberry
Bodhi
Boneset
Briony
Bromeliad
Broom
Buckthorn
Burdock
Cactus
Calamus
Caraway

Carnation
Cascara Sagrada
Castor
Cedar
Celandine
Chrysanthemum
Cinchona
Cinnamon
Cinquefoil
Clove
Clover
Club Moss
Coconut
Cohosh, Black
Cotton
Cumin
Curry
Cyclamen
Cypress
Datura
Devil's Bit
Devil's Shoestring
Dill
Dogwood
Dragon's Blood
Ebony
Elder
Elecampane
Eucalyptus
Euphorbia
Fennel
Fern
Feverwort
Figwort
Flax
Fleabane
Foxglove
Frankincense
Galangal
Garlic
Geranium
Ginseng
Gorse
Gourd
Grain
Grass

Hazel
Heather
Holly
Honeysuckle
Horehound
Houseleek
Hyacinth
Hyssop
Irish Moss
Ivy
Juniper
Kava-Kava
Lady's Slipper
Larch
Larkspur
Lavendar
Leek
Lettuce
Lilac
Lily
Lime
Linden
Liquidamber
Loosestrife
Lotus
Lucky Hand
Mallow
Mandrake
Marigold
Masterwort
Meadow Rue
Mimosa
Mint
Mistletoe
Molluka
Mugwort
Mulberry
Mullein
Mustard
Myrrh
Nettle
Norfolk Island Pine
Oak
Olive
Onion
Orris

Papaya
Papyrus
Parsley
Pennyroyal
Peony
Pepper
Pepper Tree
Periwinkle
Pilot Weed
Pimpernel
Pine
Plantain
Plum
Primrose
Purslane
Quince
Radish
Ragwort
Raspberry
Rattlesnake Root
Rhubarb
Rice
Roots
Rose
Rosemary
Rowan
Sage
St. John's Wort
Sandalwood
Sloe
Snapdragon
Southernwood
Spanish Moss
Squill
Tamarisk
Thistle
Ti
Toadflax
Tomato
Tormentil
Tulip
Turnip
Valerian
Venus' Flytrap
Vervain
Violet

Wax Plant
Willow
Wintergreen
Witch Hazel
Wolf's Bane
Woodruff
Wormwood
Yerba Santa
Yucca

PSYCHIC POWERS, to strengthen:
Acacia
Althea
Bay
Bistort
Bladderwrack
Borage
Buchu
Celery
Cinnamon
Citron
Elecampane
Eyebright
Flax
Galangal
Grass
Honeysuckle
Lemongrass
Mace
Marigold
Mastic
Mugwort
Peppermint
Rose
Rowan
Saffron
Star Anise
Stillengia
Sumbul
Thyme
Uva Ursa
Wormwood
Yarrow
Yerba Santa

PURIFICATION
Alkanet
Anise
Arabic, Gum
Asafoetida
Avens
Bay
Benzoin
Betony, Wood
Bloodroot
Broom
Cedar
Chamomile
Coconut
Copal
Euphorbia
Fennel
Horseradish
Hyssop
Iris
Lavendar
Lemon
Lemon Verbena
Mimosa
Parsley
Peppermint
Pepper Tree
Rosemary
Sagebrush
Shallot
Thistle, Holy
Thyme
Tobacco
Turmeric
Valerian
Vervain
Yucca

RAIN, to cause to fall:
Bracken
Cotton
Fern
Heather
Pansy
Rice
Toadstool

SEXUAL POTENCY, to regain or maintain:
Banana
Beans
Caper
Cohosh, Black
Dragon's Blood
Oak
Olive
Palm, Date

SLEEP
Agrimony
Chamomile
Cinquefoil
Datura
Elder
Hops
Lavendar
Lettuce
Linden
Passion Flower
Peppermint
Purslane
Rosemary
Thyme
Valerian
Vervain

SNAKES, to call:
Horsetail

SNAKES, to enrage:
Thistle, Milk

SNAKES, to repel:
Clover
Elder
Juniper
Lemongrass
Geranium
Plaintain
Rattlesnake Root
Yellow Evening Primrose

SPIRITS, to call:
Dandelion
Pipsissewa
Sweetgrass
Thistle
Tobacco
Wormwood

SPIRITUALITY, to strengthen:
African Violet
Aloes, Wood
Arabic, Gum
Cinnamon
Frankincense
Gardenia
Myrrh
Sandalwood

STRENGTH, to instill:
Bay
Carnation
Masterwort
Mugwort
Mulberry
Pennyroyal
Plantain
Saffron
St. John's Wort
Sweetpea
Tea
Thistle

SUCCESS, to attain:
Balm, Lemon
Cinnamon
Clover
Ginger
High John the Conqueror
Rowan
Wahoo
Winter's Bark

THEFT, to prevent:
Aspen
Caraway
Cumin
Garlic

Juniper
Vetivert

VISIONS, to induce:
Angelica
Coltsfoot
Crocus
Damiana
Kava-Kava

WIND, to raise:
Bladderwrack
Broom
Saffron

WISDOM, to promote:
Bodhi
Iris
Peach
Sage
Sunflower

WISHES, to manifest:
Bamboo
Beech
Buckthorn
Dandelion
Dogwood
Ginseng
Grains of Paradise
Hazel
Job's Tears
Liquidamber
Pomegranate
Sage
Sandalwood
Sunflower
Tonka
Violet
Walnut

YOUTH, to maintain or regain:
Anise
Cowslip
Fern
Myrtle
Rosemary
Vervain

GLOSSARY

AMULET: An object worn, carried or placed to guard against negativity or other vibrations. A protective object.

ASTRAL PROJECTION: The practice of separating the consciousness from the physical body so that the former may move about unhindered by time, space or gravity.

BANE: A poison; that which destroys life. 'Henbane' is poisonous to hens.

BANISH: To drive away evil, negativity or spirits.

BELTANE: An ancient folk-festival day observed by Witches that celebrates the fully blossomed spring. April 30 or May 1.

CENSER: A vessel of metal or earthenware in which incense is burned. An incense burner.

CHAPLET: A garland or wreath of flowers or leaves worn on the head, as in the chaplets given to classical Greek heroes as symbols of honor.

CLAIRVOYANCE: Literally 'clear seeing.' The ability to perceive facts, events and other data by other than the five 'normal' senses, unaided by tools.

CURSE: A concentration of negative and destructive energy, deliberately formed and directed toward a person, place or thing.

DIVINATION: The art of finding things out through means other than the five senses, using tools such as tarot cards, crystal balls, and so on.

ENCHANT: 'Sing to'. Magically speaking, a procedure whereby herbs are aligned with your magical need prior to their use.

EVIL EYE, THE: Supposed glance capable of causing great harm or fear, once almost universally feared.

FASCINATION: The art of placing other people under one's power through sounds, gazes, colors, etc.

HEX: An evil spell; a curse.

INCUBUS: A male demon or spirit which was believed to sexually tempt and abuse women; the succubus was the corresponding female demon.

INFUSION: An herbal tea.

LUGHNASADH: An old harvest festival celebrated on August 1st or 2nd in Europe, reverencing the abundant (harvested) fruits of the Earth. It is still observed by Wicca.

MAGIC: The practice of causing needed change through the use of powers as yet undefined and unaccepted by science.

MAGIC CIRCLE: A ritually-created circle (or sphere) that offers protection to the magician during magical rites.

MAGICIAN: A person of either sex who practices magic.

MAGUS: A magician.

MIDSUMMER: The Summer Solstice, usually on or near June 21st, one of the Wiccan festival days and an excellent time to practice magic.

PENDULUM: A tool of divination which consists of a heavy object suspended from a string or cord. The end of the cord is held between the thumb and forefinger; questions are asked and their answers divided by the movements of the pendulum.

PENTAGRAM: A five-pointed star which has been used in magic for centuries. Highly symbolic, it is also a protective device.

POPPET: A small doll made of various substances to influence a person's life. In herb magic, either a carved root or a cloth image stuffed with herbs. The use of poppets is known as 'image magic'.

POWER HAND, THE: The hand you write with; the dominant hand. This is a magically potent hand.

SAMHAIN: An ancient festival day marking the beginning of winter. Also known as 'Halloween' and All Hallows Eve. It is observed by Wicca with religious ceremonies.

SCRY: To gaze into a pool of ink, fire, crystal ball, etc. to awaken and summon psychic powers.

SPELL: A Magical rite.

TALISMAN: An object worn or carried to attract a specific influence, such as love, luck, money, health; as opposed to an amulet which keeps forces from its bearer.

WICCA: A contemporary religion with spiritual roots in prehistory that worships the life-force of the universe as personified as a God and Goddess. It is sometimes erroneously referred to as 'witchcraft'.

WITCH BOTTLE: A bottle or jar containing herbs, pins, shards of glass and other objects, designed to protect a person or area from evil and curses. Usually buried or placed in a window.

WITCHCRAFT: The practice of natural magic, as that of herbs, stones, and candles. Spell-casting. Still used by some to refer to the religion of Wicca.

WORT: An old word meaning 'herb'. Mugwort preserves the term.

APPENDIX I:

COLORS AND THEIR MAGICAL USES

WHITE: Protection, Peace, Purification, Chastity, Happiness, Halting Gossip, Spirituality

GREEN: Healing, Money, Prosperity, Luck, Fertility, Beauty, Employment, Youth

BROWN: Healing Animals, The Home

PINK: Emotional Love, Fidelity, Friendships

RED: Lust, Strength, Courage, Power, Sexual Potency

YELLOW: Divination, Psychic Powers, Mental Powers, Wisdom, Visions

PURPLE: Power, Exorcism, Healing

BLUE: Healing, Sleep, Peace

ORANGE: Legal Matters, Success

APPENDIX II:

MAIL-ORDER SUPPLIES

Send a self-addressed, stamped envelope for catalog ordering information.

APHRODISIA
282 Bleeker St.
New York, NY 10014
Dried herbs and essential oils.

INTERNATIONAL IMPORTS
P.O. Box 2010
Toluca Lake, CA 91602
Dried herbs, charcoal blocks, oils.

W. ATLEE BURPEE CO.
300 Park Avenue
Warminster, PA 18974
Standard Herb seeds.

NATURE'S HERB CO.
281 Ellis Street
San Francisco, CA 94102
Dried herbs and essential oils.

CAPRILANDS HERB FARM
Silver Street
Coventry, CT 06238
Herb seeds.

NICHOLS GARDEN NURSERY
1190 North Pacific Highway
Albany, OR 97321
Herb seeds, plants, books.

THE EYE OF THE CAT
3314 E. Broadway
Long Beach, CA 90803
Dried herbs, oils.

GEORGE W. PARK SEED CO.
P.O. Box 31
Greenwood, SC 29647
Common and unusual herb seeds.

GURNEY SEED & NURSERY CO.
1448 Page Street
Yankton, SD 57079
Seed plants, dried herbs.

TAYLOR'S HERB GARDENS, INC.
1535 Lone Oak Road
Vista, CA 92083
*Over 200 varieties of herbs, shipped
live.*

TRYAD COMPANY
Box 17006
Minneapolis, MN 55417
Dried herbs, charcoal blocks.

WELL-SWEEP HERB FARM
317 Mt. Bethel Road
Port Murray, NJ 07865

APPENDIX III:

THE MAGICAL PROPERTIES OF OILS

Space precludes a complete discussion of essential oils and their magical uses. However, the following list of magical needs and recommended oils is here appended due to their importance in magical herbalism.

Though many 'essential' oils are synthetic they can still be used in magic— if you are satisfied with the scent. For a more detailed look at essential oils, see MAGICAL HERBALISM. Suppliers are listed in APPENDIX II.

COURAGE:
Cedar
Musk
Rose Geranium

FERTILITY:
Musk
Vervain

FRIENDSHIPS:
Stephanotis
Sweetpea

HAPPINESS:
Apple Blossom
Sweetpea
Tuberose

HARMONY:
Basil
Gardenia
Lilac
Narcissus

HEALING:
Carnation
Eucalyptus
Gardenia
Lotus
Myrrh
Narcissus
Rosemary
Sandalwood
Violet

HEX-BREAKING:
Bergamot
Myrrh
Rose Geranium
Rosemary
Rue
Vetivert

LOVE:
Clove
Gardenia
Jasmine

Orris
Plumeria
Rose
Sweetpea

LUCK:
Cinnamon
Cypress
Lotus

LUST:
Cinnamon
Clove
Musk
Vanilla

**MAGNETIC—
TO ATTRACT MEN:**
Ambergris
Gardenia
Ginger
Jasmine
Lavendar

Musk
Neroli
Tonka

**MAGNETIC—
TO ATTRACT WOMEN:**
Bay
Civet
Musk
Patchouly
Stephanotis
Vetivert
Violet

MEDITATION:
Acacia
Hyacinth
Jasmine
Magnolia
Myrrh
Nutmeg

MENTAL POWERS:
Honeysuckle
Lilac
Rosemary

MONEY:
Almond
Bayberry
Bergamot
Honeysuckle
Mint
Patchouly
Pine
Vervain

PEACE:
Benzoin
Cumin
Gardenia
Hyacinth
Magnolia
Rose
Tuberose

POWER:
Carnation
Rosemary
Vanilla

PROTECTION:
Cypress
Myrrh
Patchouly
Rose Geranium
Rosemary
Rue
Violet
Wisteria

PSYCHIC POWERS:
Acacia
Anise
Cassia
Heliotrope
Lemongrass
Lilac
Mimosa
Nutmeg
Sandalwood
Tuberose

PURIFICATION:
Acacia
Cinnamon
Clove
Frankincense
Jasmine
Lavendar
Myrrh
Olive
Sandalwood

SLEEP:
Lavendar
Narcissus

SPIRITUALITY:
Heliotrope
Lotus

Magnolia
Sandalwood

VITALITY:
Allspice
Carnation
Rosemary
Vanilla

FOLK NAMES CROSS-REFERENCE

All folk-names listed in the encyclopedia are arranged here in alphabetical order, followed by the common name by which each plant is identified in the work.

Some folk names may apply in two or three distinct plants; when this is the case, these have been listed in alphabetical order.

In determining which plant to use (in the above situation), use logic; if a spell calls for Aaron's rod and relates to graveyards, mullein would be a better choice rather than goldenrod, which has few such associations.

A

Aaron's Rod: Goldenrod, Mullein
Absinthe: Wormwood
Achillea: Yarrow
Aconite: Wolf's Bane
Adder's Mouth: Adder's Tongue
African Ginger: Ginger
African Pepper: Grains of Paradise
Agave: Maguey
Ague Grass: Ague Root
Agueweed: Boneset
Ahuacotl: Avocado
Ajo: Garlic
Alantwurzel: Elecampane
Albahaca: Basil
Alehoof: Ground Ivy
Alhuren: Elder
Alison: Alyssum
All Heal: Mistletoe, Valerian
Alligator Pear: Avocado
Alraun: Mandrake
Alycompaine: Elecampane
Amantilla: Valerian
Amber: St. John's Wort

American Adder's Tongue: Adder's Tongue
American Dittany: Basil
American Mandrake: May Apple
Aneton: Dill
Anneys: Anise
Aniseed: Anise
Anthropomorphon: Mandrake
Appleringie: Southernwood
Aquifolius: Holly
Arabic: Arabic, Gum
Arberry: Uva Ursa
Archangel: Angelica
Arched Fig: Banyan
Armstrong: Knotweed
Arrowroot: Yarrow
Artemis Herb: Mugwort
Artemesia: Mugwort
Artetyke: Cowslip
Arthritica: Cowslip
Asphodel: Daffodil
Assaranaccara: Avens
Assear: Comfrey

Ass's Foot: Coltsfoot
Assyfetida: Asafoetida
Asthma Weed: Lobelia
Aunee: Elecampane
Autumn Crocus: Saffron
Ava: Kava-Kava
Ava Pepper: Kava-Kava
Ava Root: Kava-Kava
Awa Root: Kava-Kava

B
Baaras: Mandrake
Bad Man's Plaything: Yarrow
Bairnwort: Daisy
Baie: Bay
Balessan: Balm of Gilead
Balsam: Balm of Gilead
Balsumodendron Gileadenis: Balm of Gilead
Bamboo Briar: Sarsaparilla
Banal: Broom
Banewort: Belladonna, Pansy
Banwort: Pansy
Bardana: Burdock
Basam: Broom
Bashoush: Rue
Bat's Wings: Holly
Battree: Elder
Bay Laurel: Bay
Bay Tree: Bay
Bearberry: Uva Ursa
Bear's Foot: Lady's Mantle
Bear's Grape: Uva Ursa
Bear Weed: *Yerba Santa*
Beaver Poison: Hemlock
Bechan: Balm of Gilead
Bee Balm: Balm, Lemon
Beechwheat: Buckwheat
Beer Flower: Hops
Beggar's Buttons: Burdock
Beggarweed: Dodder
Beggary: Fumitory
Beithe: Birch
Ben: Benzoin
Benjamen: Benzoin
Bennet: Avens

Bereza: Birch
Bergamot: Bergamot, Orange
Berke: Birch
Beth: Birch, Trillium
Beth Root: Trillium
Bilberry: Blueberry
Bindweed: Morning Glory
Birdlime: Mistletoe
Bird's Eye: Pansy
Bird's Foot: Fenugreek
Bird's Nest: Carrot
Bishopwort: Betony, Wood
Bisom: Broom
Biscuits: Tormentil
Bitter Grass: Ague Root
Bitter Root: Gentian
Bizzon: Broom
Black Cherry: Belladonna
Black Cohosh: Cohosh, Black
Black Nightshade: Henbane
Black Pepper: Pepper
Blackroot: Auge Root
Black Sampson: Echinacea
Black Snake Root: Cohosh, Black
Black Tea: Tea
Blackthorn: Sloe
Black Wort: Comfrey
Bladder Fucus: Bladderwrack
Bladderpod: Liverwort
Blanket Leaf: Mullein
Blessed Herb: Avens, Pimpernel
Blessed Thistle: Thistle, Holy
Blind Buff: Poppy
Blindeyes: Poppy
Blood: Dragon's Blood
Bloodroot: Tormentil
Bloody Butcher: Valerian
Blooming Sally: Loosestrife
Blowball: Dandelion
Blue Buttons: Periwinkle
Blue Eyes: Potato
Blue Gum Tree: Eucalyptus
Blue Magnolia: Magnolia
Blue Mountain Tea: Goldenrod
Blue Violet: Violet
Blume: Dragon's Blood

Bly: Blackberry
Blye Eyes: Potato
Box: Beech
Boke: Beech
Boneset: Comfrey
Bonewort: Pansy
Bookoo: Buchu
Bo-Tree: Bodhi
Bottle Brush: Horsetail
Bouleau: Birch
Bouncing Bet: Pansy
Bour Tree: Elder
Boure Tree: Elder
Boxwood: Dogwood
Boy's Love: Southernwood
Brain Thief: Mandrake
Bramble: Blackberry
Bramblekite: Blackberry
Brandy Mint: Peppermint
Brank: Buckwheat
Bras: Rice
Bread and Cheese Tree: Hawthorn
Bream: Broom
Bride of the Meadow: Meadow-
    sweet
Bride of the Sun: Marigold
Bridewort: Meadowsweet
British Tobacco: Coltsfoot
Brittanica: Vervain
Broom: Gorse
Broom Tops: Broom
Brown Mint: Spearmint
Bruisewort: Comfrey, Daisy
Brum: Broom
Buche: Beech
Buckeye: Horse Chestnut
Buckles: Cowslip
Bucco: Buchu
Budwood: Dogwood
Buffalo Herb: Alfalfa
Bugbane: Cohosh, Black
Bugloss: Borage
Buk: Beech
Buke: Beech
Buku: Buchu
Bull's Blood: Horehound

Bull's Foot: Coltsfoot
Bumble-Kite: Blackberry
Bumweed: Pilot Weed
Burning Bush: Wahoo
Burn Plant: Aloe
Burrage: Borage
Burrseed: Burdock
Butterbur: Coltsfoot
Butter Rose: Primrose
Buttons: Tansy

C
Caaroba: Carob
Calamus Draco: Dragon's Blood
Calendula: Marigold
Calf's Snout: Snapdragon
California Barberry: Oregon Grape
California Pepper Tree: Pepper Tree
Camomyle: Chamomile
Candlewick Plant: Mullein
Cane, Sugar: Sugar Cane
Cankerwort: Dandelion, Ragwort
Cape Gum: Acacia
Capon's Trailer: Valerian
Carageen: Irish Moss
Caroba: Carob
Carobinha: Carob
Carpenter's Weed: Yarrow
Carthage Apple: Pomegranate
Carya: Walnut
Cassilago: Henbane
Cassilata: Henbane
Cat: Catnip
Catmint: Catnip
Catnep: Catnip
Catrup: Catnip
Cat's Foot: Ground Ivy
Cat's Valerian: Valerian
Cat's Wort: Catnip
Caucasian Walnut: Walnut
Cedron: Lemon Verbena
Celydoyne: Celandine
Centinode: Knotweed
Centocchiio: Periwinkle
Ceylon Morning Glory: Wood Rose
Chafe Weed: Life Everlasting

Chamaimelon: Chamomile
Chameleon Star: Bromeliad
Chanvre: Hemp
Checkerberry: Wintergreen
Chelidonium: Celandine
Cherry Pie: Heliotrope
Chewing John: Galangal
China Aster: Aster
China Root: Galangal
China Tea: Tea
Chinese Anise: Star Anise
Chinese Lovage: Lovage
Chinese Parsley: Coriander
Chocolate: Carob
Christ's Ladder: Centaury
Christ's Thorn: Holly
Church Steeples: Agrimony
Churnstaff: Toadflax
Cilantro: Coriander
Cilentro: Coriander
Circeium: Mandrake
Circoea: Mandrake
Citrus Plant: Parosela
Cleavers: Bedstraw, Fragrant
Clot: Mullein
Clotbur: Burdock
Cloudberry: Blackberry
Clove Root: Avens
Coakum: Poke
Cocan: Poke
Cocklebur: Agrimony
Cockleburr: Burdock
Colewort: Avens
Colic Root: Galangal
Common Bamboo: Bamboo
Common Fig: Fig
Common Heather: Heather
Common Lilac: Lilac
Common Thyme: Thyme
Compass Point: Pilot Weed
Compass Weed: Rosemary
Coneflower: Echinacea
Consolida: Comfrey
Consound: Comfrey
Consumptive Weed: *Yerba Santa*
Convallaria: Lily of the Valley

Cornish Lovage: Lovage
Corona Solis: Sunflower
Couch Grass: Witch Grass
Coughwort: Coltsfoot
Coumaria Nut: Tonka
Cowcucumber: Cucumber
Cow-Flop: Foxglove
Cowgrass: Knotweed
Crampweed: Cinquefoil
Crocus: Saffron
Crosswort: Boneset
Crowberry: Poke
Crow Corn: Ague Root
Crown for a King: Wormwood
Crown of Thorns: Euphorbia
Cuckoo's Bread: Plantain
Cuckowe's Meat: Sorrel, Wood
Cucumber Tree: Magnolia
Culantro: Coriander
Cumino: Cumin
Cumino aigro: Cumin
Cupid's Car: Wolf's Bane
Cutweed: Bladderwrack
Cuy: Cowslip

D
Daffy-Down-Dilly: Daffodil
Daphne: Bay
Date Palm: Palm, Date
Deadly Nightshade: Belladonna
Deadmen's Bells: Foxglove
Death Angel: Agaric
Death Cap: Agaric
Death Flower: Yarrow
Death's Herb: Belladonna
Delight of the Eye: Rowan
Delphinium: Larkspur
Desert Rue: Parosela
Deus Caballinus: Henbane
Devil's Apple: Datura
Devil's Cherries: Belladonna
Devil's Dung: Asafoetida
Devil's Eye: Henbane, Periwinkle
Devil's Flower: Bachelor's Buttons
Devil's Fuge: Mistletoe
Devil's Guts: Dodder

Devil's Milk: Celandine
Devil's Nettle: Yarrow
Devil's Oatmeal: Parsley
Dewberry: Blackberry
Dew of the Sea: Rosemary
Dhan: Rice
Digitalis: Foxglove
Dill Weed: Dill
Dilly: Dill
Divale: Belladonna
Doffle: Mullein
Dog-Bur: Houndstongue
Doggies: Toadflax
Dog Grass: Witch Grass
Dog Standard: Ragwort
Dog's Tongue: Houndstongue
Dogtree: Dogwood
Dollor: Meadowsweet
Donnerbesen: Mistletoe
Draconis Resina: Dragon's Blood
Dragon Bushes: Toadflax
Dragon's Blood Palm: Dragon's
    Blood
Dragonwort: Bistort
Drelip: Cowslip
Dropberry: Solomon's Seal
Drunkard: Marigold
Duck's Foot: May Apple
Duir: Oak
Dumbledore's Delight: Wolf's Bane
Dutch Honeysuckle: Honeysuckle
Dutch Rushes: Horsetail
Dwale: Belladonna
Dwaleberry: Belladonna
Dwayberry: Belladonna

E
Earthbank: Tormentil
Earthsmoke: Fumitory
Earth Star: Bromeliad
Easter Giant: Bistort
East India Catarrh Root: Galangal
Edellebore: Liverwort
Eerie: Yarrow
Egyptian Gum: Arabic, Gum
Egyptian Thorn: Acacia

Eldrum: Elder
Elf Dock: Elecampane
Elf Leaf: Lavendar, Rosemary
Elfwort: Elecampane
Ellhorn: Elder
Elm, Slippery: Slippery Elm
Elven: Elm
Enchanter's Plant: Vervain
Enebro: Juniper
English Cowslip: Primrose
English Elm: Elm
Englishman's Foot: Plantain
English Serpentary: Bostort
English Valerian: Valerian
English Walnut: Walnut
Euphrosyne: Eyebright
European Aspen: Aspen
European Elm: Elm
European Mistletoe: Mistletoe
European Raspberry: Raspberry
Euryangium Musk Root: Sumbul
Everlasting: Life Everlasting
Ewe Daisy: Tormentil
Eye Balm: Golden Seal
Eye of the Star: Horehound
Eye Root: Golden Seal
Eyes: Daisy

F
Faggio: Beech
Fagos: Beech
Fairies' Horses: Ragwort
Fair Lady: Belladonna
Fairy Bells: Sorrel, Wood
Fairy Cup: Cowslip
Fairy Fingers: Foxglove
Fairy Petticoats: Foxglove
Fairy's Eggs: Molukka
Fairy Thimbles: Foxglove
Fairy Weed: Foxglove
False Wintergreen: Pipsissewa
Faya: Beech
Featherfew: Feverfew
Febrifuge Plant: Feverfew
Felon Herb: Mugwort
Feltwort: Mullein

Fenkel: Fennel
Feverwort: Boneset, Centaury
Field Balm: Catnip
Field Balsam: Life Everlasting
Field Daisy: Daisy
Field Hops: Yarrow
Finnochio: Fennel
Fireweed: Dodder
Five Finger Blossom: Cinquefoil
Five Finger Grass: Cinquefoil
Five Fingers: Cinquefoil, Tormentil
Flag Lily: Blue Flag
Flannel Plant: Mullein
Flax Weed: Toadflax
Flesh and Blood: Tormentil
Fleur de Coucou: Daffodil
Fleur-de-Lis: Blue Flag
Floppy-Dock: Foxglove
Floptop: Foxglove
Florentine Iris: Orris
Flores de Cerveza: Hops
Florida Dogwood: Dogwood
Flower of Immortality: Amaranth
Flowering Cornel: Dogwood
Flowering Dogwood: Dogwood
Fluellin: Toadflax
Flukes: Potato
Flute Plant: Meadow Rue
Folk's Gloves: Foxglove
Food of the Gods: Asafoetida
Foxes Glofa: Foxglove
Fox Bells: Foxglove
Foxtail: Club Moss
Frangipangi: Plumeria
Fragrant Valerian: Valerian
Frauenschlussel: Cowslip
Frau Holle: Elder
French Wheat: Buckwheat
Frey: Gorse
Frozen Roses: Wood Rose
Fruit of the Gods: Apple
Fruit of the Underworld: Apple
Fuga daemonum: St. John's Wort
Fumiterry: Fumitory
Fumus: Fumitory
Fumus Terrae: Fumitory

Furze: Gorse
Fyrs: Gorse

G
Gagroot: Lobelia
Galgenmannchen: Mandrake
Galingal: Galangal
Galingale: Galangal
Gallowgrass: Hemp
Gallows: Mandrake
Gallwort: Toadflax
Ganeb: Hemp
Ganja: Hemp
Garclive: Agrimony
Garden Celandine: Celandine
Garden Dill: Dill
Garden Heliotrope: Valerian
Garden Lettuce: Lettuce
Garden Mint: Mint, Spearmint
Garden Purslane: Purslane
Garden Rue: Rue
Garden Sage: Sage
Garden Thyme: Thyme
Garden Violet: Pansy
Garde Robe: Southernwood
Gargaut: Galangal
Garget: Poke
Gazels: Hawthorn
Gearwe: Yarrow
Gemeiner Wachholder: Juniper
Geneva: Juniper
Genista: Broom
German Rue: Rue
Ghost Flower: Datura
Gill-Go-Over-The-Ground: Ground Ivy
Gillies: Carnation
Gilliflower: Carnation
Gin Berry: Juniper
Ginepro: Juniper
Gin Plant: Juniper
Giver of Life: Corn
Gladdon: Calamus
Goat's Leaf: Honeysuckle
Goat Weed: St. John's Wort
Golden Apple: Apricot

Golden Bough: Mistletoe
Golden Purslane: Purslane
Golden Star: Avens
Goldes: Marigold
Goldy Star: Avens
Goldruthe: Goldenrod
Gonea Tea: Goldenrod
Good Luck Plant: Ti
Goosegrass: Cinquefoil
Gooseleek: Daffodil
Goose Tansy: Cinquefoil
Gorst: Gorse
Gort: Ivy
Goss: Gorse
Gout Root: Briony
Goutberry: Blackberry
Grandilla: Passion Flower
Grape, Oregon: Oregon Grape
Grass: Hemp
Gravelroot: Joe-Pye Weed
Gravel Root: Meadowsweet
Graveyard Dust: Mullein
Graveyard Flowers: Plumeria
Great Burdock: Burdock
Greater Celandine: Celandine
Greater Pimpernel: Pimpernel
Greater Scullcap: Scullcap
Great Herb, The: Foxglove
Great Morel: Belladonna
Grecian Laurel: Bay
Greek Hay-Seed: Fenugreek
Green Broom: Broom
Green Mint: Spearmint
Green Osier: Dogwood
Green Spine: Spearmint
Grenadier: Pomegranite
Groats: Oats
Ground Apple: Camomile
Groundbread: Cyclamen
Groundeswelge: Groundsel
Ground Glutton: Groundsel
Ground Holly: Pipsissewa
Ground Raspberry: Golden Seal
Grundy Swallow: Groundsel
Guardrobe: Rosemary
Guinea Grains: Grains of Paradise

Gum Arabic: Arabic, Gum
Gum Arabic Tree: Arabic, Gum
Gum Benzoin: Benzoin
Gum Bush: *Yerba Santa*
Gum Myrrh Tree: Myrrh
Gum Mastic: Mastic
Gum Plant: Comfrey
Gypsy Flower: Houndstongue

H
Hag's Tapers: Mullein
Hagthorn: Hawthorn
Hand of Power: Lucky Hand
Hanf: Hemp
Happy Major: Burdock
Haran: Horehound
Hardock: Burdock
Harebell: Bluebell
Harefoot: Avens
Haw: Hawthorn
Haya: Beech
Haymaids: Ground Ivy
Hazels: Hawthorn
Headache: Poppy
Head Waak: Poppy
Healing Herb: Comfrey
Heart Leaf: Liverwort
Heart's Ease: Pansy
Heath: Heather
Hebenon: Henbane
Hedge Taper: Mullein
Hedgemaids: Ground Ivy
Heermannchen: Camomile
Hellweed: Dodder
Helmet Flower: Scullcap
Helping Hand: Lucky Hand
Hempseed: Joe Pye Weed
Hen and Chickens: Houseleek
Henbells: Henbane
Herba John: St. John's Wort
Herba Sacra: Vervain
Herb Bennet: Avens, Hemlock
Herb of Circe: Mandrake
Herb of Enchantment: Vervain
Herb of Gladness: Borage
Herb of Grace: Rue, Vervain

Herb of Mary: Pimpernel
Herb of the Cross: Vervain
Herb Peter: Cowslip
Herb Trinity: Liverwort
Herb Walter: Woodruff
Herbygrass: Rue
Hetre: Beech
Hexenmannchen: Mandrake
High Blackberry: Blackberry
Hildemoer: Elder
Hoarhound: Horehound
Hog Apple: May Apple
Hogsbean: Henbane
Hogweed: Knotweed
Holigolds: Marigold
Hollunder: Elder
Holm: Holly
Holme Chaste: Holly
Holy Herb: Vervain, *Yerba Santa*
Holy Thistle: Thistle, Holy
Holy Tree: Holly
Holy Wood: Mistletoe
Honey: Clover
Honeystalks: Clover
Hoodwort: Scullcap
Horseheal: Elecampane
Horse Violet: Pansy
Hreow: Rue
Huath: Hawthorn
Huauhtli: Amaranth
Hulm: Holly
Hulver Bush: Holly
Hundred Leaved Grass: Yarrow
Huran: Horehound
Hurrburr: Burdock
Husbandman's Dial: Marigold
Hylder: Elder
Hyssop Herb: Hyssop

I

Incense: Frankincense
Incensier: Rosemary
Indian Arrow Wood: Wahoo
Indian Dye: Golden Seal
Indian Elm: Slippery Elm
Indian Fig Tree: Banyan

Indian God Tree: Banyan
Indian Gum: Arabic, Gum
Indian Paint: Golden Seal
Indian Pony: Life Everlasting
Indian Root: Trillium
Indian Sage: Boneset
Indian Tobacco: Lobelia
India Root: Galangal
Inkberry: Poke
Intoxicating Pepper: Kava-Kava
Iris: Blue Flag
Irish Broom: Broom
Irish Tops: Broom
Isana: Henbane
Isopo: Hyssop
Italian Lovage: Lovage
Italian Parsley: Lovage

J

Jacob's Ladder: Lily of the Valley
Jatamansi: Sumbul
Jaundice Root: Golden Seal
Jessamine: Jasmine
Joe-Pie: Joe-Pye Weed
Johnny Jumper: Pansy
Johnny Jump-Ups: Pansy
Jove's Nuts: Oak
Joy of the Mountain: Marjoram
Jusquiame: Henbane
Jupiter's Bean: Henbane
Jalap: High John the Conqueror
Jimsonweed: Datura
John's Wort: St. John's Wort
Jopi Weed: Joe-Pye Weed
Jove's Flower: Carnation
Joy on the Ground: Periwinkle
Juglans: Oak
Juno's Tears: Vervain
Jupiter's Staff: Mullein

K

Kaempferia Galanga: Galangal
Kaphnos: Fumitory
Karan: Myrrh
Karcom: Saffron
Keckies: Hemlock

Kelp: Bladderwrack
Kenning Wort: Celandine
Key Flower: Cowslip
Key of Heaven: Cowslip
Kex: Hemlock
Kharkady: Hibiscus
Khus-Khus: Vetivert
Ki: Ti
Kif: Hemp
King Root: Bloodroot
Kinnikinnick: Uva Ursa
Kiss-Me-At-The-Garden-Gate: Pansy
Klamath Weed: St. John's Wort
Knight's Milfoil: Yarrow
Knit Back: Comfrey
Knitbone: Comfrey
Knotgrass: Knotweed
Knotted Marjoram: Marjoram
Knyghten: Yarrow
Ko: Sugar Cane
Krokos: Saffron
Kunkuma: Saffron

L

Lacris: Licorice
Ladder to Heaven: Lily of the Valley
Lady's Foxglove: Mullein
Ladies' Meat: Hawthorn
Ladies' Seal: Briony
Lad's Love: Southernwood
Lady Ellhorn: Elder
Ladykins: Mandrake
Lady of the Meadow: Meadowsweet
Lady of the Woods: Birch
Lady's Key: Cowslip
Lady's Laces: Dodder
Lady's Mantle: Yarrow
Lady's Seal: Solomon's Seal
Lady's Thistle: Thistle
Lama: Ebony
Lamb Mint: Spearmint
Lammint: Peppermint
Lapstones: Potato
Lattouce: Lettuce
Laurel: Bay
Laurier a'Appolon: Bay

Laurier Sauce: Bay
Lavose: Lovage
Leapord's Bane: Wolf's Bane
The Leaf of Patrick: Plantain
Leather Jackets: Potato
Lemon Balm: Balm, Lemon
Lemon Balsam: Balm, Lemon
Lent Lily: Daffodil
Leontopodium: Lady's Mantle
Levant Salep: Orchid
Libanotis: Rosemary
Licourice: Licorice
Lignam aloes: Aloes, Wood
Lignam sanctae crucis: Mistletoe
Lily Constancy: Lily of the Valley
Lime: Linden
Lime Tree: Linden
Ling: Heather
Link: Broom
Linseed: Flax
Lion's Foot: Lady's Mantle
Lion's Herb: Columbine
Lion's Mouth: Foxglove
Lion's Tooth: Dandelion
Lippe: Cowslip
Little Queen: Meadowsweet
Little Stepmother: Pansy
Liverleaf: Liverwort
Liver Lily: Blue Flag
Liverweed: Liverwort
Lizzy-Run-Up-The-Hedge: Ground Ivy
Llwyd y cwn: Horehound
Llygad y Dydd: Daisy
Lorbeer: Bay
Lousewort: Betony, Wood
Love Fruit: Orange
Love Herbs: Lovage
Love Idol: Pansy
Love-In-Idleness: Pansy
Love-Lies-Bleeding: Amaranth, Pansy
Love Rod: Lovage
Love Root: Lovage
Love Vine: Dodder
Love-Will: Datura
Loving Herbs: Lovage
Loving Idol: Pansy

Low John the Conqueror: Galangal
Lubestico: Lovage
Lucerne: Alfalfa
Luib na muc: Pimpernel
Lunary: Honesty
Lurk-In-The-Ditch: Pennyroyal
Lusmore: Foxglove
Lus na mbau side: Foxglove
Lycopod: Club Moss
Lycorys: Licorice
Lythrum: Loosestrife

M
Mackerel Mint: Spearmint
Mad Apple: Datura
Madder's Cousin: Bedstraw, Fragrant
Madherb: Datura
Mad Root: Briony
Madweed: Scullcap
Madwort: Alyssum
Magic Mushroom: Agaric
Maia: Banana
Maidenhair Fern: Maidenhair
Maid's Ruin: Southernwood
Maize: Corn
Male Lily: Lily of the Valley
Malicorio: Pomegranate
Mallaquetta Pepper: Grains of Paradise
Malum punicum: Pomegranate
Mandragen: Mandrake
Mandragor: Mandrake
Mandrake: May Apple
Manicon: Datura
Mannikin: Mandrake
Manzanilla: Camomile
Maracoc: Passion Flower
Marian Thistle: Thistle, Milk
Marigold of Peru: Sunflower
Marijuana: Hemp
Marjorlaine: Marjoram
Marrubium: Horehound
Marshmallow: Althea
Maruil: Horehound
Marybud: Marigold
Marygold: Marigold
Mary Gowles: Marigold

Master of the Woods: Woodruff
Masterwort: Angelica
Masticke: Mastic
Mate: Yerba Mate
Maudlinwort: Daisy
May: Hawthorn
Mayblossom: Hawthorn
May Bush: Hawthorn
Mayflower: Hawthorn
May Lily: Lily of the Valley
Maypops: Passion Flower
Maythen: Camomile
Meadow Anemone: Anemone
Meadow Cabbage: Skunk Cabbage
Meadowwort: Meadowsweet
Meadsweet: Meadowsweet
Mealberry: Uva Ursa
Melia: Plumeria
Mecca Balsam: Balm of Gilead
Medicine Plant: Aloe
Meet-Me-In-The-Entry: Pansy
Melampode: Hellebore, Black
Melequetta: Grains of Paradise
Melissa: Balm, Lemon
Michaelmas: Aster
Milfoil: Yarrow
Militaris: Yarrow
Military Herb: Yarrow
Millefolium: Yarrow
Minarta: Avens
Miracle Herb: Comfrey
Mirra Balsam Odendron: Myrrh
Mismin: Spearmint
Misseltoe: Mistletoe
Mizquitl: Mesquite
Money Plant: Honesty
Monkshood: Wolf's Bane
Moon Daisy
Moonlight on the Grove: Jasmine
Moor Grass: Cinquefoil
Moose Elm: Slippery Elm
Mortification Root: Althea
Mother of the Herbs: Rue
Mother of the Wood: Sloe
Mountain Ash: Rowan
Mountain Balm: *Yerba Santa*

Mountain Box: Uva Ursa
Mountain Cranberry: Uva Ursa
Mountain Mint: Marjoram
Mountain Tea: Wintergreen
Mousquito Plant: Pennyroyal
Muggons: Mugwort
Mum: Chrysanthemum
Murphies: Potato
Musquash Root: Hemlock
Myrtle Flag: Calamus
Myrtle Grass: Calamus
Myrtle Sedge: Calamus

N
Narcissus: Daffodil
Nard: Lavendar, Spikenard
Nardus: Lavendar
Naughty Man: Mugwort
Naughty Man's Cheeries: Belladonna
Neckweede: Hemp
Nelka: Carnation
Nepeta: Catnip
Nidor: Fumitory
Nine Hooks: Lady's Mantle
Nine Joints: Knotweed
Ninety Knot: Knotweed
Nion: Ash
Nip: Catnip
Nirvara: Rice
Noble Laurel: Bay
Noble Yarrow: Yarrow
No Eyes: Potato
Nosebleed: Yarrow
Nurse Heal: Elecampane

O
Oatmeal: Oats
Obeah Wood: Ebony
Ohe: Bamboo
Oingnum: Onion
Ofnokgi: Sumbul
Old Field Balsam: Life Everlasting
Old Gal: Elder
Old Lady: Elder
Old Man: Mugwort, Southernwood
Old Man Fennel: Mullein

Old Man's Pepper: Yarrow
Old Man's Mustard: Yarrow
Old Uncle Henry: Mugwort
Old Woman: Wormwood
Olena: Turmeric
Olibans: Frankincense
Olibanum: Frankincense
Olibanus: Frankincense
Olivier: Olive
Onyoun: Onion
Orange Bergamot: Bergamot, Orange
Orange Mint: Bergamot, Orange
Orange Root: Golden Seal
Oregon Grape Root: Oregon Grape
Organ Broth: Pennyroyal
Organs: Pennyroyal
Organ Tea: Pennyroyal
Ortiga ancha: Nettle
Osier: Willow
Ouchi: Sumbul
'Our Herb': Basil
Our Lady's Glove: Foxglove
Our Lady's Keys: Cowslip
Our Lady's Mint: Spearmint
Our Lady's Tears: Lily of the Valley
Oval Buchu: Buchu

P
Paddock Pipes: Horsetail
Paddy: Rice
Paeony: Peony
Paigle: Cowslip
Pain-de-Porceau: Cyclamen
Palma Christi: Castor
Palma Christi Root: Castor
Paraguay: *Yerba Mate*
Paralysio: Cowslip
Partyke: Loosestrife
Pas d' ane: Coltsfoot
Pasque Flower: Anemone
Passe Flower: Anemone
Passions: Bistort
Passion Vine: Passion Flower
Password: Cowslip, Primrose
Patience Dock: Bistort
Patrick's Dock: Plantain

Patrick's Leaf: Plantain
Patterns and Clogs: Toadflax
Paw-Paw: Papaya
Pearl Moss: Irish Moss
Peepul Tree: Bodhi
Peggle: Cowslip
Pelican Flower: Snakeroot
Pensee: Pansy
Pentagram Flowers: Wax Plant
Pentagram Plant: Wax Plant
Pentaphyllon: Cinquefoil
Percely: Parsley
Persea: Avocado
Persil: Parsley
Personata: Burdock
Peruvian Mastic Tree: Pepper Tree
Pesleporis: Avens
Petersilie: Parsley
Peter's Staff: Mullein
Petroselinum: Parsley
Pewterwort: Horsetail
Philanthròpos: Agrimony
Philtron: Carrot
Phu: Valerian
Pigrush: Knotweed
Pigweed: Knotweed, Purslane
Pigeon Berry: Poke
Pigeon's Grass: Vervain
Pigeonwood: Vervain
Piliolerian: Pennyroyal
Pimpinella: Pimpernel
Pinks: Potato
Pipe Tree: Elder
Pipul: Bodhi
Piru: Pepper Tree
Piss-A-Bed: Dandelion
Plumrocks: Cowslip
Pocan: Poke
Poison Flag: Blue Flag
Poison Hemlock: Hemlock
Poison Lily: Blue Flag
Poison Parsley: Hemlock
Poison Tobacco: Henbane
Polar Plant: Rosemary
Pole Cat Weed: Skunk Cabbage
Pokeberry Root: Poke

Poke Root: Poke
Polk Root: Poke
Poor Man's Meat: Beans
Poor Man's Treacle: Garlic
Poorman's Weatherglass: Pimpernel
Porillon: Daffodil
Pot Marjoram: Marjoram
Pound Garnet: Pomegranate
Prickly Broom: Gorse
Priest's Crown: Dandelion
Princess Pine: Pipsissewa
Prince's Pine: Pipsissewa
Pucha-Pot: Patchouly
Pudding Grass: Pennyroyal
Puffball: Dandelion
Pukeweed: Lobelia
Purple Betony: Betony, Wood
Purple Medic: Alfalfa
Purple Willow Herb: Loosestrife
Pussy Willow: Willow

Q
Queen of the Meadow: Meadowsweet
Queen Elizabeth Root: Orris
Queen's Delight: Stillengia
Queen's Root: Stillengia
Quick: Hawthorn
Quickbane: Rowan
Quick Grass: Witch Grass

R
Rabbits: Toadflax
Racoon Berry: Mandrake, May Apple
Radix Viperina: Snakeroot
Ragweed: Ragwort
Rainbow Weed: Loosestrife
Ramsted: Toadflax
Ran Tree: Rowan
Rapuns: Radish
Rattle Root: Cohosh, Black
Red Bearberry: Uva Ursa
Red Campion: Bachelor's Buttons
Red-Cap Mushroom: Agaric
Red Cockscomb: Amaranth
Red Elm: Slippery Elm
Red Eyebright: Eyebright

Red Eyes: Potato
Red Pepper: Chili Pepper
Red Raspberry: Raspberry
Red Legs: Bistort
Red Robin: Knotweed
Red Root: Bloodroot
Red Sage: Sage
Red Squill: Squill
Red Valerian: Valerian
Rewe: Rue
Rhizoma Galangae: Galangal
Ripple Grass: Plantain
Rob Elder: Elder
Robin-Run-In-The-Hedge: Ground Ivy
Rock Parsley: Parsley
Rocks: Potato
Rocky Mountain Grape: Oregon Grape
Roden-Quicken: Rowan
Roden-Quicken-Royan: Rowan
Roynetree: Rowan
Roman Camomile: Camomile
Roman Laurel: Bay
Rudbeckia: Echinacea
Ruddes: Marigold
Ruddles: Marigold
Rue, Meadow: Meadow Rue
Ruffett: Gorse
Run-By-The-Ground: Pennyroyal
Ruta: Rue

S
Sacred Bark: Cascara Sagrada
Sacred Herb: *Yerba Santa*
Sacred Mother: Corn
Sacred Mushroom: Agaric
Sacred Tree: Bodhi
Saffer: Saffron
Sagackhomi: Uva Ursa
Sage: Sagebrush
Sage Willow: Loosestrife
Sahlab: Orchid
Sahlep: Orchid
Saille: Willow
Sailor's Tobacco: Mugwort
St. George's Herb: Valerian
St. James' Wort: Ragwort

St. John's Plant: Mugwort
St. Joseph's Wort: Basil
St. Mary's Seal: Solomon's Seal
St. Patrick's Leaf: Plantain
Salap: Lucky Hand
Salep: Orchid
Salicaire: Loosestrife
Salicyn Willow: Willow
Saloop: Orchid
Sandberry: Uva Ursa
Sang: Ginseng
Sanguinary: Yarrow
Sanguis Draconis: Dragon's Blood
Sandal: Sandalwood
Santal: Sandalwood
Saracen Corn: Buckwheat
Satyrion: Orchid
Saugh Tree: Willow
Sawge: Sage
Scabwort: Elecampane
Scaffold Flower: Carnation
Scaldweed: Dodder
Scheiteregi: Fumitory
Scoke: Poke
Scotch Broom: Broom
Scottish Heather: Heather
Sea Dew: Rosemary
Sea Holly: Eryngo
Sealroot: Solomon's Seal
Sealwort: Solomon's Seal
Sea Onion: Squill
Sea Parsley: Lovage
Sea Spirit: Bladderwrack
Seawrack: Bladderwrack
Seed of Horus: Horehound
Seed of Seeds: Corn
Seetang: Bladderwrack
Selago: Club Moss
Semihomo: Mandrake
Sengren: Houseleek
Sention: Groundsel
Septfoil: Tormentil
Serpentary Radix: Snakeroot
Serpentary Rhizome: Snakeroot
Serpent's Tongue: Adder's Tongue
Sete Wale: Valerian

Set Well: Valerian
Seven Barks: Hydrangea
Seven Year's Love: Yarrow
Shamrock: Clover
Shave-Grass: Horsetail
Sheep Lice: Houndstongue
Shepherd's Club: Mullein
Shepherd's Herb: Mullein
Shepherd's Knot: Tormentil
Shepherd's Weatherglass: Pimpernel
Short Buchu: Buchu
Siamese Benzoin: Benzoin
Silver Bough, The: Apple
Silver Cinquefoil: Cinquefoil
Silverweed: Cinquefoil
Silver Dollar: Honesty
Simpler's Joy: Vervain
Simson: Groundsel
Skunk Weed: Skunk Cabbage
Slan-lus: Plaintain
Sleepwort: Lettuce
Slippery Root: Comfrey
Snagree: Snakeroot
Snagrel: Snakeroot
Snakebite: Plantain
Snake Grape: Briony
Snake Lily: Blue Flag
Snake's Friend: Indian Paint Brush
Snake's Grass: Yarrow
Snake's Matches: Indian Paint Brush
Snakeweed: Bistort, Plaintain, Snakeroot
Snapping Hazelnut: Witch Hazel
Sola Indianus: Sunflower
Soldier's Tea: Horehound
Soldier's Woundwort: Yarrow
Solidago: Goldenrod
Solomon Seal: Solomon's Seal
Sol Terrestis: St. John's Wort
Sops-In-Wine: Carnation
Sorb Apple: Rowan
Sorcerer's Berry: Belladonna
Sorcerer's Herb: Datura
Sorcerer's Violet: Periwinkle
Sourgrass: Sorrel, Wood
Sour Trefoil: Sorrel, Wood
Sow-Bread: Cyclamen

Spanish Arbor Vine: Wood Rose
Spanish Saffron: Saffron
Sparrow's Tongue: Knotweed
Spike: Lavendar
Spider Lily: Spiderwort
Spindle Tree: Wahoo
Spire Mint: Spearmint
Sponnc: Coltsfoot
Spotted Alder: Witch Hazel
Spotted Corobane: Hemlock
Spotted Hemlock: Hemlock
Spousa Solis: Marigold
Spurge: Euphorbia
Squaw Mint: Pennyroyal
Squaw Root: Cohosh, Black
Staggerwort: Ragwort
Stammerwort: Ragwort
Stanch Griss: Yarrow
Stanch Weed: Yarrow
Stargrass: Ague Root
Star of the Earth: Avens
Starwort: Ague Root, Aster
Stellaria: Lady's Mantle
Steeplebush: Meadowsweet
Stepmother: Pansy
Sticklewort: Agrimony
Stickwort: Agrimony, Sorrel, Wood
Stillingia: Stillengia
Stinging Nettle: Nettle
Stinking Nanny: Ragwort
Stinking Willie: Ragwort
Stinkweed: Datura, Garlic
Strangle Tare: Dodder
Storm Hat: Wolf's Bane
Stringy Bark Tree: Eucalyptus
Styrax: Liquidamber
Stubwort: Sorrel, Wood
Succory: Chicory
Summer's Bride: Marigold
Sunkfield: Cinqufoil
Suntull: Skunk Cabbage
Sureau: Elder
Surelle: Sorrel, Wood
Swallow Herb: Celandine
Swallow-Wort: Celandine
Swamp Cabbage: Skunk Cabbage

Swamp Sassafras: Magnolia
Sweating Plant: Boneset
Sweet Balm: Balm, Lemon
Sweet Balsam: Balm, Lemon
Sweet Basil: Basil
Sweet Bay: Bay
Sweet Cane: Calamus
Sweet Cherry: Cherry
Sweet Dock: Bistort
Sweet Elder: Elder
Sweet Fennel: Fennel
Sweet Flag: Calamus
Sweet Grass: Calamus
Sweet Gum: Liquidamber
Sweet Marjoram: Marjoram
Sweet Root: Calamus, Licorice
Sweet Rush: Calamus
Sweet Scented Goldenrod: Goldenrod
Sweet Scented Life Everlasting: Life
    Everlasting
Sweet Sedge: Calamus
Sweet Violet: Violet
Sweet Weed: Althea
Sweet Wood: Cinnamon
Sweet Woodruff: Woodruff
Swine Bread: Cyclamen
Swine Snout: Dandelion
Swynel Grass: Knotweed
Symphonica: Henbane
Synkefoyle: Cinquefoil

T
Tabacca: Tobacco
Tamarindo: Tamarind
Tamus: Briony
Tansy: Yarrow
Taters: Potato
Tatties: Potato
Taubenkropp: Fumitory
Teaberry: Wintergreen
Tear Grass: Job's Tears
Teasel: Boneset
Tekrouri: Hemp
Temple Tree: Plumeria
Tetterberry: Briony
Tetterwort: Celandine

Thimbleberry: Blackberry
Thormantle: Tormentil
Thorn: Hawthorn
Thornapple: Datura
Thoroughwort: Boneset
Thor's Hat: Wolf's Bane
Thor's Helper: Rowan
Thousand Seal: Yarrow
Three-Leaved Grass: Sorrel, Wood
Thrissles: Thistles
Thunderbesem: Mistletoe
Tickweed: Pennyroyal
Tipton Weed: St. John's Wort
Torches: Mullein
Tinne: Holly
Tittle-My-Fancy: Pansy
Toad: Toadflax
Toloache: Datura
Tongue of Dog: Houndstongue
Tonqua: Tonka
Tonquin Bean: Tonka
Trailing Grape: Oregon Grape
Tree of Chastity: Hawthorn
Tree of Death: Cypress
Tree of Doom: Elder
Tree of Enchantment: Willow
Tree of Evil: Walnut
Tree of Love: Apple
Trefoil: Clover, Liverwort
Trifoil: Clover
True Love: Trillium
True Unicorn Root: Ague Root
True Winter's Bark: Winter's Bark
Trumpet Flower: Be-Still
Trumpet Weed: Joe-Pye Weed, Meadow-
    sweet
Tumeric Root: Golden Seal
Tunhoof: Ground Ivy
Turnsole: Heliotrope

U
Unicorn Root: Ague Root
Unshoe-Horse: Moonwort
Unyoun: Onion

V
Vada Tree: Banyan
Vandal Root: Valerian
Vanilla Leaf: Deerstongue
Van-Van: Vervain
Vapor: Fumitory
Vegetable Sulfur: Club Moss
Velvetback: Mullein
Velvet Dock: Elecampane
Velvet Flower: Amaranth
Velvet Plant: Mullein
Verbena: Vervain
Verge d'Or: Goldenrod
Vervan: Vervain
Vetiver: Vetivert
Virginia Dogwood: Dogwood
Virginian Poke: Poke
Virginian Snakeroot: Snakeroot
Virgin Mary's Nut: Molukka
Voodoo Witch Burr: Liquidamber

W
Wallwort: Comfrey
Walnoot: Walnut
Warnera: Golden Seal
War Poison: Yellow Evening Primrose
Water Flag: Blue Flag
Water Iris: Blue Flag
Water Parsley: Hemlock
Way Bennet: Avens
Wax Dolls: Fumitory
Waybread: Plantain
Waybroad: Plantain
Weed: Hemp
Welcome-Home-Husband-Though-
    Never-So-Drunk: Houseleek
Welcome-Home-Husband-Though-
    Never-So-Late: Houseleek
Weybroed: Plantain
Whig Plant: Camomile
Whin: Gorse
White Balsam: Life Everlasting
White Endive: Dandelion
White Horehound: Horehound
White Man's Foot: Plantain
White Sandalwood: Sandalwood

White Saunders: Sandalwood
White Squill: Squill
White Thorn: Hawthorn
White Willow: Willow
Whitty: Rowan
Wicken-Tree: Rowan
Wiggin: Rowan
Wiggy: Rowan
Wiky: Rowan
Wild Ash: Rowan
Wild Cherry: Chicory
Wild Curcurma: Golden Seal
Wild Endive: Dandelion
Wild Hops: Briony
Wild Lemon: Mandrake, May Apple
Wild Oregon Grape: Oregon Grape
Wild Sage: Sagebrush
Wild Succory: Chicory
Wild Sunflower: Elecampane
Wild Vanilla: Deerstongue
Wild Vine: Briony
Wind Flower: Anemone
Wintera: Winter's Bark
Wintera aromatica: Winter's Bark
Winterbloom: Witch Hazel
Winter's Cinnamon: Winter's Bark
Wintersweet: Marjoram
Wishing Thorn: Sloe
Witchbane: Rowan
Witchen: Rowan
Witches' Aspirin: Willow
Witches Bells: Foxglove
Witches Broom: Mistletoe
Witches Grass: Witch Grass
Witches' Hair: Dodder
Witches Herb: Basil
Witches' Thimble: Datura
Witches Thimbles: Foxglove
Witch Burr: Liquidamber
Witch Herb: Mugwort
Witch's Berry: Belladonna
Witchwood: Rowan
Withe: Willow
Withy: Willow
Wolf Claw: Club Moss
Wolf's Hair: Wolf's Bane

Wolf's Hat: Wolf's Bane
Wolf's Milk: Euphorbia
Womandrake: Mandrake
Wonder of the World Root: Ginseng
Wood Aloes: Aloes, Wood
Wood Betony: Betony, Wood
Woodbine: Honeysuckle
Wood Boneset: Boneset
Wood of the Cross: Mistletoe
Wood-Rove: Woodruff
Wood Sorrel: Sorrel, Wood
Wood Sour: Sorrel, Wood
Wood Vine: Briony
Woolmat: Houndstongue
Wound Weed: Goldenrod
Woundwort: Goldenrod
Wound Wort: Yarrow
Wuderove: Woodruff
Wymote: Althea

Y
Yakori bengeskro: Elder
Yalluc: Comfrey
Yarroway: Yarrow
Yaw Root: Stillengia
Yellow Avens: Avens
Yellow Dock: Dock
Yellow Gentian: Gentian
Yellow Oleander: Be-Still
Yellow Puccoon: Golden Seal
Yellow Root: Golden Seal
Yellow Sandalwood: Sandalwood
Yerba: Yerba Mate
Yerba Buena: Spearmint
Verba del Diablo: Datura
Yerba Louisa: Lemon Verbena
Yerw: Yarrow
Yn-leac: Onion
Ysopo: Hyssop
Yssop: Hyssop

Z
Zauberwurzel: Mandrake

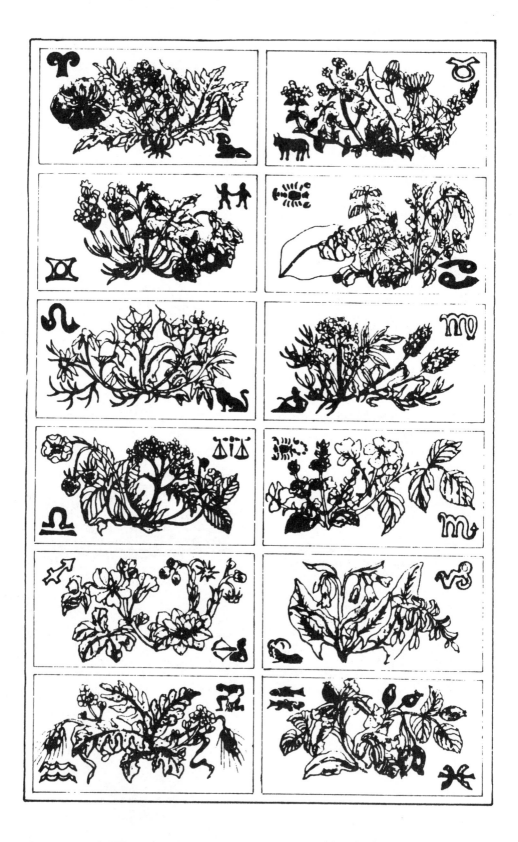

ANNOTATED BIBLIOGRAPHY

Though the literature of magic is extensive, that relating purely to the powers of herbs is limited. Few works in history have specifically concerned the subject; thus this bibliography is, for the most part, composed of books in such fields as mythology, folklore, anthropology, ethnobotany, magic and Witchcraft.

All herbals draw upon earlier writings—this one is no different. While this list of books is representative of those I have researched, it is far from complete. It is a guide for those who wish to study further.

Because of the great diversity of subject matter I have annotated this bibliography with pertinent comments. The edition cited is not necessarily the most recent; simply the one consulted. Where later editions have altered names these have been used.

287

Agrippa, Henry Cornelius: *The Philosophy of Natural Magic.*
    Antwerp, 1531. Secaucus (New Jersey): University Books, 1974.
        This neglected work is a sound introduction to natural magic, including
        that of the planets, stars, colors herbs and stones. Full coverage of divini-
        tory techniques and the elements is also included.
Aima: *Ritual Book of Herbal Spells.* Los Angeles: Foibles, 1976.
        An herbal spellbook derived mainly from contemporary voodoo herb
        magic.
Apuleius, Platonicus (or pseudo-Apuleius): *Herbarium.* Circa 400 C.E.
        One of the early herbals, interesting mainly for its curiosity.
Bailey, Liberty Hyde: *Hortus Third: A Concise Dictionary of Plants Cultivated
    In The United States And Canada.* New York: Macmillan Publishing Co.,
    1976.
        Invaluable for nomenclature.
Baker, Margaret: *Folklore and Customs Of Rural England.* Totowa (New Jersey):
    Rowman & Littlefield, 1974.
        A breezy, information-packed book of British country lore and magic.
Baker, Margaret: *Gardener's Magic And Folklore.* New York: Universe Books,
    1978.
        A delightful guide to rituals and magic concerned with the garden, as well
        as the plants contained therein.
Banis, Victor: *Charms, Spells And Curses For The Millions.*
    Los Angeles: Sherbourne Press, 1970.
        A somewhat sloppily composed collection of magical information gathered
        from many uncredited sources, this book in the infamous 'For the Millions'
        series contains some excellent herbal lore.
Barret, Francis: *The Magus, or Celestial Intelligencer.* London: 1801. New Hyde
    Park (New York): University Books, 1967.
        This classic work, mainly composed from ancient magical manuscripts,
        contains some herbal information, particularly in relation to the planets.
        Most of this work was culled from Aprippa.
Beckwith, Martha: *Hawaiian Mythology.* Honolulu: University Press of Hawaii,
    1979.
        This book contains information on the native Hawaiian's uses of plants in
        magic and ritual.
Benedict, Ruth: *Patterns Of Culture.* New York: Mentor Books, 1960.
        In this classic of anthrolopology Benedict records some of the magical
        uses of datura among the Pueblo Indians of New Mexico, as well as some
        of the Dobu islander's herb rites.
Best, Michael and Frank H. Brightman (editors), *The Book of Secrets of Albertus
    Magnus of the Vertues of Herbs, Stones, and Certain Beasts,* Also *A Book of
    The Marvels Of The World.* Oxford: Oxford University, 1973.
        A scholarly and lively discussion of (and complete presentation of) the
        famous pseudo-Albertus Magnus work. It contains some very curious
        writings concerning plants and their alleged powers.
Beyerl, Paul: *The Holy Books Of The Devas: An Herbal For The Aquarian Age.*

Minneapolis; The Rowan Tree, 1980.

A poetic herbal with practical as well as esoteric information.

Blunt, Wilfred and Sandra Raphael: *The Illustrated Herbal*. New York: Thames and Hudson, 1979.

A sumptious guide to the history of herbals, this book also includes many tantalizing extracts and full-color illustrations.

Boland, Bridget: *Gardener's Magic and Other Old Wives' Lore*. New York: Farrar, Straus & Giroux, 1976.

A charming book of plant and gardening folklore and magic.

Boland, Margaret and Bridget Boland: *Old Wives' Lore For Gardeners*. New York: Farrar, Straus & Giroux, 1976.

One more like the former.

Bolton, Brett L.: *The Secret Powers Of Plants*. New York: Berkley, 1974.

This popularized look at plants and their hidden powers contains an excellent section on magic.

Bowness, Charles: *The Witch's Gospel*. London: Robert Hale, 1979.

British folklore and contemporary Wiccan practices with a bit of plant magic thrown in.

Briggs, Katherine: *The Fairies In Tradition and Literature*. London: Routledge & Kegan Paul, 1967.

A chapter in this book is entitled 'Fairy Plants.'

Budge, E. A. Wallis: *Amulets and Talismans*. New Hyde Park: (New York): University Books, 1968.

This monumental work contains information on plants used in magic (as well as some horrendously bad line-drawings).

Budge, E. A. Wallis: *Herb Doctors and Physicians in the Ancient World: The Divine Origin of the Craft of the Herbalist*. Chicago; Ares Publishers, 1978.

An excellent work on herbalism in the middle East in ancient times. Some magical formulae are included.

Burland, C. A.: *The Magical Arts: A Short History*. New York: Horizon Press, 1966.

British and European Folk customs and magic, including that of plants.

Burris, Eli Edward: *Taboo, Magic, Spirits: A Study in Primitive Elements in Roman Religion*. New York: Macmillan, 1931.

Roman ritualistic and magical uses of plants.

Busenbark, Earnest: *Symbols, Sex and the Stars in Popular Beliefs*. New York: Truth Seeker, 1949.

Plants and sexual symbolism in early religions.

Castenada, Carlos: *The Teachings of Don Juan*. New York: Ballantine, 1973.

Though the 'Don Juan' works have come under fire regarding their authenticity, it cannot be argued that Castenada researched his subject thoroughly and knows whereof he writes. This book includes a look at the magical use of hallucinatory plants in contemporary Arizona and Mexico among Yaqui shamans.

Chappell, Helen: *The Waxing Moon: A Gentle Guide to Magic*. New York: Links, 1974.

This pleasant book contains a chapter on herb magic largely drawn from present-day voodoo practices.

Coffin, Tristram P. and Henning Cohen (editors): *Folklore in America*. Garden City (New York): Anchor Books, 1970.
Southwestern United States herb magic is included in this work.

Coles, William: *The Art of Simpling*. London: 1656. St. Catherine's (Ontario): Provoker Press, 1968.
Much information on Renaissance plant magic.

Conway, David: *Magic: An Occult Primer*. New York: Bantam Books, 1973.
This excellent (and dangerous) beginner's guide to ceremonial magic also includes some plant information, some of which could be deadly for the unprepared.

Crow, W.B.: *The Occult Properties of Herbs*. New York: Weiser, 1974.
Crow's 'shopping list' approach to writing allows him to only briefly mention topics but many of these are interesting.

Crowley, Aleister: *777*. New York: Weiser, 1973.
Crowley probably stole the bulk of this work from Samuel Mathers, whom he did not credit. It is still an amazing group of magical correspondences (including plants).

Culpeper, Nicholas: *The English Physician*. London: 1652. London: Foulsham, N.D.
This most popular (and unfortunately, least reliable) herbal contains some hints here and there on herb magic, as well as the traditional locations for finding plants (beside streams, on mossy cliffs, in fields, etc.). Later published as *Culpepper's Complete Herbal*, under which title it is still available.

Cunningham, Lady Sara: *The Magical Virtues of Candles, Herbs, Incense and Perfume*. Glendale (California): Aleph Books, 1979.
Ms. Cunningham (no relation) has produced a work of limited interest; her section on herbs is sketchy but good. Most of the rest of this work lists brand-name magical oils and incenses and is therefore of little value.

Dana, Mrs. William Starr: *How to Know the Wild Flowers*. New York; 1893. New York: Dover, 1963.
This handbook is of invaluable use in identifying American plants, and contains a few snippets of magical information.

Davis, Hubert J. (editor): *The Silver Bullet and Other American Witch Stories*. Middle Village (New York): Jonathan David Publishers, 1975.
A bit of transplanted European plant lore is included here.

de Clairemont, Lewis, *Legends of Incense, Herb & Oil Magic*. Dallas: Dorene Publishing, 1966.
As with most books 'written' by de Clairemont, this work is largely pirated, some from Leyel's excellent *The Magic of Herbs*.

De Lys, Claudia: *A Treasury of American Superstitions*. New York: Philosophical Library, 1948.
Legends and myths concerning plants.

Densmore, Frances: *How Indians Use Wild Plants for Food, Medicine and*

Crafts. Washington, 1928. New York: Dover, 1974.
> This work contains a short section on 'Plants used as Charms.'

Derlon, Pierre: *Secrets of the Gypsies.* New York: Ballantine, 1977.
> Gypsy uses of plants.

Devine, M.V.: *Brujeria: A Study of Mexican-American Folk-Magic.* St. Paul: Llewellyn Publications, 1982.
> Contemporary Mexican-American urban herb magic in the United States, written with wit and style.

Emboden, William: *Bizarre Plants: Magical, Monstrous, Mythical.* New York: Macmillan, 1974.
> An unusual collection of plant information. Some shamanistic folk uses listed.

Emrich, Duncan: *The Folklore of Love and Courtship.* New York: American Heritage Press, 1970.
> A charming collection of spells and divinations, many utilizing plants.

Faulks, P. J.: *An Introduction of Enthnobotany.* London: Moredale Publications Ltd., 1958.
> Some information on ritual uses of herbs is continued in this fascinating work.

Fettner, Ann Tucker: *Potpourri, Incense and Other Fragrant Concoctions.* New York: Workman Publishing, 1977.
> Some herb magic, and many quotes from Leyel's *The Magic of Herbs.*

Fielding, William J.: *Strange Superstitions and Magical Practices.* New York: Paperback Library. 1968.
> Superstitions related to plants, sexual symbolism.

Fisher, M. F. K.: *A Cordiall Water.* Boston: Little, Brown & Company, 1961.
> A disorganized look at herbal medicine with a smattering of magic.

Fortune, R. F.: *Sorcerers of Dobu.* New York: Dutton, 1963.
> A fascinating account of an island people's life, in every aspect of which magic plays an important role.

Fox, Helen Morgenthau: *Gardening With Herbs for Flavor and Fragrance.* New York: Macmillan, 1934.
> This delightful book contains a chapter entitled 'The Witches' Cauldron,' and details European magical herbalism. Most of the information contained herein, however, is commonly found elsewhere.

Frazer, James: *The Golden Bough.* New York: Macmillan, 1958.
> This one-volume edition is quite long enough (as opposed to the 13-volume set) and contains much information on religious and ritual significance of plants. Mr. Frazer's conclusions, however, must be taken with a large grain of salt.

Friend, Hilderic: *Flower Lore.* London, 1884. Rocktop (Maine): Para Research, 1981.
> A fabulous book brimming with herb magic, once again available. Written before the turn of the century this volume records much country herb lore that would have probably been lost otherwise. Also contains far Eastern herb magic.

Gamache, Henri: *The Magic of Herbs.* Highland Falls (New York): Sheldon Publications, 1942.
   A popular study of herbs, with an emphasis on mythological associations rather than magical uses. Almost worthless.
Gerard, John, *The Herball, or Generall Historie of Plants.* London, 1597. New York: Dover, 1975.
   This massive volume, though written by an occult skeptic, nonetheless records many examples of herb magic current at the time of its writing.
Gilmore, Melvin R.: *Uses of Plants by the Indians of the Missouri River Region.* Lincoln (Nebraska); University of Nebraska Press, 1977.
   This work contains a large amount of information regarding native American herb magic.
Goodyer, John (translator), *The Greek Herbal of Dioscorides.* 1655. New York: Hafner, 1968.
   A classic herbal preserving much magic.
Gordon, Leslie: *A Country Herbal.* New York: Mayflower, 1980.
   A beautiful book peppered with magic.
Gordon, Leslie: *Green Magic.* New York: Viking Press, 1977.
   Myths and legends surrounding plants.
Grammary, Ann: *The Witches' Workbook.* New York: Pocket Books, 1973.
   A modern spellbook containing some herb magic.
Graves, Robert: *The White Goddess.* New York: Farrar, Straus and Giroux, 1976.
   Grave's poetic account of one aspect of the Mother Goddess, although filled with wild speculation, contains some excellent mythic and ritual information concerning plants and trees.
Gregor, Arthur S.: *Amulets, Talismans and Fetishes.* New York: Scribner's, 1975.
   A popular study illustrated with many spells.
Grieve, M.: *A Modern Herbal.* New York: 1931. New York: Dover, 1971.
   A massive two-volume set edited by Mrs. Leyel from a series of pamphlets, *A Modern Herbal* contains a wealth of magical and ritual information regarding herbs.
Griffith, F. L. and Herbert Thompson: *The Leyden Papyrus.* London: 1904. New York: Dover, 1974.
   An ancient Egyptian magical book which contains a little herb magic.
Grigson, Geoffrey: *A Herbal of All Sorts.* New York: Macmillan, 1959.
   All sorts of herb magic.
Gutmanis, June: *Kahuna La'au Lapa'au. Honolulu: Island Heritage Limited,* 1979.
   A detailed account of plant medicine and magic in ancient and contemporary Hawaii.
Haining, Peter: *The Warlock's Book: Secrets of Black Magic From The Ancient Grimoires.* Secaucus (New Jersey): Citadel, 1973.
   A popularized, over-written collection of spells culled from old manuscripts.
Hansen, Harold: *The Witch's Garden.* Santa Cruz: Unity Press, 1978.
   Translated from the Dutch, this work is an investigation into some of the

poisonous plants used in magic. No practical information.

Harner, Michael J. (editor): *Hallucinogens and Shamanism.* Oxford: Oxford University Press, 1973.

A scholarly and informative collection of essays detailing psychotomimetic plants and their uses in religion and magic.

Haskins, Jim: *Voodoo & Hoodoo: Their Tradition and Craft As Revealed By Actual Practitioners,* New York: Stein & Day, 1978.

Some plant information is included in this fascinating study.

Hayes, Carolyn H.: *Pergemin: Perfumes, Incenses, Colors, Birthstones, Their Occult Properties and Uses,* Chicago: Aries Press, 1937.

Many interesting incense formulae, most of which were included in Leo Vinci's later book *Incense.*

Healey, B.J.: *A Gardener's Guide to Plant Names.* New York: Charles Scribner's Sons, 1972.

An invaluable guide to taxonomy.

Heffern, Richard: *The Herb Buyer's Guide.* New York: Pyramid 1973.

Little magical information but a great resource.

Helfman, Elizabeth S.: *Maypoles and Wood Demons: The Meaning of Trees.* New York: Seabury Press, 1972.

A children's book of tree myths and magic.

Hohman, John George, *Pow-Wows, Or the Long Lost Friend.* Dallas: Dorene Publishing, N.D.

A compilation of spells, many Christianized, which preserve some herb magic.

Hole, Christina: *Witchcraft In England.* London: Batsford Ltd., 1940.

Some information on country herb magic.

Hoyt, Charles Alva: *Witchcraft.* Carbondale (Illinois): Southern Illinois University Press, 1981.

One chapter discusses the 'pharmacological' school of Witchcraft, concentrating, as usual, on the poisonous plants.

Huson, Paul: *Mastering Herbalism.* New York: Stein & Day, 1974.

A short section on herb magic, much of which is reprinted from the author's *Mastering Witchcraft.*

Huson, Paul: *Mastering Witchcraft.* New York: Berkley, 1971.

One of the books that aided the occult craze of the late 60's and early 70's in the United States, Huson covers European herb magic fairy well, although it is scattered throughout the book.

Jacob, Dorothy: *A Witch's Guide to Gardening.* New York: Taplinger, 1965.

European herb magic is well represented, as is plant mythology and folklore.

Jacob, Dorothy: *Cures and Curses.* New York: Taplinger, 1967.

This book is a companion volume to *A Witch's Guide to Gardening* and contains a chapter on herb magic.

Jones, T. Gwynn: *Welsh Folklore and Folk-Custom.* Cambridge: D. S. Brewer, 1979.

British herb magic and folklore.

Kamm, Minnie Watson: *Old-Time Herbs for Northern Gardens.* Boston: Little, Brown & Co., 1938.
> Folk names and ritual uses by the ancients.

Kenyon, Theda: *Witches Still Live,* New York: Washburn, 1939.
> Some herb magic and folklore.

Kittredge, George Lyman: *Witchcraft In Old and New England.* New York: Russel & Russel, 1956.
> Some medieval and renaissance herb magic can be found in this work.

Kluckhorn, Clyde: *Navajo Witchcraft.* Boston: Beacon Press, 1970.
> Information relating to datura.

Krutch, Joseph Wood: *Herbal.* Boston: David R. Godine, 1965.
> European herb magic and a good article on the mandrake.

Krythe, Maymie: *All About The Months.* New York: Harper and Row, 1966.
> Herb magic is contained in some of the sections on flowers of the months.

Lathrop, Norma Jean: *Herbs: How To Select, Grow and Enjoy.* Tucson, HP Books, 1981.
> No herb magic but a delightful book of herb gardening.

Lea, H. C.: *Materials Toward A History of Witchcraft.* New York: Thomas Yoseloff, 1957.
> Herb magic taken from legal records, pamphlets, and old works.

Leach, Maria (editor): *Funk & Wagnall's Standard Dictionary of Folklore, Mythology and Legend.* New York: Funk & Wagnall's, 1972.
> A mammoth work with much plant lore.

Leek, Sybil: *Cast Your Own Spell.* New York: Pinnacle, 1970.
> Ms. Leek includes some standard herb magic in this work.

Leek, Sybil: *Herbs: Medicine and Mysticism,* Chicago: Henry Regnery Co., 1975.
> Astrological and planetary associations of herbs.

Leek, Sybil: *Sybil Leek's Book of Herbs.* New York: Thomas Nelson, 1973.
> Legends and myths surrounding herbs.

Leland, Charles Godfrey: *Etruscan Magic and Occult Remedies.* New Hyde Park (New York): University Books, 1963.
> Magical herbal information collected in Italy in the late 1800's.

Leland, Charles Godfrey: *Gypsy Sorcery and Fortune-Telling.* New York: Dover, 1971.
> Gypsy plant lore and magic.

Leyel, C.F.: *Herbal Delights.* Boston: Houghton Mifflin Co., 1938.
> Folk names.

Leyel, C.F.: *The Magic of Herbs.* New York: 1927. Toronto (Canada): Coles Publishing, 1981.
> The most-quoted book of its kind, Mrs. Leyel's work is a classic. It contains detailed spells and uses of herbs culled from ancient manuscripts in the British Museum.

Lust, John: *The Herb Book.* New York: Bantam, 1974.
> Helpful for nomenclature, particularly folk names. This book includes some magical and mythic information.

Mabey, Richard: *Plantcraft: A Guide to the Everyday Use of Wild Plants.* New

York: Universe Books, 1977.

 A bit of plant magic.

Maple, Eric: *The Dark World of Witches.* New York: Pegasus, 1970.

 This excellent work contains a chapter on folk magic.

Maple, Eric: *The Magic of Perfume.* New York: Weiser, 1973.

 A short introduction to the magical aspects of scent.

Maple, Eric: *Superstition and The Superstitious.* Hollywood: Wilshire, 1973.

 Some plant and herb magic is included in this delightful work.

Marwick, Max (editor): *Witchcraft and Sorcery.* Middlesex: Penguin Books, 1970.

 Some of the essays contain plant magic.

Masse, Henri: *Persian Beliefs and Customs.* New Haven (Connecticut): Human Relations Area Files, 1954.

 Persian (Iranian) folk magic and superstitions, some of which concerns plants.

Mathers, Samuel (translator, editor): *The Key of Solomon. New York: Weiser,* 1972.

 This work, like most grimoires, was written with the assumption that its audience was knowledgeable in the magical arts. Therefore, no lengthy instruction is given in herb magic here, for this was common knowledge. However, Mather's version (pieced together from many extant manuscripts) does include some spells involving plants.

Meyer, Clarence: *50 Years of the Herbalist Almanac.* Glenwood (Illinois): Meyerbooks, 1977.

 This collection of essays from the Herbalist almanac includes some American Indian herb magic.

Meyer, Clarence: *The Herbalist.* 1960.

 Excellent for nomenclature, especially for native American plants.

Mickaharic, Draja: *Spiritual Cleansing: A Handbook of Psychic Protection.* York Beach (Maine): Weiser, 1982.

 A somewhat peculiarly written book, *Spiritual Cleansing* offers some valuable information regarding plants and their magical qualities. Heavily Christianized.

Murphy, Edith Van Allen: *Indian Uses of Native Plants.* Fort Bragg (California): Mendocino County Historical Society, 1950.

 This book has a short section of plants used in magic and ceremonies.

Paulsen, Kathryn: *The Complete Book of Magic and Witchcraft.* New York: Signet, 1980.

 A well-researched and footnoted work, it contains a large section on plant magic, drawing on both European and native American uses.

Paulsen, Kathryn: *Witches' Potions and Spells.* Mount Vernon (New York): Peter Pauper Press, 1971.

 Spells involving plants.

Pelton, Robert W.: *The Complete Book of Voodoo.* New York: Berkley Medallion, 1973.

 Though vulgarized and popularized, this work contains one of the most complete listings of voodoo herb uses, obviously drawn for a large variety of sources.

Pepper, Elizabeth and John Wilcox: *Witches All*. New York: Grosset & Dunlap, 1977.

This compilation of the authors' annual *The Witches Almanac* includes a section on plants.

Petulengro, 'Gipsy.': *A Romany Life*. London: Metheun & Co., Ltd., 1935.

A rambling account of a Gypsy's life, with some magic and herb spells thrown in for good measure.

Pliny the Elder (Caius Plinius Secundus): *Natural History*. Cambridge: Harvard University Press, 1956.

This work, written by a Roman in the first century C.E., is a catalog of nature as Pliny knew it. In the sections on plants he records many superstitions and magical uses which were current nearly 2,000 years ago.

Porta, John Baptista: *Natural Magic*. Naples, 1558. London, 1658. New York: Basic Books, 1957.

In this classic work Porta preserves some herb magic.

Porteous, Alexander: *Forest Folklore, Mythology and Romance*. London: George Allen & Unwin, 1928.

Superstitions and magic concerning trees.

Radford, E. and M. A. Radford: *Encyclopedia of Superstitions*. Revised and edited by Christina Hole. London: Hutchinson, 1961.

British floral and herbal superstitions and magic.

Randolph, Vance: *Ozark Superstitions*. New York: Cambridge University Press, 1947.

Plant magic collected in the Ozarks.

Riva, Anna: *The Modern Herbal Spellbook*. Toluca Lake (California): International Imports, 1974.

The prolific Anna Riva relied mainly on voodoo herb magic when writing this book, though some European uses are also included. Strangely enough, cosmetic and medicinal directions are also given.

Rose, Jeanne: *Herbs and Things: Jeanne Rose's Herbal*. New York: Grosset & Dunlap, 1972.

Jeanne Rose communicates some popular herbal magic in this excellent introduction to herbalism.

Rose, Jeanne: *Jeanne Rose's Herbal Guide to Inner Health*. New York: Grosset & Dunlap, 1979.

More plant magic.

Rosengarten, Frederick: *The Book of Spices*. New York: Pyramid, 1975.

Historical legends and myths surrounding herbs.

Saxon, Lyle (editor):*Gumbo Ya-Ya*. Boston: Houghton Mifflin Co., 1945.

Louisiana voodoo herb magic.

Schmidt, Phillip: *Superstition and Magic*. Westminster (Maryland): The Newman Press, 1963.

Written by a Jesuit, this book attempts to show the horrors of the occult while revealing some excellent magical procedures. Herbal lore is included.

Schultes, Richard Evans: *Hallucinogenic Plants.* Racine (Wisconsin); Western Publishing Co., 1976.
> A popularized yet detailed account of hallucinogenic plants and the role they play in shaminism.

Scot, Reginald: *The Discoverie of Witchcraft.* London: 1584. New York: Dover, 1972.
> A classic on the subject, Mr. Scot records some herb magic in this book along with a host of spells, divinations, exorcisms and charms.

Shah, Sayed Idries: *Oriental Magic.* New York: Philosophical Library, 1957.
> Shah includes some plant magic in this excellent and entertaining account.

Shah, Sayed Idries: *The Secret Lore of Magic.* New York: Citadel, 1970.
> A compilation of ancient grimoires with some plant magic.

Shah, Sirdar Ikbal Ali: *Occultism: Its Theory and Practice.* New York: Castle Books, N.D.
> Herb magic of the West and Middle East is included in this fascinating work.

Sharon, Douglas: *Wizard of the Four Winds: A Shaman's Story.* New York: The Free Press, 1978.
> This account of Peruvian shamanism (and a Peruvian shaman) discusses some of the plants used in magic, particularly hallucinogens.

Shosteck, Robert: *Flowers and Plants: An International Lexicon.* New York: Quadrangle/The New York Times Book Co., 1974.
> Invaluable for nomenclature, this work also contains a bit of herb magic.

Simmons, Adelma Grenier: *Herb Gardening in Five Seasons.* Princeton: D. Van Nostrand Co., 1964.
> Herbal mythology and magic.

Singer, Charles: *From Magic to Science.* New York: Dover, 1958.
> Excellent coverage of English plant magic in early times.

Slater, Herman (editor): *The Magical Formulary.* New York: Magickal Childe, 1981.
> A book of incense, oil and powder formulas, mostly derived from voodoo practices.

Spence: *The History and Origins of Druidism.* New York: Weiser, 1971.
> Contains some interesting information on oak and mistletoe, but Mr. Spence is not to be trusted in his works. Too often he mistakes wild speculation for firm facts.

Spence: *The Mysteries of Britain.* London: Aquarian Press, 1970.
> More plant lore from Britain and a great deal of speculation regarding ancient British religion.

Thistleton-Dyer, T. F.: *The Folklore of Plants.* Detroit: Singing Tree Press, 1968.
> Contains much herb magic and folklore.

Thompson, C. J. S.: *The Mysteries and Secrets of Magic.* London: 1927. New York: Olympia Press, 1972.
> An invaluable book with a chapter on herbs used in magic.

Thompson, C. J. S.: *The Mystery and Lure of Perfume.* Philadelphia: J. B. Lippincott & Co., 1927.

A fascinating account of perfumery and magical oils.

Thompson, C. J. S.: *The Mystic Mandrake.* New Hyde Park (New York): University Books, 1968.
Many spells and legends concerning the mandrake, as well as general plant magic information.

Thompson, Dorothy Burr and Ralph Griswold: *Garden Lore of Ancient Athens.* Princeton (New Jersey): American School of Classical Studies at Athens, 1963.
A small booklet with ancient Greek ritual and magical plant uses.

Thorwald, Jurgen: *Science and Secrets of Early Medicine.* New York: Harcourt, Brace & World, 1963.
Herb magic as related to ancient medicine.

Tindall, Gillian: *A Handbook on Witches.* London: Arthur Baker, 1965.
This book includes a chapter on folk magic in which plants figure prominently.

Thompkins, Peter and Christopher Bird: *The Secret Life of Plants,* New York: Avon Books, 1974.
The big plant book of the 1970's. It doesn't discuss magical information but does provide an intriguing look into the hidden powers of plants.

Tondriau, Julien: *The Occult: Secrets of the Hidden World.*
Plant magic is among the 'secrets' listed herein.

Trueman, John: *The Romantic Story of Scent.* New York: Doubleday, 1975.
A book of the history of scents and oils. Little magic but much mythology.

Trigg, Elwood: *Gypsy Demons and Divinities.* Secaucus (New Jersey): Citadel, 1973.
Gypsy plant magic.

Valiente, Doreen: *Natural Magic.* New York: St. Martin's Press, 1975.
Herb magic is among the types discussed in this book.

Valiente, Doreen: *Where Witchcraft Lives.* London: Aquarian Press, 1962.
British folk magic involving herbs is mentioned briefly.

Verrill, A. Hyatt: *Perfumes and Spices.* New York: L. C. Page, 1940.
Historical sketches of herbs.

Vinvi, Leo: *Incense: Its Ritual Significance, Use and Preparation.* New York: Weiser, 1980.
A guide to incense.

Waring, Phillipa: *A Dictionary of Omens and Superstitions.* New York: Ballantine, 1979.
Plants and herbs related to superstitions and divinations are examined.

Weslager, C. A.: *Magic Medicines of the Indians.* New York: Signet, 1974.
Though not as fully covered as I would wish, this book does mention American Indian herb magic.

Wheelwright, Edith Grey: *Medicinal Plants and Their History.* New York: Dover, 1974.
A history of medicinal herbalism with some magic as well.

Whitman, John: *The Psychic Power of Plants.* London: Star Books, 1974.
Plants and modern scientific research.

INDEX

**THE COMPLETE BOOK OF INCENSE,
OILS AND BREWS**
Scott Cunningham

For centuries the composition of incenses, the blending of oils, and the mixing of herbs have been used by people to create positive changes in their lives. With this book, the curtains of secrecy have been drawn back, providing you with practical, easy-to-understand information that will allow you to practice these methods of magical cookery.

Scott Cunningham, world-famous expert on magical herbalism, first published *The Magic of Incense, Oils and Brews* in 1986. *The Complete Book of Incense, Oils and Brews* is a revised and expanded version of that book. Scott took readers' suggestions from the first edition and added more than 100 new formulas. Every page has been clarified and rewritten, and new chapters have been added.

There is no special, costly equipment to buy, and ingredients are usually easy to find. The book includes detailed information on a wide variety of herbs, sources for purchasing ingredients, substitutions for hard-to-find herbs, a glossary, and a chapter on creating your own magical recipes.

0-87542-128-8, 288 pp., 6 x 9, illus., softcover   **$12.95**

THE MAGICAL HOUSEHOLD
Empower Your Home with Love,
Protection, Health and Happiness
Scott Cunningham and David Harrington

Whether your home is a small apartment or a palatial mansion, you want it to be something special. Now it can be with *The Magical Household.* Learn how to make your home more than just a place to live. Turn it into a place of security, life, fun, and magic. Here you will not find the complex magic of the ceremonial magician. Rather, you will learn simple, quick and effective magical spells that use nothing more than common items in your house: furniture, windows, doors, carpet, pets, etc. You will learn to take advantage of the intrinsic power and energy that is already in your home, waiting to be tapped. You will learn to make magic a part of your life. The result is a home that is safeguarded from harm and a place which will bring you happiness, health, and more.

0-87542-124-5, 208 pp., 5¼ x 8, illus., softcover $9.95

MAGICAL HERBALISM
The Secret Craft of the Wise
Scott Cunningham

Certain plants are prized for the special range of energies—the vibrations, or powers—they possess. *Magical Herbalism* unites the powers of plants and people to produce, and direct change in accord with human will and desire.

This is the Magic of amulets and charms, sachets and herbal pillows, incenses and scented oils, simples and infusions and anointments. It's Magic as old as our knowledge of plants, an art that anyone can learn and practice, and once again enjoy as we look to the Earth to rediscover our roots and make inner connections with the world of Nature.

This is Magic that is beautiful and natural—a Craft of Hand and Mind merged with the Power and Glory of Nature: a special kind that does not use the medicinal powers of herbs, but rather the subtle vibrations and scents that touch the psychic centers and stir the astral field in which we live to work at the causal level behind the material world.

This is the Magic of Enchantment . . . of word and gesture to shape the images of mind and channel the energies of the herbs. It is a Magic for everyone—for the herbs are easily and readily obtained, the tools are familiar or easily made, and the technology that of home and garden. This book includes step-by-step guidance to the preparation of herbs and to their compounding in incense and oils, sachets and amulets, simples and infusions, with simple rituals and spells for every purpose.

0-87542-120-2, 260 pp., 5¼ x 8, illus., softcover   **$9.95**